STRATEGIC COMMUNICATION

Strategic Communication deals with the principles behind strategic communication planning. It covers the professional practice steps involved in researching, planning, writing, evaluating and implementing a communication strategy. This book links strategic communication campaign planning to medium and long-term business activity and to how organisations deal with issues.

This thoroughly revised third edition includes:

- New international cases and professional exercises that will enable students to work through the cases and apply theory to real-life situations;
- New discussion questions on important aspects of campaign planning;
- Chapter exercises that encourage students to think more broadly about communication strategy and work through the particular aspects of a strategy;
- In Theory panels that highlight key theories and demonstrate important links between theory and practice

Accessible and comprehensive, this is an essential text for students of professional communication and professionals transitioning into the field of Strategic Communication.

James Mahoney PhD is Adjunct Professor in Professional Communication, News and Media Research Centre, and former Head, Discipline of Communication, Faculty of Arts and Design, at the University of Canberra. He convened the Bachelor of Public Relations and the Master of Strategic Communication degrees. His research interests are in issues management and strategic communication.

Strategic Communication

Campaign Planning

Third Edition

James Mahoney

Routledge
Taylor & Francis Group

LONDON AND NEW YORK

Designed cover image: © Getty

Third edition published 2023
by Routledge
4 Park Square, Milton Park, Abingdon, Oxon, OX14 4RN

and by Routledge
605 Third Avenue, New York, NY 10158

Routledge is an imprint of the Taylor & Francis Group, an informa business

First edition published by Oxford University Press 2013
Second edition published by Oxford University Press 2016

British Library Cataloguing-in-Publication Data
A catalogue record for this book is available from the British Library

Library of Congress Cataloging-in-Publication Data
Names: Mahoney, James Scott, 1947– author.
Title: Strategic communication: campaign planning / James Mahoney.
Description: Third edition. | Abingdon, Oxon; New York, NY: Routledge, 2023. |
Includes bibliographical references and index. |
Identifiers: LCCN 2022058218 (print) | LCCN 2022058219 (ebook) |
ISBN 9781032329741 (hardback) | ISBN 9781032329734 (paperback) |
ISBN 9781003317579 (ebook)
Subjects: LCSH: Business communication. | Communication. | Management.
Classification: LCC HF5718 .M345 2023 (print) | LCC HF5718 (ebook) |
DDC 658.4/5—dc23/eng/20221215
LC record available at https://lccn.loc.gov/2022058218
LC ebook record available at https://lccn.loc.gov/2022058219

ISBN: 978-1-032-32974-1 (hbk)
ISBN: 978-1-032-32973-4 (pbk)
ISBN: 978-1-003-31757-9 (ebk)

DOI: 10.4324/9781003317579

Typeset in Akzidenz Grotesk, Minion, and Novarese
by codeMantra

For students—then, now, future. Inspiration.

Contents

Figures

Tables

Acknowledgements

One of the great joys of teaching at a university is the experience of learning from students. It happens in surprising ways, not the least of which is how they respond to questions that ask them to explain, expand and clarify. Their answers sometimes lead to explorations of new contexts for these questions, fresh interpretations of situations and new ways of looking at problems. Their experiences in answering questions that require them to say why they agree or disagree with a proposition help them to build personal confidence in their knowledge of a topic, boost their ability to debate a point and develop as people. The great reward is hearing them say at the end of a unit, especially after an exam, 'Now I understand'. Three simple words at the end of a journey in which they explore, sometimes tentatively, relatively complex topics; three words to show it all meant something: they learnt.

That context and those three words are why this book is dedicated to students. Whoever else reads it, Strategic Communication: Campaign Planning is about helping students to understand the concepts, contexts and functions of strategy-making. After all, those who have endured my 'Why?' questions about strategy over the years have taught me as much as I hope I've taught them.

Many people, friends and colleagues, influenced this book, often through opportunities they gave me to work in professional practice, to teach, in simple conversations or readings about what communication strategy is, and is not. Academic and professional colleagues supported the notion that a book on strategic communication planning from a different perspective to the normal approach would be useful—and they encouraged it. One former academic colleague influenced significantly my journey through this topic. Dr Ron Knight, a senior practitioner and at one time an academic colleague, inspired my understanding of strategy and my views of its importance to effective professional practice. Tracy Jones and Marisa Gerussi, both Public Relations Institute of Australia colleagues—Tracy a former National President—continually reinforce my view that effective strategic thinking and planning are keys to communication program success. Gai Brodtmann, Richard Buddle, Holly Castro, Associate Professor Joy Chia, Dr Leanne Glenny, Dr Tony Jaques, the late Peter Lazar, Professor Kerry McCallum, Professor Jim Macnamara, Robert Masters, Professor Sora Park, Thomas Parkes, Professor Emeritus Peter Putnis, Dr Marianne Sison, Professor Robina Xavier, and the late Professor Emeritus Warwick Blood, all academic or professional colleagues, have in significant ways contributed to this work through myriad interactions on diverse topics that always activated my own thinking.

Countless scholars have contributed to my thinking about this topic. Specifically, the works of Professor Anne Gregory, Huddersfield University, Emeritus Professor Robert Heath, University of Houston, and Professor Emeritus Kirk Hallahan, Colorado State University, have been significant catalysts for aspects of this book. So, too, has the critical scholarship of Dr Johanna Fawkes, Professor Shirley Leitch, Dr Kevin Moloney, Professor Judy Motion, Professor Juliet Roper and Professor Kay Weaver, and a range of European scholars—even though much of what is here remains in the classic, process-oriented realm of strategy-making.

Karen Hildebrandt of Taylor & Francs has supported the book from the moment the concept was presented to her and has since been an encouraging publisher, willing to advise, and always courteous. The Routledge production team has produced a terrific book.

Dr Janine Mahoney, my wife, and daughters Emma and Holly and their families have been totally supportive, as ever. I thank them for that.

To the people who read and use this book, students at all levels—whether still studying or in practice revising what they already do—enjoy, and I hope you find in it what you are looking for.

James Mahoney

The Brief

Strategic communication practice is one of the world's most exciting professions. Not only does it deal with what people believe about issues and products, how those views might be changed or how they can be convinced to buy a product, but it is also a profession in which no two days are ever the same. There is always a new challenge, new people to meet, new situations to investigate and important decisions to take. In opening this book, you are starting a journey that goes to the heart of this professional practice: exploring how to plan and write an effective communication strategy. Knowledge about why this is important, and the ability to write an effective strategy, will be one of the most important job-ready skills that will make you a highly valued employee.

So far, most of your assignments have been based on strategies developed by others so that you can enhance the technical skills you have developed. Now it is time for a new challenge that involves a quantum leap from applying your technical skills to strategic thinking and planning. In this new place, you need to be aware not only of the vast array of powerful communication tools that are available to you but to know how, why and when to use them effectively in what situations for which target publics.

The writing and technical professional practice skills you have developed, and the theoretical principles underlying communication that you have studied, now all come together to focus on why and how an organisation should communicate to people who are important to it about issues that concern both. You will now need to be interested in the world around you and the organisation you work for, and the things that are happening in your society and culture, in local, national and often international politics and in the economy.

This is the time to face the reality that what you do in strategic communication practice should be based on serious thinking about how to solve a client's issue. To be effective, it involves far more than a technical approach of issuing media releases, social media activity and all the other tactical communication tools available to you. It is planned communication based on research and rational decision-making. In the context of the war in Ukraine, former Australian Major General, Mick Ryan (2022), wrote that "Effective strategic thinking is more important than tactical excellence." That is also an appropriate way of thinking about how a strategic communication plan will help deal with a client's issues. That is, no matter how fancy the tools you decide to use are, they won't be effective if you have not thought deeply about a strategic approach that

DOI: 10.4324/9781003317579-1

uses appropriate goals, objectives, target publics, messages and communication pathways.

This book will guide you through planning a communication strategy in two ways.

First, it departs somewhat from the view that communication strategy involves an integrated approach to marketing, advertising, sales promotion, public relations and the specialisations in those professions. Instead, the book is grounded in the concept that strategic communication goes beyond the immediate bottom-line profit aims of integrated marketing communication, to deal with longer-term issues. This idea is explored through a framework that suggests communication strategy should be linked to the way in which organisations plan their business activities (see p. 45) in three time 'horizons': what they need to do now, in the mid-term and in the long term. This approach links strategic communication planning to how organisations plan their business activity. It does not ignore the need for integrated communication, but it does suggest that how organisations deal with public policy issues influences their market-related communication. Working out how issues influence organisational communication involves strategic thinking, analysis and planning. The book also suggests that strategic communication, when viewed this way, is a specialist discipline that is so important to an organisation's success that it should be the leading practice in the communication system.

Second, the book applies the classic approach to researching, planning and writing a communication strategy in the context of the horizons approach to issue management. That approach can be used, with some specific professional differences, to devise marketing communication, advertising and public relations strategies. Where it differs here, apart from some changes to terminology, is in the book's focus on issues and what is colloquially described as 'the big picture.'

AN EXAMPLE OF STRATEGIC COMMUNICATION IN ACTION

When the Australian Competition and Consumer Commission (ACCC), a national regulatory authority, advertised nationally for a General Manager, Strategic Communications, the role required a senior practitioner to:

- Provide high-level advice to the chairman and the chief executive to ensure that the ACCC's goals were underpinned by timely and relevant communication strategies
- Advise on stakeholder relations, public information and issues management
- Develop and manage the commission's internal and external communications, publications and online services
- Chair the commission's Strategic Communications Committee, which is responsible for high-level decision-making on communications and positioning.

Contenders needed substantial senior communications and issues-management experience, excellent strategic-thinking skills with a strong outcomes' orientation, first-class interpersonal and communications skills and the ability to handle complex and time-critical tasks. In the space of one advertisement, the important elements of strategic communication planning and practice were brought together to describe a senior job.

ABOUT THE BUSINESS OF ORGANISATIONS

Discussions about communication strategy focus on the notion of an organisation's business. That word, business, is used in its broadest sense. Communication practitioners are employed by corporations, not-for-profit organisations, industry associations, charities, service clubs, aid organisations, political institutions, sporting clubs, celebrities and commercial businesses and industries. Thus, business does not only have the commercial meaning of making and selling products, earning and, sometimes, losing money; it also means a person's occupation, or the things that concern or interest them. It is in this sense that charities, not-for-profit organisations, government departments and agencies and so on engage in business. Their interests are in providing services for others. Of course, all organisations need money to finance what they do, and they must be aware of, and contain, the costs of pursuing their interests. Charities, for example, raise funds to finance their activities or to support scientific research, and report annually on how those funds are spent. Most make a point of explaining how much of the money they raise is spent on the causes they support, and how little goes in administrative expenses. It is also vital for a charity to be aware of community attitudes to donating funds to support particular causes. For example, a charity would need to know whether people donate more money to support medical research on childhood diseases than they do to those organisations that provide clothing to homeless people in winter. By understanding these aspects of the context in which it operates, a charity can plan effective campaigns for fund-raising, promoting its good works and showing how it will spend the money it raises.

ASKING QUESTIONS

You will be asked a lot of questions as you work through the chapters. That's to help you develop your critical thinking skills and to look beyond what might be immediately obvious.

In researching and writing a communication strategy, you, too, should ask a lot of questions—of your client, of your co-workers, and about the research you'll need to do to write the situation analysis. The most important questions will be based on that set of simple, but fundamental, words journalists use for basic information gathering: 5Ws and H. They are, What, When, Where, Who, Why and How. For your strategic communication planning, you'll need to ask questions like,

■ What do I need to find out about the issues that affect my client's organisation?

Who is important to this organisation and the issues it faces?

■ Where will I find that information?

What kind of research will I need to use to find out about the issues?

■ Why is this information important?

When will I do that research?

■ How will the research findings be used?

And you'll probably think of others you need to ask using those words.

Later in the book you'll read about writing an evaluation plan for your strategy after it has been implemented. One way of approaching a campaign evaluation would be to use questions based on 5Ws and H to work how well it worked—but we'll see how that approach would apply in the evaluation chapter.

Writing in *The Public Relations Strategist* (Winter, 2011), US practitioner Paul Oestreicher gave some clues as to why critical thinking is important. Oestreicher (2011) drew lessons from King Arthur, Camelot and the Round Table to guide communication and leadership. He came up with ten points of 'Camelot Wisdom':

■ Get help. Always ask questions—learning never stops.

Exercise empathy. It's a strength, not a weakness.

■ Remain ethical. Openness may sometimes be restricted, but honesty never is.

Confront issues. Move past anticipation and anxiety to deal with problems and opportunities.

■ Draw boundaries. Professional and personal lives may blend but we must maintain perspective.

Plan ahead. We need time to think.

■ Involve others. We can't (and shouldn't) do it all; our power grows by using the power of others.

Use symbols. Facts and ideas become rallying points when linked to image and cachet.

■ Create balance. Think and feel; analyse and do.

Understand control. Define roles and expectations; know what you can and can't influence.

That advice is valuable for researching and writing a communication strategy, and for guiding professional, ethical practice.

So now to explore strategic communication planning. The first chapter will set out how to use the book, and the second will define the nature of strategic communication in depth. Then we'll consider the detail of how to plan and prepare the elements of strategy and some theoretical principles that will help in decision-making. Above all, enjoy the journey.

GUIDED TOUR

How to use this book

Strategic Communication: Campaign Planning is enriched with a range of features designed to help support and reinforce your learning. This guided tour shows you how to best utilise your textbook and get the most out of your study.

Introductory panel

Each chapter begins with a panel that sets out the goals and objectives that you should achieve by working through the chapter. The panel includes the principle that guides the development of the specific strategic plan element that the chapter covers and also identifies a professional practice aspect for the chapter's topic.

Key terms and glossary

Key definitions are highlighted throughout the text. The definitions are also included in a complete glossary at the back of the book for easy reference.

CHAPTER EXERCISES

Included throughout the text are Chapter Exercises. These are designed to help you revise aspects of a strategy covered in the chapter. Some of these exercises are called Strategic Plan Checklists which are designed to help you work on your strategic plan (see Chapter 1).

Cases

Case examples are provided to help you choose a strategic plan topic.

In Theory panels

Some chapters include In Theory Panels. These highlight and discuss a particular theory or theories relevant to the content.

Further reading

Each chapter will suggest further reading as a guide to broadening your understanding of the topics covered in the book.

Evaluation panels

Each chapter concludes with an evaluation panel which uses case-method questions to help you review what you have learnt from the chapter content.

Chapter 1
What this book is about

Goal: To introduce this book and explain how to benefit from it.

Objectives: At the end of this chapter, you should:

1. Understand how the chapter topics work together to build your knowledge of the principles behind, and practice of, planning and implementing a strategic communication plan

    ■ Be aware of the basic framework for a strategic communication plan

2. Choose a topic to begin building a strategic communication plan you will prepare as you work through this book.

Principle: All strategic communication should be based on a detailed plan.

Planning: Researching the positive and negative issues facing an organisation is the first step in planning a communication strategy.

Practice: Professional practitioners use strategic plans to achieve goals and objectives for their clients.

Planning a communication strategy is a major task. A strategy sets the direction for all activities, from the simplest door-stop media interview, marketing communication or regular communication with employees, through to a major political lobbying campaign or an ongoing program to make sure an organisation's brand reputation is maintained. In the context of the western alliance's withdrawal from Afghanistan, the senior Australian practitioner, and former military officer, Bob Crawshaw, wrote

> Strategy is the framework from which all else hangs.
> *Canberra Times*, 3 September 2021

A strategy—or strategic plan—makes sure communication activities have clear purposes and have the best possible chances of achieving positive, measurable outcomes. Some dictionaries use "master plan" as a synonym for "strategy" and that is a good way of describing a strategic communication plan. It is a master plan setting out what is needed to achieve clearly defined goals and objectives.

Successful communication strategic plans, whether for advertising, public relations, or integrated communication, ensure that nothing is implemented without a reason.

Strategic communication deals with how strategic communication plans are prepared by exploring the principles that underpin this important professional work. We examine the professional practice steps involved in, and after, this planning: researching, writing and implementing a communication strategy. I use the term strategic communication to describe a range of professional practice specialties: corporate communication; community relations; financial and investor relations; public affairs, government relations and lobbying; internal communication; marketing communication; public relations; public sector communication. The framework set out here can be used for planning specific communication strategies for each of these specialisations or for specific projects. For example, the framework could be used to prepare the investor-relations communication plan for a major retail company, or it could be used for the retailer's new share offer. The framework is also appropriate for the top-level strategy that would set the directions for an organisation's entire professional communication effort, and to which each specialisation and functional area would link specific project strategic plans.

Strategy the term used to describe what organisations or individuals will do to achieve goals, usually over the long term.

Senior practitioners—either the managers of communications teams or those who specialise in strategy—are responsible for planning the details of what, how and why their organisations communicate with their target publics. This planning reflects their experience and their regular, sometimes daily, interactions with top management. An organisation's most senior managers (known as the "dominant coalition") need to know how communication activities can enhance business performance. That requirement means senior communicators must understand almost as much about the organisation, the market environment in which it operates and the potential impact of socio-economic and political issues on its operations as do members of the dominant coalition. But it is important for all those who work in a strategic communication function to understand how to research, write and implement a strategic communication plan. Being able to do this gives new graduates enhanced skills that make them more employable.

Dominant coalition the most influential people in an organisation in a specific situation.

Strategic plans should be prepared for an individual project, like the launch of a new product, or to set a cohesive and integrated framework for all the components of the organisation's continuing communication program.

For example, when a manufacturer launches a new product, perhaps a new mobile phone model, its public relations staff or its external consultants will plan a communication strategy to make sure the relevant news and specialist media, potential customers and retailers are aware of the new product. This strategic plan might include a special event to launch the new phone, a program of visits to retailers to explain the new model's advanced features, and a media kit that includes a news release and other material, like technical information, for specialist journalists who write about telecommunications. Importantly, the plan will outline why the manufacturer needs the strategic communication plan, what it aims to achieve, who the target publics are, the messages that need to be communicated and how messages will be delivered. It will also outline the resources (people, funds and technology) needed to make the plan work and set out how success will be measured. Detailed planning makes sure that advertising, sales and public relations efforts are integrated so that goals, objectives and messages are consistent. This approach also means that everyone involved in communicating messages knows what they have to do, when they have to do it and to whom their messages will be directed.

Strategic communication plan a document that describes how an organisation will achieve its communication goals and objectives.

Strategic communication plans have clear links to an organisation's business strategy. All successful organisations have strategic business plans that set out what they want to achieve and how they'll go about pursuing goals and objectives. Strategic business plans include a great deal of financial and operational information, and they are used to guide all parts of the organisation in planning their activities and how they'll achieve, for example, production and sales targets. The company's strategic communication plan will reflect and support those goals and objectives by listing activities designed to establish and maintain positive relationships with a range of people, including staff, who are important to the company's success. Many organisations have strategic plans that set out how they will deal with advertising, marketing communication, public relations and employee relations.

When you are writing a strategic communication plan, think of it as a stepwise process, one in which all the elements progress in a series of distinct stages, but are nevertheless linked. For example, you cannot set objectives until you have identified goals; messages can't be delivered to specific target publics until you work out what pathways will be needed and what tools you'll use. And, the most important point of all: every step in the planning stages relies on an adequately researched situation analysis that sets the scene for deciding what follows in the strategy. Researching and writing that analysis will begin with a brief from your client that sets out what they want to achieve. Figure 1.1 shows the steps you'll need to follow in this process and explains what each step involves.

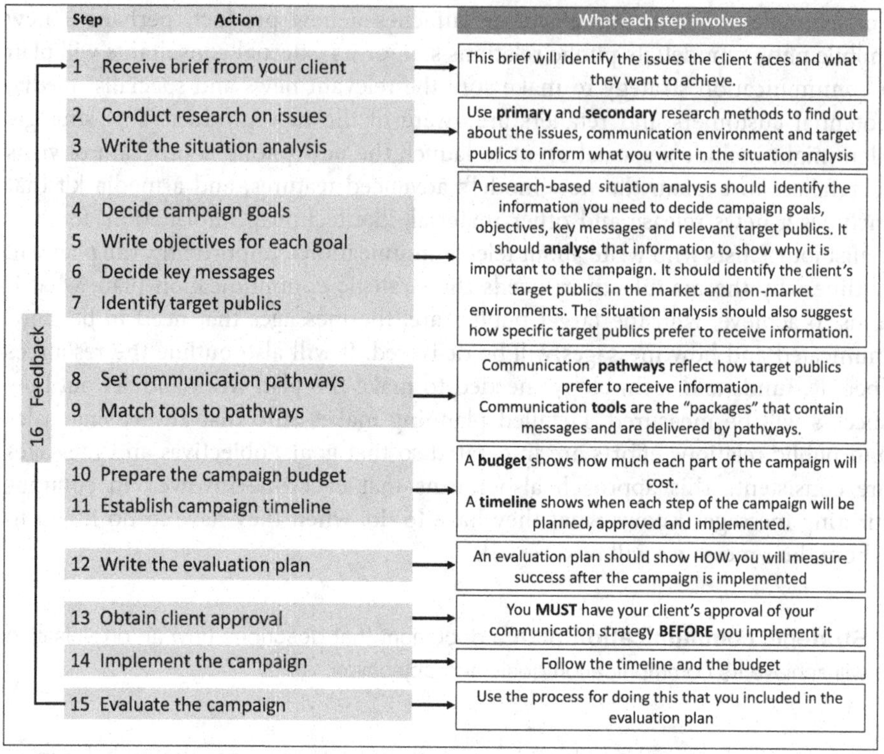
Step
Action
What each step involves
1 Receive brief from your client
This brief will identify the issues the client faces and what they want to achieve.
2 Conduct research on issues
3 Write the situation analysis
Use primary and secondary research methods to find out about the issues, communication environment and target publics to inform what you write in the situation analysis
4 Decide campaign goals
5 Write objectives for each goal
6 Decide key messages
7 Identify target publics
A research-based situation analysis should identify the information you need to decide campaign goals, objectives, key messages and relevant target publics. It should analyse that information to show why it is important to the campaign. It should identify the client's target publics in the market and non-market environments. The situation analysis should also suggest how specific target publics prefer to receive information.
8 Set communication pathways
9 Match tools to pathways
Communication pathways reflect how target publics prefer to receive information.
Communication tools are the "packages" that contain messages and are delivered by pathways.
10 Prepare the campaign budget
11 Establish campaign timeline
A budget shows how much each part of the campaign will cost.
A timeline shows when each step of the campaign will be planned, approved and implemented.
12 Write the evaluation plan
An evaluation plan should show HOW you will measure success after the campaign is implemented
13 Obtain client approval
You MUST have your client's approval of your communication strategy BEFORE you implement it
14 Implement the campaign
Follow the timeline and the budget
15 Evaluate the campaign
Use the process for doing this that you included in the evaluation plan
16 Feedback

Figure 1.1 Strategic planning steps

A NOTE OF CAUTION

Some of the terms used in this book, like strategy, messages and target publics, do not sit comfortably with some academics. Critical analysis of communication strategy by academics and some professional practitioners has led them to express concern that working with these terms, and planning how they will be used, suggests a one-sided approach to communication that does not include genuine attempts to engage in transparent discussions with people who are interested in an issue. That is because people are targeted with messages delivered through communication tools. It can seem as though organisations use their greater power to win a debate because they have more resources than individuals do; a more equitable approach would be to engage in a transparent conversation between equals based on their shared interests.

In a world dominated by social media and in light of discussions about how this phenomenon has enabled people to access and use information, critics argue that planning communication in this way demonstrates an old-fashioned, mass-media approach to professional communication. Social media are not about messaging, nor are those who access their myriad applications "targets" for anything: they are equal participants in conversations about things and issues in which they have a mutual interest. Organisations who want to understand those social media conversations ought to be on their best behaviour and to listen before contributing. Perhaps they won't need to contribute at all but will simply become aware of what people say about them.

These important issues will be dealt with later in *Strategic Communication*. But two points need to be made. First, we must be aware of legitimate criticisms of planned communication and understand that personal and professional ethical standards should always guide the way in which we practise all aspects of strategic communication. Second, all professions have schemas, or frameworks, for the way in which they approach their work. Doctors, for example, have protocols for medical examinations and use specific terms to define what it is they do, how they do it and what they find; lawyers, accountants, business managers and pilots have similar systems and discipline-specific terms that help them do their jobs.

The strategic communication framework examined in *Strategic Communication* is the schema, including discipline-specific terminology that professional communicators use to plan, implement and evaluate the work they do for internal and external clients. Sometimes, to do this, individual practitioners develop their own language or terminology based on their professional experience. Many communication consultancies (or agencies) do this. As we'll see later in the chapter, sometimes this terminology varies according to the communication discipline in which a practitioner works.

It is also important to recognise that in our profession, "plan" and "strategy" are often interchangeable words that describe the document that sets out what an organisation needs to achieve its goals. That is why you'll become familiar with terms like "strategic communication plan," "communication strategy" and "strategic plan" in your studies and professional practice.

HOW THE CHAPTERS WORK

Strategic Communication is structured to help you research and plan a communication strategy as they work through the chapters. To do that, each reader should select a topic for which they will write a strategic communication plan (for help doing this, See Section "Choosing a topic for your strategic plan project"). Each chapter deals with how you can plan a specific element for your communication strategy and with the principles and relevant theories that inform that part of the strategy. Each chapter shows how the principles and planning are brought together in professional practice. Together, the chapters build an integrated framework for researching, planning and writing a communication strategy.

INTRODUCTORY PANELS

As you saw at the start of this one, each chapter begins with a panel that sets out the goals and objectives that you should achieve by working through the chapter. As you work through *Strategic Communication*, you will learn that goals and objectives have important specific—and different—roles in a strategic communication plan. The panels include the principles that guide the development of the specific strategic plan element that the chapter covers. For example, the principle for the chapter dealing with target publics addresses the need to identify clearly and precisely who these people are. Each panel also identifies a planning step (sometimes, steps) and a professional practice aspect for the chapter's discussions.

EXERCISES AND THE CASE METHOD

Exercises—sometimes in the text, sometimes at the end of the chapter—are designed to help you to develop your chosen strategy project. The exercises are an adaptation of the case method of learning pioneered and developed at Harvard University's Business and Law schools and used widely throughout the world. In the case method, students face real-life, sometimes ambiguous, situations (cases) and work as decision-makers to resolve them. Sometimes cases are taken from real life; sometimes lecturers invent cases to apply the business or legal principles being investigated. If you've seen the movie *Legally Blonde,* you'll have an idea from the university classroom scenes how it works. Similarly, many medical series on television show specialist doctors leading students through patient examinations and asking them questions. The principles that underpin aspects of a case, or a decision that needs to be made, aren't always learnt by attending lectures or listening to a recorded version—but can always be found in relevant textbooks. Before they go to class, students read about the principles, and they read through the case (sometimes there's more than one for each formal session). Then they use their class time to work through the issues they believe need to be resolved. Classroom discussions are led by lecturers, who pose questions like:

Eliseo, why is that issue important?
How could the organisation address that question?
What else could the organisation do, and why?
Sam, do you agree with Valentina's answer, and why?
Jorja, when would it be important for the organisation to do what Sam has
    suggested?

If you are working in a class based on the case method, don't expect your lecturer to say whether your answer is correct or not. If you ask a question, especially if you ask whether your original answer was correct, the response is likely to be, "What do you think, and why?" And after you've answered, the lecturer might say, "Thomas, do you agree with William's answer?" And once Thomas replies, the lecturer is likely to ask, "Eliseo, how would you approach this issue?" And so it goes. Throughout a semester, everyone in the class will be required to answer questions. By working in this way, the lecturer is probing students' understanding and application of the business, legal or medical principles involved in the case. Sometimes the case method frustrates students because questions are not always resolved—just like in real life. But that's OK: it just means students will (or should) go away from the class to further explore the principles and their application. Normally students work outside class in small groups to help each other understand the next week's cases and the principles that will be explored, and to anticipate the questions that might be asked of them. That helps their learning.

In *Strategic Communication*, the case approach has been adapted to pose questions based on the principles covered in each chapter, which should be applied in the context of the strategic planning project that you are developing. Use the questions to work through the decisions you need to make about each element of the strategy you are preparing. For example, in the chapter on situation analysis, you'll need to ask at least the following questions about your project:

- What external issues are important to the situation the organisation is facing?
  Why are they important?
- Who else is interested in them, and why are they interested?
  How can I find out more about these issues and their impact on my organisation?

In some chapters, the exercises focus on actual cases, for which summaries are provided. Where this occurs, the case method is used to guide readers through a critical analysis of why certain decisions were taken. For example, in a case dealing with political communication, questions might be:

Why would an uncontrolled communication channel be chosen to distribute information via the mass news media?
Do you agree with that decision, and why?
What would be an alternative way of delivering information in this situation?

Answering those questions requires an understanding of the situation that the strategy is dealing with; the goals and objectives that have been set for the strategy; the target publics and the ways in which they prefer to receive information—all topics dealt with in previous chapters. The principles needed to answer most of these questions can be found somewhere in the text; answering others may require wider reading

Your lecturers may apply the case teaching method to their classes about advertising, marketing communication or public relations strategic planning because it works really well with the problem-solving needed in these classes.

EVALUATION PANELS

Each chapter concludes with an evaluation panel. These use case-method questions to help you review what you have learnt from the chapter content.

A STRATEGIC COMMUNICATION PLAN FRAMEWORK

All professional communication disciplines use the same basic framework for strategies. Some names for individual elements of the strategic plan vary—for example, "target audiences" for advertising, and "target publics" for public relations. No matter how strategic planners in advertising, marketing communication or public relations describe each element, there's a common purpose: the need to be as precise as possible about what they mean.

Strategic Communication adapts the classic framework for researching and preparing a public relations strategy because it is a straightforward approach to communication planning that covers all the required, and easily defined, elements for an effective plan. The framework is set out in Table 1.1, in which elements of a strategy are listed and briefly defined. Later chapters will expand on the definitions.

Two specific changes have been made: the classic "message delivery strategies" element has been renamed "communication pathways"; the traditional term "tactics" that describes the things practitioners produce has been replaced by "communication tools." Both adaptations simplify what these elements of a plan mean and more clearly link the concept of having to first reach a target public

Table 1.1 Strategic communication elements and definitions

Element	Definition
○ **Situation analysis**	○ This is a narrative that provides a detailed analysis of the communication issues and opportunities facing an organisation. The analysis is based on formative research.
○ **Goals**	○ Broad statements of what the organisation hopes to achieve with its communication strategy, goals reflect an organisation's business strategy and deal with reputation, relationships or tasks. A plan can have one or more goals – but for efficiency, don't write more than three.
○ **Objectives**	○ These are precise and measurable statements of what an organisation needs to do to achieve a goal. Regard objectives as steps towards achieving a goal. Objectives express exactly what needs to be achieved in a defined time frame. They deal with raising awareness, or building acceptance, or convincing publics to take action in support of the organisation. Each goal can have one or more objectives.
○ **Messages**	○ These convey information to target publics to create awareness about a client's product or views about an issue, to build credibility or to persuade a target public to take some action that will support the client's interests. Messages can be informative or persuasive. Formative research will help to identify gaps in knowledge among specific target publics and therefore messages that might be needed to increase their awareness.

Table 1.1 continued

Element	Definition
○ **Target publics**	○ These are the people who receive messages to raise awareness, generate acceptance and promote action. Formative research for a public relations plan will help you identify your client's target publics.
○ **Communication pathways**	○ Sometimes described as "message delivery" or "communication" strategies, these are the methods that explain how messages will reach target publics. For example, in this book actually talking to someone, or a group, in person—at a meeting, or in one-to-one conversation—about an issue facing your organisation would be described as "an interpersonal communication pathway."
○ **Communication tools**	○ These are the communication products that target publics see or experience or use. They are the "packages" used to deliver messages. Common examples of communication tools are websites, blogs, podcasts, tweets, videos, displays, publications, meetings, media releases, posters, annual reports, speeches and special events. In some texts, the traditional term "tactics" is used to describe these communication tools.
○ **Implementation**	○ This describes the details of the financial, human and technological resources needed to put the strategy into action. Preparing this part of the strategy includes planning a timeline for when things need to be done and creating a checklist of actions and responsibilities.
○ **Evaluation**	○ This explains how the success of the strategy will be measured. Among the basic questions for an evaluation are: did we achieve our goals and objectives? Did the target publics take the action we sought? Was the plan completed on time and within budget? In each case, ask: if not, why not? Can we do it better next time? What stopped us from achieving our goals and objectives? An evaluation should compare outcomes and outputs with objectives.

(through a communication pathway) before being able to deliver a message with an actual product (or tool). This also avoids confusing when the terms "strategy" and "tactical" are used elsewhere in communication planning. If you think the use of "pathways" could be clearer, you could use "message delivery pathways."

CHOOSING A TOPIC FOR YOUR STRATEGIC PLAN PROJECT

Now you are ready to choose a case for the strategic communication plan project on which you'll work as you progress through *Strategic Communication*. You could choose an organisation that you are involved with (perhaps you work there) or a public issue about which you are personally concerned. It is important that you choose a case that you can research with the resources available to you, so that your strategy project will be manageable. You can find valuable information through desk research using an organisation's website, especially its annual report, mission statements and other information under the "About us" or "Investor relations" tab and in the "Media centre," especially in the media releases, the annual report, factsheets, senior managers' speeches, and other corporate information likely to be published there. This desk research will help you understand the organisation, the industry in which it is involved, the issues that concern it and its attitude towards the people who are important to it. This, in turn, will enable you to prepare a situation analysis—the important first step in developing a strategic communication plan.

The vast resources of the internet—including the sites of public opinion research companies; government agencies (especially those that collect census and other official statistical data); the research sections of congressional, parliamentary, and other important libraries; and industry associations—can help in this formative research. Reading, watching or listening to the news media and perusing online news sites will enable you to build your awareness of current economic, political and social issues and the background to them.

As you work with the book from here, imagine that you are a senior professional who is writing a strategic communication plan for your organisation. Think about that plan in three dimensions:

- What needs to be done now to meet the organisation's current communication requirements
- The emerging issues that might affect the organisation in 12 months to 5 years
- How the organisation can communicate its long-term plans and deal with issues that it may face five to ten years from now.

Working in these dimensions means you need to identify current and emerging social and economic issues and analyse their potential impact on your organisation. You need to ask questions. For example, if you had just started working as a senior communication practitioner for a mining company, you'd need to rapidly understand the kinds of issues it faces: What government environmental policies does the company need to be aware of? What are the company's views on those issues? Does it have a view? Does it need a view? (Most will, of course.) What effect do the company's operations have on climate change? How many people does it employ? Where does it sell its minerals: only domestically or to export markets? Is the company profitable? What social and economic issues affect the company's performance now, and what issues are likely to emerge in the next five years? What political issues concern the company now—or will the next time there's an election? How would you prioritise these issues?

Here are some examples of possible project topics that you could use as cases as you work through the book. All can be researched from public sources such as the internet but the names of the organisations are fictitious.

CHAPTER EXERCISE

Analysing an issue

Visit the website of your state's largest newspaper to find and read an article that deals with an issue. Maybe it is about delays in completing major road-works, falling literacy rates in secondary schools, obesity or a proposed new sporting complex to be built on parkland.

Identify and list the categories of people for whom this is an important issue. Segment your list so that the categories are clear. For example, don't just write "the media." Be specific about which media you mean: sports journalists for sports topics; political reporters and commentators for politics; police reporters for crime stories. And don't say "the general public." Be specific about who in "the general public" you mean.

Answer the following questions:

- Why would the people in your list be interested in this topic?
  How many people are likely to be affected by the issue?
- What is the background to the issue?
  Is this issue important? Why?
- Does the article have all the information that the people on your list would need to make up their minds about the issue?
  What other information would they need to make up their minds?
- Which group is *directly affected* by this issue? Which is *indirectly affected* but may *influence* the first group? Which group is *not affected* by the issue at all but can *influence* the others?

Product tampering

For this project, assume that you work for High Health, a company that produces complementary health products—that is, non-pharmaceutical tablets such as vitamin pills. You've been asked to write a communication strategy that the company could implement if it was subjected to a claim that someone had tampered with its products, thus making them unsafe for human consumption. This would be planning for communication in a crisis. The principles you use to write this strategy would be the same as those you'd use to write a strategy promoting the health benefits of, say, vitamin B, except you'd be researching and planning for a situation that, you hope, would not occur. You would have a strategy to set out what you would need to achieve and how you would go about it. For this project, let's assume that we are planning for the possibility of someone ringing the company anonymously to claim that they had tampered with the company's unbottled stock of echinacea tablets by spreading rat poison in the bins in which the tablets are stored. How would the company manage this situation? With whom would it need to communicate? What messages would it have for its target publics? How would it deliver them? When?

Convincing young Americans to register to vote

Your strategic communication consultancy, Right Direction Communication, has its headquarters in the capital city of an American state (choose one). The Secretary of State is concerned at the low level of young people in the State who are eligible to register to vote—and later to vote—who have not registered, especially as there are elections due next year. Right Direction Communication has been contracted to help the Secretary of State resolve this issue and because you are a mid-twenties rising star in the consultancy you've got the job of writing a strategic communication plan. However, you've never registered to vote, so you need to research the election law to find out as much as you can before you start to plan the strategy. That research has convinced you to register as the experience will help in your strategic planning.

Sudden infant death syndrome and sleeping posture

This is a serious worldwide problem that affects thousands of families. You are the communication manager for Sleep Tight, a new charitable organisation that promotes safe sleeping practices for babies up to 18 months old and that raises funds for research into sudden infant death syndrome. You've been asked to prepare a communication strategy that promotes safe baby sleeping practices. To whom do you need to give the essential messages? How would you do that? What goals and objectives would you need to pursue?

You could change the topic for this case to another serious childhood disease: Neuroblastoma, which receives relatively little research funding in comparison to other childhood diseases. If you take on this case, research neuroblastoma and assume you are the Communication Director of your State''s Neuroblastoma Foundation (not an actual name) that is about to start a fund-raising campaign to contribute to research for a cure for this disease. It is seeking a million dollars during the campaign, which will last two years. You have been asked to research, plan and implement communication plan for the campaign.

Light rail planned for your city

Your state government is responsible for public transport infrastructure. It has decided that your capital city needs a light rail system to reduce traffic congestion caused by the ever-increasing use of cars. The new metro will be built and operated by a private company, Integrated Metro Lines Inc. The company has bought the right to be the sole operator for US$800 million and has experience in building and running light rail in other cities and overseas. The first line for your city's "Rapid Metro" will take four years to build but will serve 100,000 residents when it is operational. Not everyone in your city agrees with the light rail project. Environmental, residents' and business groups argue it will cost too much, destroy native trees along the route and cause huge disruptions to traffic flow while it is being built. The state government argues that the US$1 billion construction cost is the average cost for such a metro system, that it will create jobs and boost the state economy. It says the US$500 million paid by Integrated Metro Lines will offset construction costs. The government's research has found that the native trees, which were planted 40 years ago, were not appropriate for the area, are dying anyway, and that the new landscaping included in the project will introduce more appropriate and healthier trees. The government concedes that normal traffic and pedestrian flows will be disrupted during the construction phase but argues that the metro, once extended across the city, will be a cost-effective solution to growing traffic gridlock.

You work for a local communication consultancy that has been hired to research and write a strategic plan for a campaign to promote the government's views to residents of your city. What issues would be included in the situation analysis? What would the goals and objectives be for this campaign, and who would be the target publics? How would you reach them and what communication tools would you recommend? What messages would be used in the campaign?

Road safety–young women driving with mobile phones

The government has told your boss, Angela Morrison, the chief executive of the State Transport Authority, that it wants a strategic communication program aimed at preventing people driving while using their mobile phones, especially young people and especially young women aged 18–25. It's now your job to research and plan the program. Who would be your primary, secondary and tertiary target publics—and why? What do you know about them, their attitudes and how they access information? How would you reach them with the campaign messages? What would you say to them?

A community consultation

For 50 years, a ten-hectare block of rural land in the outer-suburban council area of Woolamarook has been a waste management facility. The city council has decided to rehabilitate the land, in the historic, semi-rural suburb of Ferrytown, and to build a new community centre that will have meeting facilities, a hall and kitchen for social functions, a small library and a child-care centre. The suburb was one of the earliest farming areas settled in the state and it is on the site of the first ferry crossing on the Perch River—a crossing that enabled products from rural areas on the other side of the river to be transported to the state's capital city, 100 kilometres to the east. Ferrytown has a population of 3,000 and, even though it is growing as a dormitory suburb for the capital city, it is surrounded by dairy farms. As the council's communication manager, you've convinced the chief executive that because US$25 million will be spent on the project, the Woolamarook Council should begin a community consultation process with the townspeople and surrounding farmers. What would you need to achieve with this consultation process? What would you need to say to the townspeople and farmers? How would you say it? How would you go about consulting with the townspeople?

Getting rid of plastic waste in Thailand–helping a 12-year-old girl

You have just arrived for a two-year posting to the Bangkok bureau of your international communication consultancy, Strategic Communication Solutions. Your first job is to work on a project being funded by a well-known international philanthropist, Tim Thompson, whose father was a champion of Thai silk manufacture, wants to fund a major initiative in Thailand to clean up plastic waste. Mr. Thompson read about the problem of plastic waste in Thailand when he was on holiday recently in Australia. He was so inspired by 12-year-old Lilly who is trying to rid Bangkok of plastic waste that he decided to fund an organisation, Let's Clean Up Plastic, to help. Lilly will become the spokesperson for the new organisation; Tim Thompson will be the chair.

To start your research, go to the news story Mr. Thompson read:

https://www.abc.net.au/news/2020-01-01/meet-thailands-answer-to-greta-thunberg/11817228

WHAT NEXT?

As you work through *Strategic Communication*, the chapter topics and exercises will help you to apply various elements of the strategic communication plan to your project. You will need to research widely, ask yourself questions about what you are doing and think about how, when and why you propose to do what you recommend.

Chapter 2 will start that process by discussing the nature of strategic communication and will introduce the concept of planning communication in the three dimensions mentioned earlier in this chapter.

CHAPTER EVALUATION

Answer the following questions to evaluate how much of the content in this chapter you now understand:

1. Do I understand how *Strategic Communication* will lead me through the strategic communication planning process?
2. Am I aware of the basic framework of a strategic communication plan?
3. Have I selected a topic for my strategic communication plan?
4. Do I understand how the chapters work?

Notice how these questions reflect the objectives set for the chapter. That is a principle we will cover in the chapters dealing with goals, objectives and evaluation.

Chapter 2
The nature of strategic communication

Goal: To explore what strategic communication means.

Objectives: This chapter will help you to:

- Appreciate the importance of analysing the potential impact of external issues on an organisation
  Understand how issues analysis and strategic communication are linked
- Recognise that strategic communication works in the mid- and long terms

Principle: Strategic communication addresses issues and supports organisational goals.

Planning: Researching and writing a communication campaign strategy involves careful planning to make sure it meets organisational goals and objectives.

Practice: Strategic communication advances organisational goals.

Strategic communication is about planning how an organisation will respond to issues that concern it. This chapter examines how that happens.

All professional communication should be based on a plan designed to manage responses to important social, economic, and political issues. Issues might be current—that is, happening now—or they might be longer-term issues that will affect what the organisation plans to do in five or more years. In both cases, the organisation needs to be aware of them so that it can work out how to deal with them. Our focus in this chapter is on how communication strategies deal with mid- and long-term issues—those that impact beyond the day-to-day operations of an organisation. These are the strategic horizons for planning communication programs. This does not mean that current issues—promoting products or services to customers, or organisational advocacy about an issue that is "happening now"—are unimportant to communication strategy. All are vital because they directly affect an organisation's profitability and its reputation. Generally, though, how an organisation deals with current issues is tactical practice. Product promotion, for example, is the tactical task of people working in marketing communication, and one for which there will be a specific plan linked to the organisation's business, communication,

DOI: 10.4324/9781003317579-3

and marketing plans. Similarly, day-to-day media relations—like writing and issuing media releases, conducting press conferences, updating the website newsroom and briefing journalists about current issues and events—will reflect the goals and objectives of an overarching communication strategic plan. In this book, the term used for these activities is **communication tools**.

> **Communication tools** are what practitioners produce in a campaign. They are what target publics see or experience including websites, blogs, podcasts, tweets, infographics, videos, displays, email, old-style snail-mail letters, publications (including regular employee newsletters posted on the web or, sometimes, in hard copy), meetings, media releases, posters, speeches, annual reports, staff meetings, face-to-face meetings with target publics and special events. These tools help achieve strategic outcomes.

The idea that communication practitioners must think beyond day-to-day tactical market considerations (product promotion, daily media relations) by working out what issues might emerge in a year or more and planning programs to deal with them is the key to effective communication. Richard Buddle, a senior international advertising expert, describes this approach as the "strategy you have before you have a strategy."

This process begins with issues analysis and management.

ISSUES ANALYSIS AND MANAGEMENT

Robert Heath and Michael Palenchar, American scholars of strategic issues management, highlight how important this process is by describing it as "an ancient business and communication practice" (2009, p. 5). Their "ancient" practice uses formal and informal research to work out what issues should concern an organisation, what they mean, what the organisaton's views about them might be, and what might be done about them. This is the start of both a business plan and a communication strategy. The American business professor Richard Rumelt explains the process this way: a strategist's key job is to find out the crucial factors in a situation and to design a way to coordinate and focus actions to deal with them (2011). That key job definition applies as much to communication strategy as it does to business strategy.

Let's look at what an issue is. The simplest explanation is that an issue is the subject of a debate. Issues are usually about things external to the organisation. For organisations, issues could involve changes in a government policy, or levels of customer satisfaction with a product or service, or the environment, or traffic problems, or the costs of health care, or the need to make target publics aware of a new product.

> **Issue** "a point in question; an important subject of debate" (Australian Concise Oxford Dictionary, 2004).

Issues of this kind create public debates and internal discussion about what they mean for an organisation. Heath and Palenchar view these debates about issues as routine in business management and communication practice. They argue that positive or negative outcomes in these debates can affect how organisations are managed. That is why they say that issue management must be performed strategically if organisations are to achieve corporate public policy and strategic business planning goals (2009, p. 121). The Australian expert Tony Jaques notes that not every issue is strategic, but that "all issue management should be strategic in its approach and implementation" (2009a, p. 21).

Boundary spanning what practitioners do when they interpret the external environment to an organisation's senior management and the organisation to external target publics. This involves environmental scanning (see below) to monitor, identify and analyse external and internal issues and the opportunities and threats those issues pose for organisations.

Counselling what senior practitioners do when they advise top management on communication solutions to current, emerging or potential issues.

Environmental scanning identifying and interpreting complex and changing environments—or business contexts—for clients.

This kind of analysis is part of strategic issues management. It identifies changes in the environment in which an organisation operates and how these changes will affect the organisation and its activities.

In professional communication, finding out about issues and advising on communication responses to deal with them is most often a task for the organisation's senior public relations practice leader. This responsibility reflects the dual roles of senior communication practitioners as **boundary spanners** and **counsellors**. Both are strategic roles, in which practitioners use formal and informal research techniques in their **environmental scanning** to identify issues and opinions target publics have about their organisations.

Boundary spanning has long been recognised as playing an important strategic role in program planning and management. Martha Lauzen (1997) observes that as a result of the environmental scanning involved in boundary spanning, communication counsellors develop significant knowledge of the world views and values of internal and external organisational constituencies, and that this knowledge represents a unique contribution to issue analysis and management. Ansgar Zerfass and Simone Huck (2007) make the important point that the strategic communication that follows this investigation of issues helps prepare organisations for uncertain futures.

ISSUES MANAGEMENT PROCESS

In this "quicksand of duelling definitions" about what an issue is, three distinct constructs have emerged (Jaques, 2009b). These constructs view issues in the contexts of dispute, expectation and impact themes, which Jaques (2009b) argues have broad scholarly and professional agreement.

The special significance of strategic issues management is that it gives an organisation a rational process through which it can work out the opportunities and threats that issues present by understanding:

- What the issues are
  who is promoting the issues—and why
- Who opposes the issues
  whether they are emerging issues or have an immediate impact
- What that impact might be
  whether there is strong support for the issues in the broad community
- After that analysis, the organisation can plan how, and when, to deal with an issue using strategic communication techniques.

IN THEORY: SOME ISSUE DEFINITIONS

In professional communication, issues are defined as disputes between two or more people (Hallahan, 2001), or as "unsettled matters," or points of conflict between an organisation and one or more of its publics (Cornelissen, 2005, p. 26). Others define issues as "controversial inconsistencies" caused by gaps between the expectations of corporations and those of their stakeholders or target publics, or as political and social problems (Dougall, 2008, p. 4; Grunig and Repper, 1992; Regester and Larkin, 2005).

Organisational issues are also described as external matters that could "positively or negatively affect [an organisation's] prosperity or survival" (Moloney, 2006, p. 37). Organisations, their stakeholders, and other constituencies may be concerned about the same issue but rarely share the same perspective (Dougall, 2008). Issues are strategic because they "compel" an organisation to deal with them when there is a conflict between two or more identifiable groups (Van Riel and Frombrun, 2008, p. 203). Bigelow and colleagues (1993) draw on the earlier work of other scholars (Ansoff, 1979; Bucholtz, 1988; King, 1982; Mahon and Bigelow, 1992; Mintzberg et al., 1976) to note that public issues are developments that will affect organisational performance. This means they are important for resource acquisition and the ability to meet objectives (Bigelow et al., 1993). Dougall (2008) notes that issues management "divine[s] and determine[s] the existence and likely impacts of these contestable points of difference" (p. 4) for organisations.

Hallahan (2001) argued that the origins of issues could be traced to "the moment" a person identified a situation to be problematic; that is, when it posed negative consequences for one or more people (p. 28). Such situations were attributed to the unfair or risky actions of others and emerge only when people share problems through communication, and analyse, define, delimit and label problems (Hallahan, 2001).

Hallahan (1999, 2001) notes that interpretations of how a problem or concern is understood, or explained, are at the heart of most issues and that disputants vie to have their preferred interpretation dominate. That is, issues involve disputants airing differing views in attempts to influence others by "altering their knowledge, attitudes, or actions" (Hallahan, 2001, p. 29). Such disputes usually arise over the allocation of resources or the treatment or portrayal of groups in society and frequently mean an extensive public discussion (Hallahan, 1999). That argument reflects Grunig and Hunt's (1984) view that publics form around issues. In an issue context, publics are defined by Hallahan (2001) as groups with which "an organisation wants to form a relationship" (p. 29).

It is these points about disputes over differing views, about how stakeholder relationships are built and about organisations and stakeholders having an interest in the same issues that create a core principle underpinning strategic issues communication. That is, stakeholder opinions need to be identified by professional issues analysis and appropriate responses to them planned in a strategic way.

Issues emerge when publics or stakeholders or both raise problems they believe need to be resolved in their interests (Pang, Jin and Cameron, 2010). That reflects Heath and Palenchar's (2009) argument that an issue is not what everyone believes but what some people strongly believe. In this view, people who strongly believe in something exert pressure for their views to be heard in public policy debates. Van Riel and Frombrun (2008) hold that the sooner a potential threat of an issue to an organisation's ability to achieve its business goals is recognised, the more likely the organisation is to take action on that issue. In Heath and Palenchar's (2009) view, debates about issues are routine in business management and communication practice and that the positive or negative outcomes of these debates can affect how organisations are managed. Thus, an issue is worthy of attention when it can have an impact on an organisation (Heath and Palenchar, 2009).

In summary, issues occur in an organisation's external environments when there are inconsistencies between its views on a socio-economic or political subject and those of one or more of its stakeholders. They are about disagreements that occur in public and they are often debated by the population, considered by governments and reported in the news media (Hallahan, 2001). Organisations are compelled to deal with issues because of the potential impact they could have on their operations, even the organisation's survival, and on their stakeholder relationships. In this sense dealing with them is a strategic practice. Issues are raised by people who strongly believe the issue should be resolved in their interests. Similarly, organisations raise and publicly address issues when they hold strong views about them and believe they should be resolved in the organisation's interests.

Lobbying attempts to influence someone or convert them to a particular point of view. Lobbying often happens in political contexts and involves meetings with bureaucrats and politicians about issues; submissions to formal inquiries; media releases on the organisation's views; and other public relations tasks.

Lobbyist specialist communication practitioner, often with experience in politics, who engages in lobbying on behalf of individual organisations and industry associations.

Industry associations organisations set up to represent the common interests of all the businesses in one industry. Sometimes they are formed as interest groups (e.g. environmental activists) to give them a united and stronger voice in public debates.

Here is an example of how this works. What would an ice cream manufacturer do if the government proposed a new health rule that increased the amount of fresh milk that must be included in its products? This would be both a political and economic issue for the company: political because it would involve government regulation; economic because it would have a financial cost to the business. The company would need to work out what that financial impact would be, as would other companies in the ice cream industry. Senior communication counsel would advise on what companies should say publicly, and how that should be done. They would also advise on how this issue should be raised with their staff. Together, the companies might find that implementing the regulation would be enormously expensive, meaning that the cost would have to be passed on to ice cream lovers through higher prices at the supermarket. That would probably lead the ice cream industry to **lobby** the government with an argument about why the new regulation would be bad. And they may decide to take their argument to their customers with a communication campaign. Other interests, perhaps community health groups, might oppose the industry and support the government's proposal on the basis of its health benefits. This would create a dynamic issues debate in which each participant would respond to the arguments of the others. If you scan your daily news source, you'll find examples of this in action. They might be a community group in the United States arguing for a tightening of gun-ownership laws; an environmental group urging a government to stop a planned urban development because it would destroy a fragile habitat for native animals; or the mining industry arguing against a new tax on its products. In each case, you will identify people and groups with different views advancing their opinions and perhaps refining them as the debate progresses.

Chong and Druckman's (2007) theory of competitive framing effects helps to explain the dynamics of issue debates and the complexities of issues analysis and management. Issue dynamics and complexities mean that "virtually all public debates involve competition between contending parties to establish the meaning and interpretation of issues. When citizens engage an issue … they must grapple

IN THEORY: ISSUE DYNAMICS

Public issue debates are dynamic in the sense that they change as the debate progresses. This is an important consideration for strategic communication planning; reading about theoretical principles will help you to understand the process.

Issues sometimes emerge unexpectedly, and the ways in which they are framed, and affect organisations, alter as others (often described in this context as social actors) join the debates about them. In these situations, professional communication practitioners' primary and subsequent decisions about advocating an organisational position, or stance on an issue, reflect the dynamics of issue debates. Heath and Palenchar (2009) extend this idea by noting that issue dynamics are not simply those that occur when organisations and activist groups engage in debate: issue dynamics also occur in industries, between activist groups and between government agencies (p. 120). They argue that in this "array of players, issues managers are wise to be concerned about understanding the dynamics of the various publics and the dynamics that motivate them" (Heath and Palenchar, 2009, p. 120).

Hallahan (2001) also views issues as complex, dynamic and as involving more than merely a dispute between two parties. In a reflection of classical issues management practice, Hallahan (2001) argues that to deal effectively with an issue, organisations and their managers need to develop an understanding of claims made and the context in which a particular issue evolves (p. 48). This understanding occurs as a result of environmental scanning and subsequent issues analysis, all of which contributes to a situation analysis.

The use of contingency theory in management and communication scholarship grew out of scholars' application of general systems theory to better understand organisational structures (Donaldson, 2006; Hatch and Cunliffe, 2006). In this view, organisations are complex systems involving dynamically interacting parts in which a change in one part can affect the behaviour of other parts (Beinhocker, 1999). Hodge and colleagues (2003) argue that contingency theory helps to model how organisations' constituent parts and external factors interact to achieve organisational goals and that these complex systems are path dependent.

It is in this perspective that contingency theory helps to understand how social, political and economic issues act as independent variables that influence organisational decisions on strategic communication directions. That is, while communicators must deal with an organisation's short-term needs (Argenti et al., 2005) in the market environment, the decisions they take about mid- to long-term strategy for the non-market environment are influenced by their analyses of the dynamics of issues beyond a tactical day-to-day approach.

Luoma-aho and Vos (2010) conceptualised issue arenas as the spaces in which organisations and their stakeholders dealt with multiple common issues. This concept is similar to Bach and Allen's (2010) argument about issue debates occurring in a non-market environment. However, Luoma-aho and Vos (2010) argue that practitioners and academics should focus on identifying the different issues facing organisations, and issue dynamics, before "trying to define stakeholders and their preferred ways of communicating" (p. 20). In their view, "Today, it is issues and topics, not organisations that are at the centre of communication" (Luoma-aho and Vos, 2010, p. 4).

In a reflection of the arguments of Bach and Allen (2010) about the importance of non-market environments, Luoma-aho and Vos (2010) propose that their concept is a paradigm shift from an organisation-centred focus on relationship management towards "monitoring and dialogue on issue arenas that are outside the organisation's control" (p. 15).

with opposing frames that are intended by opinion leaders to influence public preferences" (Chong and Druckman, 2007, p. 100).

Luoma-aho and Vos (2010) reflect the role of public affairs when they argue that organisations need to actively participate in various issue arenas so that they are "involved as a major player in co-producing outcomes" (p. 18). While this point resonates with the concept of dialogic communication, Luoma-aho and Vos (2010) note that the "underlying assumption is that if an issue arena is identified early on, the organisation has a better chance of becoming one of the major actors" (p. 18) in an issue debate.

While communicators must deal with an organisation's short-term needs (Argenti et al., 2005), the decisions they take about mid- to long-term strategy are influenced by their analyses of issues beyond a tactical day-to-day approach. This presents a professional practice challenge because issues evolve, sometimes as an organisation responds, or as publics, the news media and governments give them attention (Hallahan, 2001). Guth and Marsh (2006) locate issues in the evolution of public opinion, which, they argue, forms after a public debate leads to consensus and public policy. That is, public opinion begins to evolve when an issue is "injected" into public consensus and public and private debates over the issue ensue (Guth and Marsh, 2006, p. 155). Bigelow and colleagues (1993) describe this as the "path" of an issue that is affected as stakeholders engage and disengage in an issue debate (p. 22). Harrison (2011) describes issues as dynamic. Heath and Palenchar (2009) argue that as those involved in a dialogue advocate opinions, facts, evaluation and conclusions, issues take on content.

Issue dynamics are usually discussed in the context of issue life cycles that describe the way in which issues move, broadly, from public opinion formation to policy formulation to public policy implementation. Of course, issue life cycles are more complex than simple diagrams showing how they work. Generally, as issues may evolve over weeks, or years, an organisation's ability to influence them as public concerns about an issue rise over time declines. The normative four stages in an issue's life cycle are:

- ■ Defining the issue
  shaping the debates
- ■ Limiting or containing the issue
  shaping regulations, standards, plans.

In the first two stages, as public expectations change, an organisation's ability to define and shape issues is high. As an issue becomes politicised, and, say, government involvement decides the outcome, the organisation's ability to continue defining and shaping an issue debate declines. This illustrates how important it is for organisations to monitor current and emerging issues, plan responses to them, and to contribute to issue debates that concern them as soon as possible.

Issue identification is difficult because they are often complex, and many variables affect how they emerge and evolve. That means analysis becomes more demanding when:

- ■ Positions are ambiguous and complex
  many issues are being tackled and many participants are promoting their views and
- ■ An issue has not been well defined.

Because issues are dynamic, the ways in which they are framed and impact on organisations alter in the context of debates about them. Heath and Palenchar (2009) note that issue dynamics are not simply those that occur when an organisation and an activist group debate the issue, but also occur in industries, between activist groups, and between government agencies. In this array of players, issues managers need to understand the dynamics of the various publics and the dynamics that motivate them.

The dynamic nature of issues and the fact that they are often more complex than disputes between two parties, organisations and their managers need to understand the context in which a particular issue evolves (see Hallahan, 2001). They need to understand, too, that their organisation's strategic orientation results from the complex interaction of many internal and external factors, including multiple stakeholders.

In their critical analysis of the linearity inherent in traditional issue life cycles, Bigelow and colleagues (1993) deal with issue dynamics by arguing that issues may be at different stages of evolution depending on the perspectives and activities of each stakeholder. They argue that an issue's evolution begins before "stakeholders have established positions" and that public issues "may be resolved in arenas other than governmental ones" (p. 21). Thus, the resolution of public issues is more complex than that for other strategic issues (in their example, seeking a limited number of stakeholders' support for a strategic decision to introduce a new product: see Bigelow et al., 1993, p. 21). In their typology of issues evolution, Bigelow and colleagues (1993) suggest that not all issues move sequentially through all the stages implicit in a traditional issue life cycle. This is because issues "may be buffeted by a number of forces outside the control of any one organisation or stakeholder" (p. 21), causing deviations from the traditional issue life cycle model's linear, sequential path. These dynamic forces can be caused by facts, stakeholders, other issues and an inability to resolve an issue. Bigelow and colleagues (1993) argue "new facts and other issues may create a need for stakeholders to reinterpret issues and subsequently redefine their positions. The inflexibility of some stakeholder positions may stymie attempts to achieve resolution" (p. 23).

Bigelow and colleagues' (1993) typology of issues evolution suggests that some issues follow a recursive path "cycling back and forth through the stages" (p. 24) of the traditional issues cycle, and may never be resolved. The evolution of other issues skips stages or is interrupted by new facts, stakeholder actions or other issues attracting attention. The typology also proposes that some issues are enduring because of "an added complexity that makes resolution elusive" (Bigelow et al., 1993, p. 25). For a recursive issue, such complexity may reflect stakeholder diversity, the cost of solutions or the range of values about ethical dimensions of the issue (p. 25). Bigelow and colleagues (1993) argue their typology challenges traditional life cycle models that suggest all issues follow similar paths. They contend that issues have their own distinct dynamics that are more complex than issue life cycle models suggest. This approach is reflected in Heath and Palenchar's (2009) view that no organisation can dominate the course that an issue takes and that issue resolution becomes dialogic (in Heath's terms, this is *rhetoric* as he regards communication, especially public relations, as rhetorical practice; see Heath, 2001, pp. 31–50). When different people in an organisation's non-market environment have different levels of knowledge about an issue, the organisation is obliged to assert its point of view and to offer reasons for why it holds that view.

Lauzen (1997) argued that the knowledge of the worldviews and values of internal and external organisational constituencies that communication counsellors develop as a result of their environmental scanning make a unique contribution to issue analysis and management. In other words, understanding issues and their importance to an organisation contributes to how the organisation is managed.

ISSUES AND STRATEGY

Many issues are about organisations' reputations and their relationships with target publics, including customers, employees, governments, regulators, suppliers and competitors. Dealing with reputational and relationship issues is not a short-term, tactical pursuit. It requires consistent professional communication that links directly to mid- to long-term organisational aspirations, goals and objectives. This in turn requires an understanding of what strategy really is, how it is influenced by external factors and internal debates, how the non-market environment works, and of how organisations, represented by their public spokespeople, are social actors when they deal with public issues. Hence, strategic communication should be planned to reflect business-planning time frames. Strategic communication can appropriately apply not only to commercial business but also to public sector and not-for-profit organisations, as well as in a party-political context, because it is concerned with issues that occur at a level above the immediate tactical approach of public relations, mass media advertising, media relations, public affairs and corporate and political communication.

Volkswagen's embarrassing admission that it had fitted computerised devices to some of its diesel engine models to change performance and generate better results when its vehicles had emissions tests is an example of a major issue. This involved a significant international corporation and millions of cars and drivers across the world. (For a detailed explanation of this issue, see 'Volkswagen: The scandal explained' at www.bbc.com/news/business-34324772.) Volkswagen faced not only huge financial costs to fix the software and legal ramifications but the company also suffered severe reputational damage. In its communication response to the crisis that this issue generated, the company may have turned to the lessons corporations learnt from the 2008–11 global economic crisis. In the years after that crisis, business and communication scholars focused on how business should deal with the issue of damaged corporate reputations in the mid- and long term. This included identifying issues—like breaches of corporate and individual ethics, loss of customer trust and breaking the law—that arose during the crisis. The reputations of some of the world's biggest banks, especially of many that provided housing loans, were seriously affected by their less-than-rigorous lending practices before the crisis, and some have closed down as a result of losing huge amounts of money and because of their damaged reputations.

Resolving issues like these can take a long time and is similar to the challenges of post-crisis communication: not only repairing damaged reputations but also dealing with anger from people who have been affected, negative word of mouth about the organisation, and executive and organisational accountability for misconduct (Coombs and Holladay, 2009). The people affected by these crises are customers and other important **stakeholders** like suppliers, utilities, governments and employees.

....

Stakeholder "someone with an interest or concern in something" (*Australian Concise Oxford Dictionary*, 2004). Stakeholders are those who help the organisation to go about its business, have an interest in (or receive a benefit from) what it produces, regulate it or have some impact on its market and non-market environments.

....

ENHANCING REPUTATIONS

The management scholar Pankaj Ghemawat (2010) has argued that a crucial area for business to focus on as it recovers from crises is how organisational identities and reputations could be enhanced. That would require senior executives to spend more time focusing on the problems and to make greater efforts to manage their relationships with government. That is an important task because, since the world economic crisis, many governments, especially in the United States, have an expanded role as investors, customers, regulators and tax collectors as a result of having bought shares in companies to help them survive. In any event, there is almost always some government role in crisis resolution.

Managing an organisation's relationships with local, state and national governments is a strategic communication activity. Building these relationships requires a major effort; improving and maintaining them involves consistent engagement over many years. Most large companies have senior professional communication executives who work at this full-time; they are supported, when necessary, by the chief executive and other members of the dominant coalition. This is often described as public affairs, a specific public relations specialisation.

This approach is not restricted to companies and their relationships with governments. It is equally important that positive relationships are built with other stakeholders on all issues they face. Government agencies need to take a similar strategic approach to their communication with stakeholders, as do community groups and not-for-profit organisations.

Understanding the issues means that organisations can, as Lauzen (1997) put it, know, understand and, more effectively, interact with their environments.

THE EXTERNAL ENVIRONMENT

In all their work, communication practitioners need to understand an organisation's *external* environment. (They also need to be aware of the organisation's *internal* environment—how policies are decided, who makes decisions, who manages particular areas, the make-up of the workforce, internal issues—because what happens inside the organisation can affect its ability to achieve its business goals. We will deal with this in detail in Chapter 4.)

Traditionally, analysing an organisation's external environment has involved considering:

- Changing public attitudes towards the organisation, its products or services, and the industry in which it operates
- Customer expectations about its products and the organisation itself; laws and regulations that determine what it can and can't do
- Investor expectations of the organisation's performance what its competitors are doing
- The impact of technological change on its ability to do what it does aspects of the current and future political environment that may affect the organisation
- The socio-economic environment—for example, a booming economy or one in recession, or pressure for greater action on climate change mass news media interest in the organisation, its products or services, the industry in

■ Which it operates and the issues that surround both the organisation and the industry.

Some experts view organisational environments in a different way. They argue that business planners and communication practitioners should view an organisation's external environment from the perspective of both the "**market**" **environment** and the "**non-market**" **environment** (See Figure 2.1).

Categorising relationships in this way will help you to be precise when you identify those you will need to reach (see Table 1.1 in Chapter 1), and in what contexts, when you plan a communication strategy. For example, market environment relationships with customers and suppliers suggest an immediate marketing communication approach. Managing a non-market environment relationship about an emerging issue identified through environmental scanning and issue analysis suggests the need for a mid- to long-term strategic approach.

Non-market environment all the relationships an organisation has beyond the market that nevertheless affect its ability to reach its objectives. Non-market issues are social, political and economic.

Market environment involves an organisation's relationships with customers, suppliers and competitors.

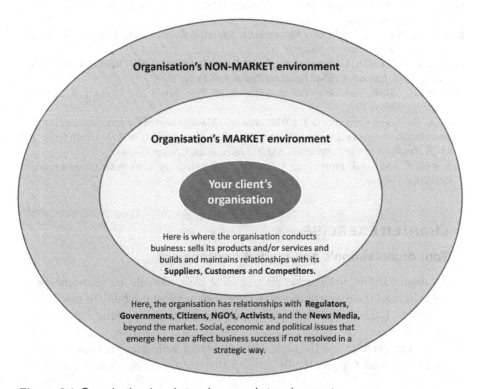

Figure 2.1 Organisational market and non-market environments

Strategic issues analysis and strategic communication are most often undertaken to deal with issues in an organisation's "non-market environment." This is the approach taken in *Strategic Communication* because the issues in the "non-market" environment generally deal with strategic mid- to long-term public policy questions, while the market environment is more concerned with immediate factors that decide annual performance.

FURTHER READING

Bach, D. and Allen, D.B. (2010), What Every CEO Needs to Know about *Non*market Strategy, *MIT Sloan Management Review*, 51(3), pp. 41–8.

Bigelow, B., Fahey, L., and Mahon, J. (1993). A Typology of Issue Evolution, *Business and Society*, 32 (Spring), pp. 18–29.

Dougall, E. (2008), Issues Management, *The Science beneath the Art of Public Relations*, Institute for Public Relations, online topics at http://www.instituteforpr.org/ topics/issues-management, accessed 28 December 2013.

Hallahan, K. (1999), Seven Models of Framing: Implications for Public Relations, *Journal of Public Relations Research*, 11(3), pp. 205–42.

Hallahan, K. (2001), The Dynamics of Issues Activation and Response: An Issues Process Model, *Journal of Public Relations Research*, 13(1), pp. 27–59.

Heath, R.L. and Palenchar, M.J. (2009), *Strategic Issues Management: Organisations and Public Policy Challenges*, 2nd edn, SAGE, Los Angeles, CA.

Jaques, T. (2009a), Integrating Issue Management and Strategic Planning: Unfulfilled Promise or Future Opportunity? *International Journal of Strategic Communication*, 3(1), pp. 19–33.

Jaques, T. (2009b), Issue and Crisis Management: Quicksand in the Definitional Landscape, *Public Relations Review*, 35(3), pp. 280–6.

Jaques, T. (2014), *Issue and Crisis Management: Exploring Issues, Crises, Risk and Reputation*, Oxford University Press, Melbourne.

Lauzen, M.M. (1997), Understanding the Relation between Public Relations and Issues Management, *Journal of Public Relations Research*, 9(1), pp. 65–82.

Moloney, K. (2006), *Rethinking Public Relations: PR Propaganda and Democracy*, 2nd edn, Routledge, Milton Park.

Pang, A., Jin, Y. and Cameron, G.T. (2010), Strategic Management of Communication: Insights From the Contingency Theory of Strategic Conflict Management, in R. L. Heath (ed.), *The SAGE Handbook of Public Relations*, SAGE, Los Angeles, CA, pp. 17–34.

Van Riel, C.B.M. and Frombrun, C.J. (2008), *Essentials of Corporate Communication*, Routledge, London.

CHAPTER EXERCISE

Your organisation's non-market environment

An organisation's non-market environment comprises all the relationships it has beyond the market but which nevertheless affect its ability to reach its objectives. Issues in this environment are about are social, political and economic matters.

For this exercise, use the topic you selected for your strategic plan project when you read Chapter 1. To develop that strategic plan, you'll need to identify and analyse issues that are important to your organisation before you work out goals, objectives and the other elements of the strategy. To start that process, and to help identify specific issues, it will be useful to set up a framework for your organisation's market and non-market environments. This exercise is designed to help you do that.

Use the format shown in Tables 2.1 and 2.2 to set up two Word tables: one for your organisation's market environment and one for its non-market environment. In each table, include a row for each of the elements of the environment, as in the examples. Some pointers for doing this are included in the table.

In the relationships column of your table, list who the relationships are with, and what political, economic or social issues are associated with the relationships. Relationships could be with specific stakeholders. For example, in the non-market table, you will need to identify specific media that are appropriate to your organisation, along with governments, regulators, groups of citizens and so on. In other words, unless your organisation is involved in sports, it is highly unlikely that sports journalists would be interested in it.

Be precise in identifying the relationships and issues. "The media" is not an appropriate relationship because it is not clear enough; "business journalists" is appropriate if your organisation is a commercial business.

These are important tables because you will use them in Chapter 5 to help you analyse your organisation's communication needs, and in Chapter 6 to identify specific target publics by refining broad stakeholder groups.

As you compile the two tables, ask yourself:

1. Who is important to the organisation in this context?
2. Why are they important?
3. What issues are they interested in, and why?

Table 2.1 Market environment for [name of your organisation]

Element	Relationships
Customers	Are these retail customers? Do you mean individuals or corporate customers?
Suppliers	Which suppliers? Those who provide services like electricity or the resources your organisation needs to make its products?
Competitors	Who are they? Are they multinational or domestic? What is their unique selling point? How do their products differ from yours—or are they the same? How does their product pricing relate to yours?

Table 2.2 Non-market environment for [name of your organisation]

Element	Relationships
Regulators	What agencies regulate your industry and what issues do you need to talk to them about?
Governments	Which governments? The national government? Regional or local governments? All of them? Remember that "the government" means the ministers who have specific responsibilities, so you'll need to be specific about which are important to you. Identify the issues that are important at each level of government and for each specific minister. Remember, too, that civil service agencies have policy responsibilities and their officials advise ministers. It is important to remember that the appropriate agency officials are briefed on your organisation's views
Citizens	
Activists	
NGOs	Research the concept of non-government organisations. Which of these are important to the issue you need to deal with?
Media	Which specific media? Who are the specific journalists? What issues do you want them to know about?

STRATEGIC COMMUNICATION

When they introduced the first edition of the *International Journal of Strategic Communication* in 2007, Kirk Hallahan and his colleagues noted that this was a new area not only for academic research but also for professional practice. They described strategic communication as purposeful and designed to help an organisation fulfil its mission. This new communication discipline evolved from specialisations like public relations, advertising, corporate communication, financial public relations and community relations, which had been practised as "crafts." They characterised it as "an immature science" but made a vital point: "Strategic communication differs from integrated communication because its focus is how an organisation communicates across organisational endeavours. The emphasis is on the strategic application of communication and how an organization functions as a social actor to advance its mission" (p. 7). In this view, organisations are participants in the economic, political, social and environmental debates that affect how they go about their business. That means they have something to say about the issues and say it. These debates take place around broad issues in the non-market environment (See Figure 2.1). In their role as **social actors**, ___ organisations use informational, persuasive, discursive and relational communication to pursue goals and objectives.

Social actors people who participate in public discussions and debates about social, economic and political issues.

In other words, strategic communication is about far more than day-to-day media relations, product advertising and sales promotion. Examples of this occur almost every night on television public affairs programs when people representing companies, charities, industry associations and other organisations debate issues with activists, commentators, academics, politicians and journalists. An industry association president might be making points about matters that affect his or her industry, or an environmental activist may have raised concerns about native forests, or community groups could be pointing out how a proposed government policy will prevent them from delivering services. For their part, governments at all levels are always involved in public debates about policy, not only in the day-to-day hurly-burly of daily politics that are reported in the 24-hour news cycle, but in efforts to explain new or changed policies to citizens. In Australia, for example, state governments conduct regular "community cabinet" meetings in which ministers meet with citizens at venues across the state to discuss policies that affect specific regions, and issues that are the focus of daily politics.

SOME STRATEGIC COMMUNICATION DEFINITIONS

The argument in this book is that strategic communication involves analysing big-picture issues that help or harm an organisation's ability to do its job and working out how to deal with them. Scholars have examined the growing focus on strategic communication and have proposed some definitions that help to explain it.

Falkheimer and Heide (2018) suggest strategic communication is a conscious activity aimed at reaching an organisation's overall long-term goals, not, as for tactical communication, a tool for disseminating information and facilitating internal organisational discussions. Accepting that strategic communication helps organisations reach set goals, Falkheimer and Heide (2018) propose a range of functional tasks set in a frame of the practice being "...about doing the right things" and which includes all forms of internal, external, formal, and informal communicative action which occurs at all levels of an organisation (p. 74).

For others, strategic communication is defined not as practice, but as "the study" of how communication is used purposefully to achieve organisations' missions (Frandsen and Johansen, 2017, cited in Falkheimer and Heide, 2018, p. 57). Yim (2021) recognised the reality of the definitional discourse about strategic communication by describing it as a "still-evolving" concept (p. 69).

Swaran Sandhu (2009, p. 72–92) describes strategic communication as multi-disciplinary and intentional communication in which an organisation is a purposeful actor making rational and deliberate decisions. James Grunig (2006) regards strategic communication as a "bridging activity" between organisations and their stakeholders that should be standard procedure—that is, institutionalised. This approach reflects the notion of two-way symmetrical communication in public relations practice.

Paul Argenti and colleagues (2005) describe strategic communication as imperative for businesses. They argue that strategic communication should be "aligned with a company's overall strategy, to enhance its strategic positioning." In their view, although strategic communication has a long-term orientation, practitioners must meet short-term needs but stay focused on the long-term issues facing organisations. In his book on corporate communication, Joep Cornelissen (2005, p. 99) argues that the scope and involvement of strategic communication as a management function is more substantial when it stretches beyond a set of functional goals and tactics (our tools) to corporate and business unit levels. For Cornelissen, strategic communication is a critical management function in which practitioners must respond to business needs and concerns. This view is shared by Falkheimer and Heide (2018), who, in the context of their discussion of strategic communication as practice, describe it as "...a fundamental part of an organisation's management function" (p. 73).

Johnson and Glenny (2021) say that when the term strategy is applied to communication, it "...provides consistency, structure and cohesiveness" (p. 180). And they argue that all strategies "...need to align with other parts of an organisation..." and that

> No amount of rhetoric about your organisation's position on the environment will work if the actions of the organization don't follow through and support the strategy.
>
> (p. 184)

In Chapter 3, we will look at why definitions like these mean strategic communication plans must be linked to an organisation's business (or strategic, or corporate) plan.

WHAT DRIVES STRATEGIC COMMUNICATION?

Argenti and colleagues (2005, pp. 82–9) note some broad categories of issues that "drive" strategic communication. That is, three factors in organisations' non-market environments lead them to think about their communication approaches in a strategic way. These factors, or drivers, are government regulations, organisational complexity and the need for business, especially, to increase credibility.

New, or amended, government regulations mean companies must review their communication strategies and practices to take account of the new external regulatory environment. Because organisations are complex, their communication strategies must be consistent in helping employees and other stakeholders understand its business, products and services, and where it stands on issues that affect its ability to continue to be successful. It takes a major effort to build an organisation's reputation; once that reputation is damaged, management teams face formidable challenges to restore credibility both in the market and non-market environments.

These are significant issues that need strategic solutions over long time frames even though day-to-day tactical tools would be used to pursue some goals and objectives. Issues like an organisation's reputation, its relationships with external stakeholders, and the regulatory environment in which it operates are important at any time. This also applies to the not-for-profit and charity sectors, government agencies, industry associations, and political parties and executive governments. These issues play out in what we briefly looked at earlier as the "non-market" environment.

FURTHER READING

Hallahan, K., Holtzhausen, D., Van Ruler, B., Verčič, D. and Siramesh, K. (2007), Defining Strategic Communication, *International Journal of Strategic Communication*, 1(1), pp. 3–35.
Falkheimer, J. and Heide, M. (2018). *Strategic Communication: An Introduction*, Routledge, Milton Park, esp. Chp. 3.
Mahoney, J. (2022). *The Strategic Communication Imperative For Mid- and Long-Term Issues Management*, Routledge, Milton Park, Oxon and New York, esp. Chp. 3.
Zerfass, A. and Huck, S. (2007), Innovations, Communication, and Leadership: New Developments in Strategic Communication, *International Journal of Strategic Communication*, 1(2), pp. 107–22.

Reputation, values, relationships, and change

While strategic communicators must be concerned with the values of their organisations, and stakeholder perceptions of their reputations, they must also consider the impact of change on their companies, agencies, community groups or charities. Changes in a commercial company's market and non-market environments can have major consequences for its ability to maintain profitability or to deliver effective services. So, too, can changes in these two environments affect a charity's ability to raise funds for its essential work, or an NGO's service delivery, or a government agency's ability to be seen as an effective service provider.

Reputation and values

Cornelissen (2005, p. 83) describes reputation as a "perceptual construct" that is often associated with organisational behaviour. This construct is formed by stakeholder groups, who evaluate the multiple characteristics of organisations based on perceptions of behaviour and demonstrations of corporate values. These stakeholder perceptions are a significant concern of communication management. The people who study organisational change, especially significant restructuring, identify a common theme: the need for leaders to set the values and objectives of their organisations.

Way back in the 1980s, Tom Peters and Robert Waterman (1984), who wrote a significant book about research into why some companies performed better than others, found that in their so-called "excellent" companies, senior managers paid

explicit attention to **organisational values**. They concluded that the greatest contributions a leader could make were clarifying the organisation's value system and
"breathing life into it." Excellent companies were clear about what they stood for
and were serious about value-shaping, attention to organisational values. They
concluded that the greatest contributions a leader could make were clarifying the
organisation's value system and "breathing life into it." Excellent companies were
clear about what they stood for and were serious about value-shaping, leading
Peters and Waterman to question whether it was possible for a company to be
excellent without clarity on values.

> **Organisational values** the beliefs on which the organisation bases its policies
> and actions.

Laura Nash (1995) says that influencing organisational values requires a range
of coordinated efforts, from the chairman's personal interest and commitment through to discussion, debate, widespread dissemination of information, monitoring, effective communication channels, arbitration of grey-area
problems or non-compliance, enforcement and rewards. Many of these
findings were reflected in the findings in the Excellence in Public Relations and
Communication Management study led by James Grunig (1992).

Relationships and change

Some management researchers who study how organisations work, argue that
changes, sometimes small ones, sometimes unexpected, influence the way
organisations are formally structured and work. They use complexity theory to
explain this. This theory views organisations as systems. It holds that because
organisational systems are complex, and have equally complex relationships with
stakeholders, changes in the system affect the organisation. A metaphor for this is
the commonly used example in which the air movement generated by a butterfly
flapping its wings in a Brazilian rainforest might become so great that it would
affect the weather in Europe or other distant locations. In other words, small
changes outside an organisation—a system—affect its environment.

IN THEORY: SYSTEMS, COMPLEXITY, AND CONTINGENCY

Scholars use systems, complexity, and contingency theory to investigate how
communication works. Many view organisations as systems operating in
a bigger system (our market and non-market environments, for example).
Systems are, of course, complex things, so using complexity theory is also an
important way of examining communication. Using complexity theory in
this way means investigating how the things that make organisations complex
(like internal structures) affect their ability to communicate.

Contingency theory attempts to explain how internal and external factors (independent variables) influence organisations' abilities to do what they do, and it is used by scholars to explore how such factors influence communication. This approach is often contested, but it is a useful tool with which to examine the potential impact of political, social and economic issues on organisations, especially given that these issues play out in the "non-market" environment but nevertheless have an impact on day-to-day operations.

Let's look at this concept by starting with systems theory. The notion that organisational environments have an impact on management decision-making grew out of scholars' application of systems theory to better understand organisational structures. In this view, organisations are complex systems that comprise dynamically interacting parts; a change in one part can affect the behaviour of other parts (Beinhocker, 1999).

Hodge and colleagues (2003) argue that this approach helps to explain organisational structures and how their constituent parts interact with each other, and with external factors, to achieve organisational goals. These complex systems are "path dependent" (Beinhocker, 1999, p. 49), meaning that, like the Brazilian butterfly, random changes produce unrelated outcomes. In this strategic systems model (Hodge et al., 2003), an organisation's structure is contingent on the contexts it faces. Steve Mackey (2009, p. 60) notes that many complex contexts "support, enable, change and threaten" a system or organisation. This notion that complex systems like organisational structures are affected by internal and external variables has led scholars to apply contingency theory to communication practice. Jinae Kang and I-Huei Cheng (2008) argue that contingency theory pays "close attention" to the influence of variables (external factors) on how practitioners select a stance and communication strategy that is best for an organisation (p. 4). For example, they found that legal and regulatory factors were contingent variables affecting issue management. Other public relations scholars (for example, Murphy, 2000; Reber and Cameron, 2003; Shin et al., 2006) have used contingency theory to argue the limitations of the two-way symmetrical model of public relations theorised by Grunig and colleagues. Research by these scholars has found that practice moves along a continuum from advocating a point of view on an issue to a point where, depending on circumstances, organisations begin to accommodate the views of others on the issue. These scholars use contingency theory to understand the internal and external dynamics that could affect the stance an organisation takes on a particular issue (Pang, Jin and Cameron, 2010). Research grounded in contingency theory found that 87 internal and external variables impact on practitioners' abilities to do their jobs (see, for example, Pang, Jin and Cameron, 2010). Amanda Cancel and others (1997) argue that strategic communication is practised on a continuum from pure advocacy to pure accommodation depending on the circumstances (contingent variables) the organisation faced.

This idea has important implications for strategic communicators. Anne Gregory (2000), an internationally renowned communication scholar, argues that small incremental and insignificant changes in an organisation's internal and external environments create disturbances that, through their own increasing dynamics, start major change. For communicators, this means that seemingly insignificant comments and actions can escalate rapidly into hot issues and crises, with what Gregory (2000) describes as their own uncontrollable lives. Understanding this leads senior communicators to build and maintain positive relationships with stakeholders, and to identify other people and groups with which the organisation should have regular dialogue. Understanding what stakeholders know about an organisation, and their views on issues important to it, is one of the keys to ensuring that good relationships are maintained. It is also important that communicators are aware of the views of people who might oppose the organisation's policies so that differences can be at least discussed. An example of this might be the intervention of a labour union in relation to changes to workers' entitlements. The organisation might normally have a good relationship with the union but, if changes to workers' entitlements are proposed, this might change for the worse and perhaps even escalate into Gregory's "hot issue" or crisis.

FURTHER READING

Beinhocker, E.D. (1999), On the Origin of Strategies, *The McKinsey Quarterly*, (4), pp. 47–57.

Cancel, A.E., Cameron, G.T., Sallot, L.M. and Mitrook, M.A. (1997), It Depends: A Contingency Theory of Accommodation in Public Relations, *Journal of Public Relations Research*, 9(1), pp. 31–63.

Hodge, B.J., Anthony, W.P. and Gales, L.M. (2003), *Organization Theory: A Strategic Approach*, 6th edn, Prentice Hall, Upper Saddle River, NJ.

Kang, J. and Cheng, I-H. (2008), Application of Contingency Theory Frameworks to Issue Management: A Case Study of the Restaurant Industry's Obesity Issues Management, paper presented at the annual meeting of the National Communication Association, 94th Annual Convention, San Diego, CA, 20 November 2008.

Mackey, S. (2009), Public Relations Theory, in J. Johnston and C. Zawawi (eds), *Public Relations Theory and Practice*, 3rd edn, Allen & Unwin, Sydney, pp. 47–77.

Murphy, P. (2000), Symmetry, Contingency, Complexity: Accommodating Uncertainty in Public Relations Theory, *Public Relations Review*, 26(4), pp. 447–62.

Pang, A., Jin, Y. and Cameron, G.T. (2010), Strategic Management of Communication: Insights from the Contingency Theory of Strategic Conflict Management, in R.L. Heath (ed.), *The SAGE Handbook of Public Relations*, 2nd edn, SAGE, Los Angeles, CA, pp. 17–34.

Reber, B.H. and Cameron, G.T. (2003), Measuring Contingencies: Using Scales to Measure Public Relations Practitioner Limits to Accommodation, *Journalism and Mass Communication Quarterly*, 80(2), pp. 431–46.

Shin, J-H., Cameron, G.T. and Cropp, F. (2006), Occam's Razor in the Contingency Theory: A National Survey on 86 Contingent Variables, *Public Relations Review*, 32(3), pp. 282–6.

CHAPTER EXERCISE

Organisational reputation and issues affecting it

This exercise is to help you to see how issues and target publics are related.

Select an organisation in your region that is facing a reputational crisis. Research the organisation and how it is managing—or has resolved—the reputational crisis. Using the information you have read so far in this book, draw a mind map (if you are not sure about mind maps, check out Susan Gregory, How to Make a Mind Map—The Basics, www.youtube.com/watch?v=wLWV0XN7K1g) that shows the issues that affect that organisation's reputation. You can do this by hand. On the mind map, and using what you prepared in the previous Chapter Exercise, link to each issue the specific elements, which we will now call target publics, in the organisation's non-environment (Figure 2.1).Then, prepare a three-column table that lists (in column 1) the specific target publics, (in column 2) prioritises the issues associated with those target publics (priority 1 being the most important, priority 2 the second and soon), and (in column 3) identifies in dot point form some important information each target public would need to know about each issue. It doesn't matter if different target publics share issues.

STRATEGIC COMMUNICATION LEADERSHIP

Strategic communicators are also concerned with organisational leadership, management and their specialist role as counsellors. In the latter function, they counsel (that is, advise) management about how to respond to political and social issues, protect reputations, and manage and communicate in crises; they also counsel about long-range organisational positioning. We'll look more closely at the counselling function of senior communicators in Chapter 13. In this high-level work, senior communicators apply all the communication disciplines and their associated communication tools to advance top-level strategic goals and objectives (Cornelissen, 2005). Of course, they need to know about communication pathways and tools and how they can be best used to reach target publics, but their focus is on the big picture and on ensuring that the day-to-day tools of the communication disciplines are applied in a consistent way.

James Grunig and his colleagues have spent many years studying and commenting on how public relations practice works. In 2009, Grunig used this work to examine two paradigms for public relations practice as it relates to campaigns designed to generate behavioural outcomes. Most of the time, strategic communication is about just this: generating behavioural outcomes, like working to make sure that stakeholders or target publics understand an organisation's point of view on an issue. Grunig argues that practitioners working in the "symbolic, interpretive" paradigm of marketing communication "generally" believe publics can be persuaded by messages that change their understanding and beliefs about a situation. He believes this approach devotes excessive attention to the tactical role of communication in negotiating meaning by emphasising messages, publicity, media relations and media effects. A contrasting "strategic management, behavioural" paradigm would build relationships with stakeholders. This paradigm facilitates what Grunig and his colleagues have earlier described as two-way communication and dialogue and includes a framework of research and listening (environmental scanning) that would result in an organisation's messages reflecting the information needs of its stakeholders as well as its own need to advocate a point of view about particular issues.

Chief executives have an important role as communicators. The Australian scholar Donald Alexander (2006) examined how chief executives communicated with external stakeholders. He argued that organisational leaders needed to be competent communicators and to understand communication practice at a high level to manage the myriad interests and publics that impact on business goals.

In a commentary about the companies that Peters and Waterman described as "excellent," Laurie Wilson (1994) notes that a key element of business success is open and honest communication. One of the five attributes these companies displayed was internal and external relationships built on respect, trust and human dignity, not on profit or personal gain. The other attributes were long-range vision; commitment to community, not just to profit; strong corporate values that in some way emphasise the importance of people; and a cooperative approach to management problem-solving (Wilson, 1994). Each of these is an important factor to consider when you plan a communication strategy and its goals and objectives.

FURTHER READING

Grunig, J.E. (2009), Paradigms of Global Public Relations in an Age of Digitalisation, *PRism* 6(2). www.prismjournal.org/fileadmin/Praxis/Files/globalPR/GRUNIG.pdf

Grunig, J.E. and Repper, F.C. (1992), Strategic Management, Publics, and Issues, in J.E. Grunig (ed.), *Excellence in Public Relations and Communication Management*, Lawrence Erlbaum Associates, Hillsdale, NJ.

Hamel, G. (1996), Strategy as Revolution, *Harvard Business Review*, 74(4), pp. 69–82.

Wilson, L.J. (1994), Excellent Companies and Coalition-Building among the Fortune 500: A Value- and Relationship-based Theory, *Public Relations Review*, 20(4), pp. 333–143.

COMMUNICATING ABOUT ISSUES

So far, we have looked at the nature of strategic communication and why it is important for organisations to deal with issues over the mid- and long term. Organisations need to consider how they protect their reputations and deal with a range of issues that occur in their non-market environments, such as regulation, the views of activists, how the mass news media is dealing with the organisation and its industry, what politicians are proposing, and the impact of socio-economic changes. The next section discusses the time frames—or horizons— in which communication strategy can be planned and implemented.

Communicating in three horizons

Linking communication plans to corporate business plans (see Chapter 3) is not new. Public relations scholars especially have researched this topic for many years but have argued that more should be done in professional practice, and in academic research, to make those links explicit. Some argue that, as communication is regarded as a management practice, the ways in which it is researched, planned and implemented, should be through the frame of business theory and principles. For example, Karla Gower (2006) notes that a great deal of research about professional communication has focused on what practitioners do, rather than on the business drivers of practice, and argues that this does not keep up with the way that "thinking about strategy" has evolved in the management literature. In *Strategic Communication*, strategic communication planning is directly grounded in the idea that businesses should plan for growth in three horizons.

The idea of business planning in three horizons came from research by the management scholars Mehrdad Baghai, Stephen Coley and David White. They explain their research in an important book, *The Alchemy of Growth: Practical Insights for Building the Enduring Enterprise*, published in 2000. In their view, business growth can be managed across "three horizons" simultaneously to distinguish between the embryonic, emergent, and mature phases of a business' life cycle. They explain the horizons this way:

> *Horizon 1*: extending and defending core business. This horizon covers the businesses that are at the heart of an organisation and with which customers and analysts most readily identify. Horizon 1 is critical to near-term performance because it is in this horizon that the money and skills needed to provide resources for growth are generated. One of the primary management challenges is to shore up competitive positions aided by, among other tasks, marketing.
>
> *Horizon 2*: building emerging businesses. In this horizon, business leaders are concerned with the emerging stars of the company, because they transform companies. Horizon 2 is about building new streams of revenue, which may be extensions of current business or moves in new directions.
>
> *Horizon 3*: seeding options for future businesses. Horizon 3 is the longer-term future, in which real activities, such as research projects, test market pilots and alliances, mark the first steps towards actual businesses that, if they prove successful, will be expected to reach the profitability of those in the Horizon 1 stage of growth (Baghai et al., 2000, pp. 4–7).

The focus of each horizon and its associated outputs are shown in Table 2.3. Baghai and colleagues say that planning for each horizon should be separated to avoid a natural tendency for people to concentrate on the things that need to be

Table 2.3 Planning in three horizons

	Horizon 1	Horizon 2	Horizon 3
Focus	Executing to defend, extend and increase profitability of existing businesses	Resourcing initiatives to build new businesses	Uncovering options for future opportunities and placing bets on selected options
Outputs	Annual operating plan: tactical plans, resourcing decisions, budgets	Business-building strategies: investment budget, detailed business plans for new ventures	Decisions to explore: ○ initial project plan ○ project milestones

Source: Baghai et al. (2000), p. 130.

done immediately in Horizon 1 rather than what has to be done in the other two horizons.

This is the critical point about grounding strategic communication in the three-horizons approach to managing. Earlier we looked at Argenti and colleagues' argument that strategic communication has a long-term orientation but that practitioners must deal with short-term needs while staying focused on long-term issues. Planning communication in a three-horizons paradigm enables that to happen. In the next section, we will look at how.

CHAPTER EXERCISE

Communicating about your organisation's issues

For this exercise, you need to think about the topic you selected in Chapter 1 and for which you prepared the tables in the first exercise in this chapter. Use the non-market environment table. You will need to do some research about the kind of organisation you selected, and the industry in which it operates, to do this exercise. The suggested organisations in the list in Chapter 1 are fictional, so you won't find references to them, but the topics are real and you will find references to product tampering, sudden infant death syndrome, driving while using a mobile phone, and waste management.

Make some detailed notes as you answer these questions—and keep the notes for future exercises:

1. Which of the issues you identified apply in *each* of the three horizons?
2. Why do they apply in those horizons?
3. In terms of what your organisation does, which issue is the most important, and why?

4. Who else is interested in these issues, and why?
5. Do these issues affect other organisations? Which ones, and why?
6. What, if any, regulations have you discovered that apply to your topic? Who has an interest in those regulations?

When you have made your notes, you should have some detailed and useful information that will help you as you work through the exercises in the following chapters.

ALIGNING STRATEGIC COMMUNICATION WITH THE THREE HORIZONS

Strategic communication helps ensure that goals are met, whether an organisation is a commercial business, a charity, a community group, an industry association, an activist group, a government agency or a political party. All are concerned to achieve significant results over the long term, not just to sell their products and services or to meet the demands of today's 24-hour news agenda. For example, political parties have their eyes firmly fixed on winning the next election and they plan policies that are explained over a number of years to do that, just as a charity continually keeps its donors aware of what it is doing and why it is doing it, beyond its annual fund-raising effort. Mobile phone networks want you to sign up to a contract today but they also promote their services over the longer term to attract new business. Environmental activists try to convince governments to introduce policies to protect endangered species, encourage alternative energy sources and ensure a sustainable future but they also argue their case over many years knowing that, say, a demonstration this week (in communication terms, a "tactic") won't win what is a long-term debate.

The drivers of strategic communication—regulation, organisational complexity, the need to increase credibility, and other potential issues—are all mid- to long-term considerations. It is a task of communication practitioners to plan how their strategic plans explicitly align to the horizon-management approach. That is, it's their job to write goals and objectives, plan important messages, identify target publics, work out how to reach them, prepare communication tools to do that, and apply them in each horizon:

Horizon 1, the focus of which is extending and defending the core business to increase profits. This focus consolidates the vital role of integrated marketing communication. Horizon 1 provides an explicit link to management decision-making on the immediate tactical activities involved in issues and crisis communication, event management, and some of the corporate communication functions—political lobbying, for example—of public relations

Horizon 2, where the focus is on organisational efforts to strategically enhance reputations, to counsel on the public communication aspects of regulatory issues and to manage relationships with internal and external publics in the context of business-building strategies

Horizon 3, where the focus is on long-term public-issues identification, strategic counselling and associated communication program planning.

Table 2.4 shows some communication output examples in the three horizons.

Chapter 3 will examine how strategic communication is linked to business goals and objectives.

What categories of issues would you identify as the most important in strategic communication planning?

Table 2.4 Horizons for strategic communication

	Horizon 1 *Now*	**Horizon 2** *Mid-term (up to 5 years from now)*	**Horizon 3** *Long-term (more than 5 years from now)*
Focus	Current business	Emerging business	Future business
Outputs	Day-to-day media	Issue identification	Strategic issue identification
	Crisis communication	Policy development	Strategic communication through relationship management, ongoing government relations, community relations
	Marketing communication	Tactical lobbying	

Source: Based on Baghai et al. (2000), p. 130.

CHAPTER EVALUATION

These questions will help you review this chapter:

What characteristics define strategic communication? Why are those characteristics important?

Why are issues important considerations in planning communication activities?

How important is it for a strategic communicator to identify external issues that an organisation faces in its non-market environment?

Why does strategic communication need to deal with external issues in the mid- and long-term horizons?

Chapter 3
Communication strategy and business planning

Goal: To understand the link between business strategy and communication.

Objectives: This chapter will help you to:

- Recognise the need to link an organisation's business and communication strategies
- Understand how communication strategies reflect the organisation's business directions
- Appreciate that strategic planning is a dynamic process.

Principle: All communication activities support organisational goals.

Planning: Preparing a strategic communication plan follows a specific process.

Practice: Communication strategists ground their plans in the organisation's business plan.

Few of us ever take a vacation without thinking through where we want to go, and why; how we'll get there; how long we'll spend away from home; what we'll do while we are away; how much money we'll need. The vacation plan that comes out of this thinking, and discussions with family or friends, provides us with a kind of road map for reaching our holiday destination that helps us identify how much it will all cost. Once we know those details, we can plan what we'll do on vacation and settle on a budget for travel, food and entertainment. This vacation road map gives us directions for achieving what began as a great idea for taking a break from work or study.

Each time a large international corporation announces a sporting team sponsorship, support for an international aid project after a natural disaster or funding for a new playground in the city where it has a manufacturing plant, it is directly implementing an aspect of a **business** strategy. None of these projects, or myriad others, will be about direct profit growth but they will be part of strategic objectives to enhance the corporation's reputation. The communication tools they use to announce these projects will be directly linked to the corporation's business

DOI: 10.4324/9781003317579-4

strategy, as will those they implement when they announce quarterly profit results or new infrastructure projects, or when they comment on issues in their market and non-market environments.

Communication strategies set out why these activities are important and how they link up with the organisation's overall directions.

STRATEGIC DIRECTIONS

An organisation's directions are written down in a corporate business plan or "strategy." These documents—reviewed regularly, but usually planned for three- or five-year periods—set out the organisation's mission and goals, and details about how they will be achieved. For example, the mission (or vision) statement in a charity's strategic plan would set out the values that inform its work; a union's mission would explain how it represents workers' rights; that of an environmental group might talk about the importance of protecting native flora and fauna. In each organisation, the strategic plan would list its goals and the things it needs

---

Case: Mission statements, goals and objectives

Mission statements, goals and objectives are linked. Here's an example. The International Red Cross and Red Crescent Society, created in 1863 under the Geneva Conventions, operates under international law. On its website, the following is included as part of its **mission** statement:

> The International Committee of the Red Cross (ICRC) is an impartial, neutral and independent organization whose exclusively humanitarian mission is to protect the lives and dignity of victims of armed conflict and other situations of violence and to provide them with assistance.
> The ICRC also endeavours to prevent suffering by promoting and strengthening humanitarian law and universal humanitarian principles.

The ICRC directs and coordinates the international activities conducted by the Movement in armed conflicts and other situations of violence.

The Geneva Conventions list the following six goals for the Red Cross:

- To monitor compliance of warring parties with the Geneva Conventions to organise nursing and care for those who are wounded on the battlefield
- To supervise the treatment of prisoners of war
- To help with the search for missing persons in a war (tracing service)
- To organise protection and care for normal people
- To make peace between groups in war.

Each goal has objectives supported by a broad range of programs that help the Red Cross achieve these goals.

---

to do to achieve them. Commercial businesses use the same approach, and their corporate strategies, or business plans, set out the range of financial, production, research and development, marketing, sales and human resource actions that will support the directions the plan sets.

Mission a person's task or goal; the general principles that an organisation says guide its operations (adapted from *Australian Concise Oxford Dictionary*, 2004).

Top-level strategic plans are developed from research that enables an organisation to decide its business directions, and to identify what it needs to do to achieve them, and how it can measure success. This information comes from an analysis of the organisation's market and non-market environments, competitive position, equipment, staff and financial needs and the views of senior managers about the organisation's future. Top-level strategic plans are used by business, not-for-profit groups, charities, government agencies and organisations like the United Nations' various commissions.

What an organisation does in its advertising, public relations and sales activities has a direct linear link to its business strategy in much the same way that a family tree shows the paths that our genes have travelled from earlier generations to our immediate family members and to us. These direct links are made because every aspect of an organisation's business is grounded in a top-level strategic plan. Financial and investment strategies are geared to managing the organisation's resources in cost-effective ways that support the directions senior management

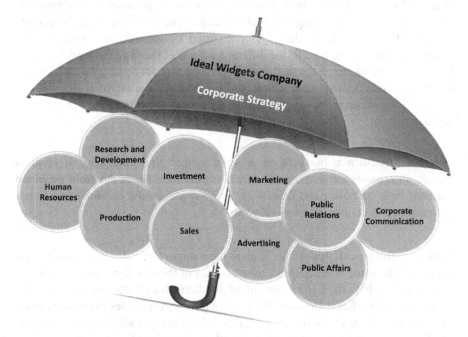

Figure 3.1 Corporate strategy and operational plans

and the board of directors have set for the business, just as the production, sales, research and development and employment plans reflect those directions. They all link up under the umbrella of the organisation's top-level strategic plan, and they all have a direct linear link to the goals of that plan (see Figure 3.1).

The most important link for strategic communication practice is the formal "genetic" pathway from the goals of the business plan to the communication activities that reflect them. This pathway ensures that there is always a reason for communication action. As we'll see in Chapters 4–7, communication goals reflect an organisation's goals, and communication activity reflects the need to address the issues the organisation faces with the people who matter most to it.

STRATEGIC COMMUNICATION AND ORGANISATIONAL STRUCTURES

Formal structures, or hierarchies, differ from organisation to organisation. Companies, clubs, schools, sporting associations and other organisations have formal hierarchies that enable work to be carried out, instructions to be communicated, and business to be managed as efficiently as possible. Most organisational structures have different levels of management, each with its own degree of authority over the area for which it is responsible. In large organisations, management structures can be complicated, and there is continuing scholarly debate about which model is the best fit for each type of organisation. At the top of the structure, the board of directors is legally responsible for everything the organisation does and sets the major strategic business directions. A chief executive officer (CEO, also known as a managing director or president) is responsible for overall day-to-day management of the organisation in line with the board's policies. At the next level, the CEO is assisted by general managers or vice-presidents, who are responsible for different aspects of the organisation's business. A number of managers at the next level are responsible for specific work teams. If you research one or two organisations on the internet, you might notice similarities in their structures, but also differences, depending on their size, industry or business type.

Formal structure a hierarchy or ordered system that identifies the ways in which an organisation is managed. Each organisation has a structure designed to best meet its needs and objectives. Large organisations generally have more complicated structures than smaller ones.

Strategic communication practice leaders have important roles in organisational hierarchies. In some organisations, they are part of the senior management team, reporting directly to the CEO or president; in others, they report through another senior executive. Regardless of their formal reporting lines, senior practice leaders almost always have direct, sometimes daily, contact with the CEO, unhindered by hierarchy. Chapter 13 will discuss this counselling function.

CHAPTER EXERCISE

Identifying organisational directions

Select a large organisation. It might be a big company that produces sports equipment or exports minerals, a car manufacturer, a computer software company, or it might be a government agency that delivers services to veterans, or a water or electricity utility. Find and explore the organisation's website and locate its latest annual report.

Answer these questions:

1. What does the organisation's website, and its annual report, say about its values and business directions?
2. Why are those values and directions important?
3. How does the organisation's vision, or its mission statement, relate to its values and business directions?
4. Does the annual report illustrate how the organisation has followed its values in achieving its business objectives or goals?
5. Does the information you have identified from this research indicate that the organisation is dealing with issues that are broader than its immediate bottom line? How?

SPECIALIST PRACTICE AND STRATEGIC COMMUNICATION

While decisions about an organisation's direction are based on research, the ultimate key to success is the ability of managers to engage in what Peggy and Carl Brønn (2002) describe as insightful and creative strategic thinking. They say that while organisations provide the framework for decision-making, it is individuals who think strategically, not the organisation. They are writing about decision-making in relation to how organisations should address issues, but their points about issues and creative thinking apply equally to the role of strategic communication planners.

Organisational communication has often been included the marketing communication function. The underlying principle is that all organisational communication, including product promotion, sales, direct selling, advertising and public relations, needs to be coordinated so that it always follows the same goals and objectives with consistent messages. Integrated marketing communication was the result. As we saw earlier, in the middle of the first decade of the twenty-first century, scholars began to think about the role of communication beyond a marketing context and to explore how a longer-term, strategic focus explains a range of other activities. Communication practice specialties like issues management, community relations, investor relations, lobbying and employee communication are regarded as having this longer-term focus because they are more likely to be practised in non-market environments. These specialties are grouped under broader functions like corporate communication and **public affairs** (see box) that deal with how communication happens at a corporate, rather than a tactical product, level. This reframing does not ignore the importance of all forms of communication to advancing the financial bottom line, but it does differentiate between what needs to be done today and how the organisation will communicate with vital non-market stakeholders in the longer term to address broader issues. It is this notion that has led scholars to focus on how communication strategy should be linked to mid- and long-term business goals and objectives. A great deal of the modern literature on public relations, public affairs and corporate communication has explored this notion, including the factors that drive strategic communication decisions, and why and how such strategic communication should occur.

Public affairs a communication specialty that primarily deals with issues management. Like many such terms, there is no one, clear definition.

Senior public affairs practitioners are especially suited to strategic planning communication roles. This is a natural fit because these practitioners have a wide remit in organisations through their role as boundary spanners. By identifying and analysing the socio-economic and political issues that play out in the external environment, senior public affairs practitioners have a sound understanding of the organisation's business, the issues that are important to it, and the people who care most about those issues.

Some scholars and practitioners view public affairs as a communication specialty that deals with external **public policy** challenges; others regard public affairs as interchangeable with public relations; still others see it as lobbying; and in some countries, "public affairs" is the functional description of the communication sections of government agencies. McGrath, Moss and Harris (2010) suggest that public affairs involves all the corporate functions that relate to the management of an organisation's reputation with external publics. They describe public affairs as seeking to influence public policy in an organisation's favour and to ensure that issues of importance to the wider world are reflected within the organisation's thinking.

Public policy the decisions governments make about issues that are important to the way a society functions. In most countries public policies deal with, for example, health care, pensions, immigration, industrial relations and education. These are all issues that relate to an organisation's external environment, which is why strategic communicators are interested in them, and their impact on organisations. And it is why organisations contribute to discourses on public policy issues in their role as "social actors."
    The professional-practice functions covered by public affairs include corporate communication; issues management; crisis communication; media relations;

employee communications; and community, stakeholder, government and media relations.

Here, the terms *strategic communication*, *corporate communication* and *public affairs* are interchangeable because they are each practice functions that deal with issues management.

For some further reading on what public affairs involves, see C. McGrath, D. Moss and P. Harris (2010), The Evolving Discipline of Public Affairs, *Journal of Public Affairs*, 10(4), pp. 335–52.

The definitions that scholars apply to public relations in its strategic role are appropriate to public affairs in the context in which it is used here. They also provide a prism through which the development of strategic communication as a corporate function can be viewed.

Scott Cutlip and his colleagues (2006) define public relations as both a management art and a science, and as an organisational management function. They argue that public relations is inescapably tied, by nature and necessity, to top management, a relationship in which public relations staff provide counsel and communication support. That is the role of strategic communication. The eminent US scholar Robert Heath (2001) also sees public relations as a management function that seeks to achieve what he describes as mutually beneficial relationships between organisations and their publics through the use of rhetoric. Heath's definition, and his use of rhetoric as a tool, illustrates the argument of David Bach and David Allen (2010) that organisations are social actors who need to advance their interests in public discourses about issues. Fraser Seitel (2007), another eminent US scholar, argues that business management courses should include the theoretical and practical underpinnings of public relations because its practice is an integral part of an organisation's daily workings and relationships. Seitel includes companies, churches, schools and governments as examples of organisations. The British scholar Emma Wood (2009, pp. 51–2) notes that a key dimension of corporate communication is its relationship to overall organisational strategy. Wood says that linking the two is vital if communication is to be taken seriously by the highest levels of management.

FURTHER READING

Cancel, A.E., Cameron, G.T., Sallot, L.M. and Mitrook, M.A. (1997), It Depends: A Contingency Theory of Accommodation in Public Relations, *Journal of Public Relations Research*, 9(1), pp. 31–63.

Grunig, J.E. (2006), Furnishing the Edifice: Ongoing Research on Public Relations as a Strategic Management Function, *Journal of Public Relations Research*, 18(2), pp. 151–76.

Mahoney, J. (2011), Horizons in Strategic Communication: Theorising a Paradigm Shift, *International Journal of Strategic Communication*, 5(3), pp. 143–53.

Sandhu, S. (2009), Strategic Communication: An Institutional Perspective. *International Journal of Strategic Communication*, 3(2), pp. 72–92.

HIGH-LEVEL DECISION-MAKING

Interpreting the potential impact of external socio-economic and political issues, and counselling internal and external clients on ways to respond to them, is a strategic management function. These issues are most likely to play out in an organisation's non-market environment (see Chapter 2). It is their ability to interpret non-market issues that helps qualify strategic communicators for what many describe as "a seat at the management table," where they are able to participate in high-level discussions about corporate strategy, business planning and performance as well as communication opportunities.

Writing about the links between public affairs and strategic business planning, including in major companies like General Motors, Thomas Marx (1990) notes that in comprehensively analysing current and future socio-political environments, public affairs staff must be able to:

- Detect and assess changing social values and attitudes, and emerging social expectations
- Not just predict the future, but also understand the forces that cause change
- Understand the potential policy implications of those changes
- Identify the opportunities and risks that the changes would create for an organisation.

Marx is arguing for the integration of public affairs strategic planning into business strategic planning. Earlier, in 1986, Marx had written that the challenges posed by the global integration of the world's economies, and by social integration of human economic and social needs, meant that organisations' public affairs and strategic planning staff needed to establish the legitimacy of business participation in public policy issues.

That integration is a reality in many organisations, and business participates in public policy discourses. Anne Gregory (2005) suggests the appointment of senior strategic communicators to high-level decision-making positions is institutionalised. That is, senior management understands that strategic communication adds value to corporate decision-making at a level that transcends the bottom-line contributions of the product communication functions, which focus on the day-to-day market environment. That added value is the ability to identify, analyse and address the mid- and long-term issues that will impact on how organisations go about their business.

The senior people in these strategic roles understand not only the context in which their organisations operate, but also how they are managed. Good management is about leadership and about guiding an organisation to achieve its objectives in a constantly changing environment, but good managers responding to, or driving, change need to communicate effectively with shareholders, external authorities, staff, customers and suppliers (Tymson et al., 2006). Once the business direction and strategy have been decided, every decision and action will involve a cause and effect and will result in an outcome. Much of this will be determined by how well decisions are communicated and understood (Tymson et al., 2006), which is why the link between a strategic communication plan and the organisation's strategic business plan is so important.

FURTHER READING

Gavetti, G. (2011), The New Psychology of Strategic Leadership, *Harvard Business Review*, 89(7–8), pp. 118–25.
Kim, S. and Rader, S. (2010), What They Can Do Versus How Much They Care: Assessing Corporate Communication Strategies on *Fortune 500* Web Sites, *Journal of Communication Management*, 14(1), pp. 59–80.
Northhaft, H. (2010), Communication Management as a Second-Order Management Function: Roles and Functions of the Communication Executive—Results from a Shadowing Study, *Journal of Communication Management*, 14(2), pp. 127–140.

FOLLOWING THE GENETIC CODE

In addition to the formal links to a business strategy or plan, multiple discussions between practitioners and senior staff enhance communication strategies. These include the functional hierarchical arrangements we've already looked at, and personal working relationships between communicators and management.

James Grunig and his colleagues found in their "Excellence" study that when public relations was sublimated to marketing or another management function (say, "operations"), it lost its unique role in strategic management (Grunig, 2006). This is also true for the new professional practice of strategic communication.

When an organisation's board agrees on a strategic business plan, everyone in the organisation needs to know about it, as do external target publics like shareholders, the stock exchange, customers, suppliers and financial journalists. Thus the "genetic" link between a business strategy or plan and strategic communication means that communication goals, objectives, pathways and tools reflect the directions in which the organisation is heading. Accordingly, the fundamental starting point for the strategic communication plan should be how it will help achieve strategic business goals. For example, if the fictitious company Ideal Widgets Pty Ltd decides on a new strategic business goal to produce the safest widgets on the market, the strategic communication plan will reflect that by including:

- A broad-based *goal* that identifies an over-arching purpose for the plan precise, measurable communication *objectives* aimed at increasing knowledge of the safety benefits of Ideal's widgets among customers by, say, 50 per cent over six months, and other communication steps needed to achieve the goal
- Communication *messages* that include references to the fact that the widgets exceed safety standards and that they cost less than competitor products

communication pathways (or *message delivery strategies*) indicating how the messages will be delivered to *target publics*

■ An outline of the *communication tools* (or *tactics*) that will implement the strategy.

We'll look more closely at these elements of strategic planning in the following chapters.

As noted earlier, Wood (2009) identifies the link between communication activities and a strategic business plan as vital if the highest levels of management are to take communication seriously. Robert Dilenschneider, a senior American practitioner, put it more bluntly. He told an international public relations

CHAPTER EXERCISE

Public affairs and managing issues

This exercise will help you to explore how organisations use public affairs activities when they address issues. It also introduces some of the steps involved in identifying and analysing the situations addressed by strategic communication plans, which will be discussed in the next two chapters.

■ First, reflect on the discussion earlier in this chapter about public affairs and the strategic role it has in organisational communication. Then return to the organisation that you used for the first exercise in this chapter (see page 53).

■ From the annual report, and any other information you can find on your organisation's website, list the issues that would be managed through public affairs activities.

■ Do these issues relate to the organisation's values and business directions? Why?

■ Using a search engine, research two of the issues you've identified to discover what other organisations or groups are interested in them. Which groups have an interest in these issues, and why are they important to them?

■ Are the mass news media interested in these issues? Which mass news media? Why are they interested?

■ What did the organisation do to address the two issues you identified? Were these activities within the definition of public affairs?

■ Why did the organisation use these activities?

■ Does the organisation's annual report explain whether its activities to address issues were successful? If so, why did it say they were successful or unsuccessful?

■ Were the issues linked to the strategic directions of the organisation? Why?

conference in Australia in 1988 that CEOs wanted people who, among other things, helped them make money, and tied strategic planning to business objectives (in White, 1989). While Dilenschneider was talking more than three decades ago, his views are still valid today, and current strategic communication scholarship reflects research on topics related to what he had to say.

FURTHER READING

Hamrefors, S. (2010), Communicative Leadership, *Journal of Communication Management*, 14(2), pp. 141–52.

Rumelt, R. (2011), The Perils of Bad Strategy, *McKinsey Quarterly*, online topics at http://www. mckinseyquarterly.com/The_perils_of_bad_strategy_2826/, 8 July 2011

Silver, D. (2011), Overcoming Groupthink in the Boardroom, *The Public Relations Strategist*, 17(1), spring, pp. 25–6.

Steyn, S. and Niemann, L. (2010), Enterprise Strategy: A Concept that Explicates Corporate Communication's Strategic Contribution at the Macro-organisational Level, *Journal of Communication Management*, 14(2), pp. 106–26.

Zerfass, A. (2009), Institutionalising Strategic Communication: Theoretical Analysis and Empirical Evidence, *International Journal of Strategic Communication*, 3(2), pp. 69–71.

BUILDING RELATIONSHIPS WITH SENIOR EXECUTIVES

Practitioners and scholars argue strongly for a strategic communication input into the development of a strategic management plan. John Allert and Clara Zawawi (2004) write that a practitioner's input into the design of a strategic business plan can influence how well it is understood by the organisation's publics; if it cannot be understood by these publics, they write, it will be unworkable.

To achieve that kind of input, strategic communication practice leaders must build relationships with executives at all levels of an organisation and be able to advise them about how they can communicate with their staff and external publics. This is an important function, whether the practice leader reports directly to the CEO or to someone else. Building these relationships and making sure that similar cross-functional working relationships occur at other levels is vital to strategic communication success. Good relationships provide opportunities for identifying interesting people, activities and research and development discoveries that can be used to promote the organisation. They also ensure access to people at all levels, often when it is needed urgently, and generate requests for advice on communication opportunities.

These relationships, and the trust associated with them, are vital when senior practitioners counsel senior executives on a particular course of action, say in a crisis. They are equally vital in the day-to-day decision-making of the organisation when senior practitioners are working at a strategic level. Grunig and his colleagues helped us understand why this would be so when their research identified involvement in strategic management as a critical characteristic of communication excellence. They argued that unless it was "empowered to be heard,"

CHAPTER EVALUATION

Review your understanding of this chapter by answering these questions:

1. Why is it important to link strategic communication plans to an organisation's strategy?
2. How does strategic communication reflect the organisation's overall goals?
3. Why do communication practice leaders need to think strategically?
4. Do you agree that organisations need to be aware of the potential impact of public policy on their operations? Why?
5. Is it more important for organisations to deal with market issues or non-market issues? Why?
6. In what circumstances would an organisation use strategic communication to deal with non-market issues?

the strategic communication function would have little effect on organisations (Grunig, 2006). Strategic communication won't be heard, and thus empowered, if its practitioners do not build effective relationships and demonstrate that they are capable of contributing to management decisions by linking strategic communication to organisational strategy.

Chapter 4 outlines the framework elements of communication strategies and explains terminology, definitions and structure. It will discuss similarities and differences between the strategic plan frameworks used in the communication disciplines and expand on the framework used in this book.

TIME OUT: ON THE IMPORTANCE OF THEORY

On a journey of discovery like this exploration of strategic communication, taking time out to reflect on what else is involved, beyond the process, is a useful way of understanding the context in which practitioners do what they do.

In exploring the nature of strategic communication and why it has a special role in dealing with public policy issues, we're concerned with what is involved in a strategy and how all that links to business planning (understanding "business" broadly as not just being about commercial things). This involves all the elements of a communication strategy, such as researching organisational communication needs, and planning and writing the important parts of a strategic communication plan: a situation analysis, target public segmentation, and goals and objectives.

This research and analysis build the core foundations on which the rest of the strategy is based. Knowing what needs to be done; why it needs to be done; who is important in that situation; what they know, don't know or need to know about the issue and the organisation; the goals and objectives—all this preparation puts what follows on a solid foundation. And what follows in strategic communication planning is decision-making about messages: how to deliver them, the resources that will be needed and how to evaluate success.

All this is grounded in theoretical principles, mostly adapted from other disciplines, like sociology, psychology, the sciences, political science and philosophy. The *In Theory* panels in this book explain relevant theoretical principles and illustrate where and how they apply. The theoretical honeycomb diagram in Time Out Figure 1 illustrates some of the theories and practice that can inform strategic communication planning decisions. It suggests that after an issues analysis, consideration must be given to whether communication will be informative or persuasive, or perhaps both, for the situation being addressed; the theories might help in making those decisions; and the selection of messages, communication pathways and tools that will be applied.

Outside the academy, few people spend much time pondering the theoretical concepts that drive professional communication. For some, theories about how and why people communicate, process information, participate in discourse about the affairs of the day, or can be persuaded of something, are irrelevant, no matter how soundly based they are. For them, this is the concern of scholars and their students; busy practitioners have little time left for theory after dealing with their daily tasks. This is a rather head-in-the-sand attitude because scholars regularly publish research results which have major implications for modern, up-to-date, professional practice.

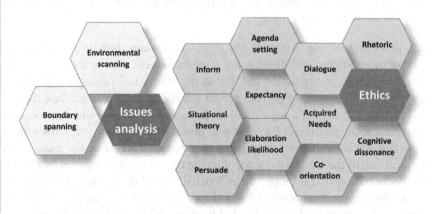

Time Out Figure 1 A honeycomb of theory

Joep Cornelissen (2000) has written about the need for practitioners to inform their work with theory and research. He describes those who do this as reflective practitioners, and says they are able to work out how to adapt to changing circumstances instead of relying on intuition and trial and error. Cornelissen's view is that theory is a resource to help practitioners continually question what they do and to make sense of situations they are asked to address. Understanding theory makes professional practice more effective.

Reflective practitioners do not exist in ivory towers, wondering only about theoretical principles. They are usually experienced, adept at using a full range of communication practice skills, and curious about knowing how and why each tactic is appropriate for target publics. They are people Cornelissen would describe as pragmatic professionals who adopt ideas from the rich pool of academic theory, but only where it is relevant to their practice.

Cornelissen's three models of translation

Cornelissen (2000) identifies three ways by which theories and concepts are translated into practice.

- The *instrumental* use of theory is a traditional problem-solving approach in which academic theory and research provide rational solutions to managerial problems in a direct and instrumental way.
- In a *conceptual* model, abstract academic knowledge is applied to practical cases through generalisations, concepts and ideas.
- The *translation* model suggests that theory and practice are intertwined as mutually influential entities in the generation of knowledge. It recognises that scientific knowledge is hardly ever used unchanged in a practical setting, since practitioners transform and interpret research outcomes in the context of professional understanding.

In fact, practitioners use theory all the time, even when they do not recognise it. For instance, writing and distributing a media release, no matter how serious or trivial the topic, is a practice task based on theoretical principles. A simple media release applies principles from **media effects theory**, two-step flow theory, agenda setting, target public segmentation, news writing theory and the selection of communication pathways. For example, media effects theory explains why it is important for an organisation to have its messages carried in the mass news media, and one of the traditional ways of trying to get that to happen is by producing a media release that is picked up by journalists and turned into a news story. Some scholars argue that media effects theory overestimates the impact of the mass media, because people are subjected to other influences that also build their awareness and understanding of an issue and that influence their behaviour—that is, the action they take. Nevertheless, the somewhat simplistic view that your message is most effectively conveyed to target publics via the mass news media persists and provides a great deal of work for public relations practitioners. It is almost certain that the adage about the media setting the agenda for public discourse about issues still applies; what is unclear is the extent to which an *output* like, say, newspaper coverage of an organisation's media release achieves an *outcome* like a change in behaviour (see the case on pp. 47–8).

Media effects theory the idea that the mass media have a powerful direct influence on people's awareness and understanding of an issue, and that people change their behaviour because of exposure to messages delivered via this communication channel.

Other tasks—using social media applications in a strategic communication campaign; goal and objective setting; identifying target publics; writing messages; selecting communication pathways and tools; and effective evaluation—are similarly based on theoretical principles. For example, Chapter 6 deals with why target publics matter in strategic communication and uses **resource dependency theory** to explain one aspect of relationship building. It also cites Kirk Hallahan's exploration of issues dynamics and his typology of publics as examples of the importance of target public segmentation (2000, 2001). Scholarly endeavours to understand how and why communication works has even led to a theory about the kind of practitioner who doesn't use communication theory at all but works from intuition.

Resource dependency theory the idea that organisations depend on, and manage, external resources to do the things they do. In strategic communication, building good relationships with suppliers (of electricity, water and raw materials, for example) assists in the acquisition of resources.

Dan Lattimore and colleagues (2004) suggest that individual practitioners should build a set of theories to help their practice. Many advertising and public relations agencies do precisely this when they utilise specific theories to explain their recommendations to clients. The chosen theory is not heavily emphasised but is treated broadly by pointing out to the client that research by distinguished scholars has shown that people in this target public are likely to process information in this particular way—and that's the approach that backs up these recommendations for the campaign.

The most important theoretical principles are those that help explain how and why professional communication works: why dialogue is important; definitions and segmentation of publics; why considering situations organisations face is important; systems, **contingency** and **complexity theory**; the relationships between organisations and their publics; and rhetoric. Some of these are outlined in Chapter 8.

Contingency theory an attempt to explain how internal and external factors (independent variables) influence organisations' abilities (the dependent variable) to do what they do. It is used by scholars to explore how such factors influence communication.

Complexity theory the idea—derived from the physical sciences—that all systems, natural and human-made, are continually changing, often in small ways. Some scholars use complexity theory to study interactions and relationships in organisations.

Often senior communication practitioners know what will work in a particular situation based on their experience. David Dozier (in Oliver, 2007) describes this approach as *individualistic*, meaning communication activities are prepared using internalised professional standards of quality. Sometimes, especially in a crisis, working in this way helps to resolve urgent matters. Dozier defines the alternative to this approach as *scientific*—an approach to planning based on learning about publics from scientifically derived knowledge. That means using recognised research methods to analyse situations.

Recognised methodologies deliver effective situation analyses. **Quantitative research**, for example, will provide numbers—for example, how many people believe this, do that, go there, are in a particular age range, get married every year, live in the suburbs, smoke cigarettes, work, go to school, have kids, swim twice a day, play tennis and will vote for the government at the next election. This data can be sorted by any or all of those variables to build a demographic picture of target publics. **Qualitative research** findings will help to interpret the numbers by providing reasons why people do things.

Quantitative research reports its results as numbers.
Qualitative research is concerned with finding people's attitudes and opinions about something. It can be used to explain quantitative results.

The following case illustrates how research and theory can be used to address an issue.

Case: Linking research to strategy

Research for an Australian government agency sought to find out why so many university students still smoked cigarettes after being exposed to anti-smoking campaigns from their time at pre-school through to tertiary studies. The research found that almost two-thirds of the 234 university students (75 per cent were female) had smoked cigarettes at some stage of their lives, but that only 36 per cent still smoked. More females (74 per cent) still smoked compared with males, almost the same percentage as those who said they had ever smoked. More than half of those who still smoked thought about quitting, or cutting down, every day or at least weekly. Almost everyone recalled hearing anti-smoking messages from teachers at school and in the mass media and could list the messages. The students were asked their reasons for smoking. None said they smoked because they did not believe health warnings, but more than half the smokers said they did so because it relaxed them, or they enjoyed it, or because their friends smoked. The students were asked to rank on a scale of 1–8 their preferences for receiving anti-smoking messages. Among all smokers, and also among current smokers, the number-one preference was to receive these messages from medical people like doctors, as it was for females. Male smokers and non-smokers preferred to receive these messages from television and radio advertising, but rated doctors as their second preference. Messages on cigarette packages were the third most preferred option, while messages designed to scare people from smoking were least preferred. Messages from parents and teachers were well down the preference scale, especially as students saw teachers smoking shortly after talking about anti-smoking.

This information was interesting, but it also has implications for communication strategies designed to promote anti-smoking health objectives. The researchers suggested that fear-based messages are generally ignored, and that campaigns to convince young people not to smoke may not have adequately taken account of the ways in which they process information. They recommended that campaign designers consider using elements of content and process communication theories to inform future strategies. These theories include:

- Richard Petty and John Cacioppo's (1984) elaboration likelihood model, discussed in Chapter 8
  David McClelland's acquired needs theory (see, for example, the discussion in Kitchen, 1999, pp. 146–8), which assists in profiling the "needs" that motivate an individual's behaviour. The relevance to anti-smoking campaigns is that McClelland found that people with a high need for achievement prefer individual responsibility and challenging but achievable goals. They also prefer interpersonal relationships and opportunities to communicate: doctors delivering anti-smoking messages would respond to that need.
- Victor Vroom's expectancy theory (see, for example, Kitchen, 1999, pp. 156–60), which suggests people calculate the benefits of behaving in certain ways after they assess the effort involved, and the probability of a rewarding outcome. Applied to anti-smoking campaigns, expectancy theory would allow campaign designers to prepare persuasive messages for people who smoke because, for example, it relaxes them, by arguing there is no value in continuing the habit but high value for their health if they stop.

Sources: J. Mahoney and A. Burrell (2007), *A Puff of Smoke: The Effectiveness of Anti-Smoking Campaigns among Young Canberrans*, a pilot study for the ACT Department of Health; J. Mahoney (2010), Strategic Communication and Anti-smoking Campaigns, *Public Communication Review*, 1(2), pp. 33–48.

Chapter 4
Elements of a communication strategy

Goal: To understand the elements of a strategic communication plan.

Objectives: This chapter will help you to:

- Learn the strategic communication framework
  Familiarise yourself with the terminology used to describe strategy elements
- Be aware of the similarities and differences between advertising, marketing communication and public relations strategic plans.

Principle: Successful strategic communication planning is based on both theoretical and practical principles.

Practice: Professional practitioners apply a framework to plan strategic communication.

Practitioners in each of the major professional communication disciplines—advertising, marketing communication and public relations—use time-tested frameworks to plan what they need to do for clients. While the frameworks used by each discipline vary in some ways, like terminology, they are similar in that they are about maximising opportunities and minimising problems. As previous chapters have pointed out, strategic communication plans set out what needs to be done for a client, how it will be done and how a practitioner will know that it has worked. The British academic Anne Gregory (2006) tells us that this kind of planning won't make a poorly conceived program successful but will make it more likely that the program will be well conceived.

HOW MANY STRATEGIES CAN ONE ORGANISATION HAVE?

Cees van Riel and Charles Fombrun (2008) describe communication as the life-blood of organisations. They say that an organisation's success in acquiring the resources it needs to produce its products or services successfully, and to influence the context in which it operates, depends heavily on how professionally it

DOI: 10.4324/9781003317579-5

communicates. They write that the multiple strategic and tactical communication activities in which organisations engage build a **communication system**.

System a set of connected things, or parts, that work as a whole. The *Australian Concise Oxford Dictionary* explains systems using, as examples, the human body, and the group of related hardware and program units that make up a computer.
Communication system the overall structure or system through which an organisation communicates with target publics, and in which each piece fits with others to make up the overall picture, a bit like a jigsaw puzzle. Effective communication systems are integrated so that people working on each part follow the same goals and objectives and use the same messages.

A communication system includes functions like advertising, investor relations, community relations, marketing, marketing communication, public relations, public affairs, sales and employee (or internal) communication. Large commercial organisations are likely to have a communication system that includes all these functions. Smaller organisations usually have communication systems in which staff are proficient in one area and employ external consultants when additional expertise is needed. Figure 4.1 illustrates a communication system visualising integration between marketing, marketing communication, advertising and public relations. In this system, for example, mass media advertising is about selling products in the market environment. Outcomes from mass media advertising have appropriate, significant and most often immediate impacts on an organisation's financial bottom line. Corporate advertising, sometimes called "advocacy advertising," is a longer-term activity. It promotes the organisation itself, its values and reputation and advocates its position on the issues it faces. It works in tandem with public relations and public affairs activities and doesn't have an immediate impact on the organisation's financial bottom line.

Here's an example of the differences between the two advertising approaches working in a communication system: most automobile manufacturers use paid advertising in the mass media to promote sales of their cars, trucks and other vehicles. These advertisements are based on extensive market research that identifies how potential purchasers react to new models and respond to draft advertisements. Television, social media, radio and press advertisements are developed by skilled creative practitioners and production teams, usually in external advertising agencies, using information from market research. From time to time, the manufacturers also produce advertisements that are not designed to immediately convince potential customers to buy a new car, but rather to tell audiences about the company's good works, or views on a public issue. In both approaches, other specialists in the communication system work in tandem with advertising staff. For product advertising, marketing people will have identified pricing, logistics and distribution options; sales staff will have developed the material needed to help buyers make decisions; public relations people will have been involved in their marketing communication role of developing and writing supporting material. **Corporate** or **advocacy advertising**

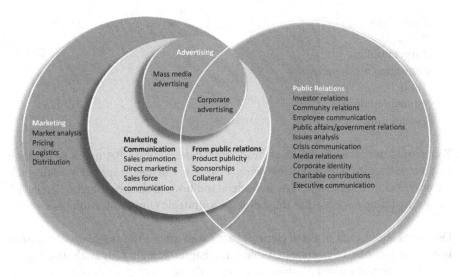

Figure 4.1 A communication system

will be planned from information identified in issue monitoring carried out by the public affairs or corporate communication teams. This monitoring will alert communicators to current and emerging issues—perhaps in a corporate social responsibility context—that the organisation needs to address. The organisation's advertising agency will produce these advertisements.

Corporate advertising, advertising that promotes the organisation itself rather than its products.
Advocacy advertising, advertising that deals with an organisation's position on public policy issues.

The key piece in an organisational communication system is a big-picture, corporate-level strategy, directly linked to the organisation's business plan. Each of the communication functions in the system will have specific plans linked directly to this top-level strategy. These describe how goals and objectives for advertising, marketing communication and the sub-disciplines of public relations (like, for example, investor relations, community relations, public affairs and employee communication) will be achieved. From time to time, particular circumstances—a product launch, or a special event, or the need to lobby a government for a change to a policy or a regulation—will require a communication plan just for that activity.

STRATEGIC COMMUNICATION PLAN FRAMEWORK

The classic strategic communication plan framework used in this book was outlined in Chapter 1. The elements of the framework are:

- A situation analysis
  goals

- Objectives
  messages
- Target publics
  communication pathways
- Tools
  implementation
- Evaluation.

You should use these elements as headings for describing what needs to be done in your strategic plans. The following chapters will deal separately with each element, but it is important now to understand how all this fits together. Table 4.1 shows the framework used in this book for a strategic communication plan.

Decisions about each of these elements are taken after a thorough **situation analysis**, which is not, of course, in Table 4.1. Chapter 5 deals with analysing organisational communication needs—situation analysis.

Situation analysis narrative that provides a detailed analysis of the communication issues and opportunities facing an organisation. The analysis is based on formative research.

From left to right, the top six columns in Table 4.1 show how the elements of a strategic plan cascade. *Goals* dealing with the organisation's reputation, or its relationships or tasks that need to be completed to implement the strategy, set the broad direction. *Objectives*, which are about changes to awareness, acceptance and generating action, are a step towards achieving the goals. *Messages* are what the organisation needs to say to its *target publics*, and *communication pathways* are the methods by which target publics can be reached with *tools* which carry messages. The *implementation* section of the plan outlines all the steps that are needed to prepare and apply it; the *evaluation* part sets out in detail how the plan's success will be measured. The results of an evaluation, whether it's for a top-level corporate communication strategy or the plan for a product launch, provide valuable information that can be used to prepare the next version of the plan, or to help formulate the next steps. Chapter 12 deals with evaluation.

Implementation putting a decision or a plan into effect. In strategic communication, this means deciding what needs to be done, writing a plan to do that, working out the resources—money, people and technology—that are required, and preparing a timeline showing the dates by which all the activities will be completed and who will be responsible for them.

If a practitioner does not understand what the organisation does, the issues it faces and why those issues are important, there is little chance that the strategic plan elements will be appropriate. Figure 4.2 shows the broad areas that need to

Table 4.1 Strategic plan framework

Goals	Objectives	Messages	Target publics	Pathways	Tools
Goals acknowledge the situation or issue and broadly set out how the organisation wants to deal with it.	These are clear, measurable statements that indicate changes the organisation wants to achieve over a period of time to meet the goals.	Messages are the things that the organisation needs to say to its target publics to achieve objectives	Target publics are the people who need to know the organisation's messages to help it achieve its goals and objectives	Communication pathways indicate how the organisation can reach its target publics	Communication tools carry messages and are what target publics see. They are delivered by communication pathways
Goals deal with: ○ reputation ○ relationships ○ tasks (outputs)	**Objectives** are steps to implement goals and deal with changes to: ○ awareness ○ acceptance ○ action. Objectives are to achieve **outcomes**. Objectives are precise and **measurable**—they must include numbers that **indicate the amount of change** needed **Output** objectives deal with tasks	**Messages** are written to make publics: ○ **aware** of the organisation ○ **accept** the organisation's point of view ○ take **actions** that support the organisation	**Target publics** can be classified as: ○ **primary**—those directly affected ○ **secondary**—indirectly affected publics who can nevertheless influence primary publics ○ **tertiary**—publics that can influence others	**Communication pathways** deal with the mechanisms by which this will be done, for example: ○ controlled media ○ uncontrolled media ○ building alliances ○ special events ○ sponsorship ○ interpersonal dialogue ○ interactive media	**Tools** are **outputs** like: ○ websites ○ social media ○ displays ○ printed material ○ meetings ○ interviews ○ media releases ○ funding from sponsorships ○ factsheets

(continued)

Table 4.1 continued

Goals	Objectives	Messages	Target publics	Pathways	Tools

Implementation

Implementation applies to all phases of your strategy. It is the section that identifies all the logistical things that will be needed to make the strategy work. The implementation section should include:

○ a timeline covering all the steps that you will need to take to deliver your communication pathways and tools, including formative and summative research

○ the resources (money, technology, people) you will need

○ a checklist that indicates who in your team will be responsible for doing which parts of your strategic planning and implementation, which can also be used to check progress

○ the financial budget

Evaluation

Evaluation also applies to all parts of a communication strategy. An evaluation plan should clearly indicate how you are going to show your client that the plan worked. That is, you will need to show whether:

○ the goals and objectives were achieved on time and within budget

○ the communication strategies were appropriate for reaching target publics, and the tools worked with the communication pathways

○ the target publics received, understood and acted on the messages delivered by the communication tools.

An evaluation tests whether the situation analysis identified the relevant issues that needed to be covered by the strategy—and whether the decisions you took in writing goals and objectives, and in selecting messages, publics, pathways, tools and how and when you implemented it, were correct.

○ If your goals and objectives are based on a sound situation analysis, and are correctly written, the evaluation will likely mean successful outcomes for the strategy.

If the plan is not successful, you need to ask, "Why wasn't it?"

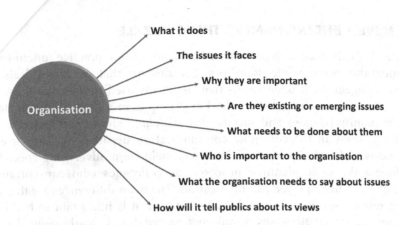

Figure 4.2 Strategic communication plan focus

CHAPTER EXERCISE

Strategies and issues

First, think about the discussion so far in this chapter, and relate it to what was covered in the previous chapters. Then, answer the following questions:

1. Why do organisations need a strategic plan?
2. What do strategic plans do?
3. What is the key to a strategy? Why is that the most important part of a strategy?
4. Why are activities in the organisation related to strategy?
5. Why do organisational leaders need to be communicators?
   Next, go back to the exercises you did in Chapters 2 and 3. Apply your thoughts in those exercises to the organisation you selected for your strategic communication plan. Then, answer these questions:
6. What is the main issue facing your organisation? Why is it important from a communication perspective?
7. How might a communication strategy help to resolve the problems you've identified? Why did you answer in that way?

be addressed in researching and writing a plan. Chapter 5, on situation analysis, includes a discussion about researching issues.

FURTHER READING

Cornelissen, J. (2005), *Corporate Communications: Theory and Practice*, Sage, London.
Oliver, S. (2007), *Public Relations Strategy*, 2nd edn, Kogan Page, London.
Van Riel, C.B.M. and Fombrun, C.J. (2008), *Essentials of Corporate Communication: Implementing Practices for Effective Reputation Management*, Routledge, London.

THE NEVER-ENDING NAMING THING PUZZLE

Chapter 3 briefly dealt with professional communication practice functions and explained the role of public affairs as a specialisation that, generally, deals with issues management. It often seems that the terms used to describe these specialist functions are interchangeable. For example, in a large company, terms like *community relations* and *investor* (or *shareholder*) *relations* describe specialist functions in the corporate communication department. They use the same skills and techniques, sometimes seek help from advertising specialists, and follow the same planning processes as colleagues who concentrate on public affairs and employee communication. The main differences are that they concentrate on specific target publics with whom it is important to build and maintain special relationships. Employees are vital and clearly defined target publics for all organisations, just as shareholders are important to companies. In this sense, the seemingly never-ending puzzle about how communication functions should be described is important mainly for functional and operational reasons. All these functions share the same basic strategic planning principles and elements.

COMMUNICATION STRATEGY AND THE MARKET AND NON-MARKET ENVIRONMENTS

We've explored how strategic communication:

- Is for specific purposes and specific situations
  is planned, rational and deliberate
- Links organisations with their stakeholders, especially on common issues—those they share with their publics
  advances an organisation's goals and objectives
- Involves thinking about the future as much as working on immediate tactical functions
  includes a range of specialist functions.

Chapter 2 proposed that strategic communication works in the contexts of an organisation's market and non-market environments, as well as in the three business-planning horizons proposed by Baghai and colleagues. Remember that Horizon 1 is concerned with the organisation's current business; Horizon 2 focuses on the mid-term (the period up to five years from now); Horizon 3 is about the long-term future (beyond the next five years). In each horizon, strategic communicators are concerned with identifying issues that may impact on the organisation, and with developing communication plans to deal with them. The realities of our dynamic world mean that the time parameters for Horizons 2 and 3 may shorten, especially when new or improved technology speeds up the construction of the infrastructure needed to produce goods, or to deliver services. Strategic communicators need to be aware of this, especially how issues are **dynamic**—that is, changing and evolving—and how changing circumstances

Table 4.2 Communication functions, environments and principal horizon focus

Communication function	Environment	Principal horizon focus
Community relations	Non-market	2 and 3
Corporate advertising	Both	2 and 3
Corporate communication	Non-market	All
Crisis communication	Both	1
Employee communication	Internal	All
Investor/financial relations	Market	All
Issues management	Non-market	2 and 3
Marketing communication	Market	1
Mass media advertising	Market	1
Media relations	Both	1 and 2
Public affairs	Non-market	2 and 3
Public relations	Both	1 and 2

and different aspects of issues will impact on strategic plans. Table 4.2 gives some examples of how this might apply.

Dynamic changing and evolving, sometimes over a long period; not static.

Hallahan's approach to dynamic issues

The scholar Kirk Hallahan—who proposed a typology of organisational target publics that helps communication practitioners work out who they need to build, and maintain, relations with, and why (we'll explore the typology in Chapter 6)— argues that issues are dynamic. Hallahan says issues involve opposing viewpoints, aired by people who attempt to influence the behaviours of others by altering their knowledge, attitudes or actions. He says most organisations deal with issues on multiple fronts and should tailor how they do this to their different target publics. Sometimes, after analysing issues, an organisation might decide not to respond to particular issues at all.

Hallahan has proposed 16 strategies organisations can use to respond to issues. For further reading, see K. Hallahan (2001), The Dynamics of Issues Activation and Response: An Issues Processes Model, *Journal of Public Relations Research*, 13(1), pp. 27–59.

AND NOW TO POLITICS

The discussion so far has been about strategic communication in an organisational context. But the concept that strategic communication deals with current and emerging issues suggests that it can also apply in politics.

In all democratic countries, politicians need to convince voters to elect, then re-elect, them to office. Politicians and their staff claim they do that through communication strategies. Often, however, these are only formally planned when an election campaign looms, even though politicians at all levels use communication techniques (often wrongly described as "strategies") throughout their terms to convince voters that they are doing a good job, are addressing issues that concern people, and know what needs to be done in their next term.

However, most political communication is tactical, not strategic. That is, it is focused on the issues of the day and on generating mass news media coverage of politicians' messages. Several factors explain this tactical approach to political communication.

First, politicians focus on issues—either by proposing new policies, legislation, regulations, or programs to resolve them, or by reacting to issues raised by their opponents. Second, politicians survive by being well known and by ensuring that voters understand what they believe in. Therefore, politicians want their messages, and faces, on the nightly television news, or on page 1 of the daily newspaper, supported by social media, including several daily tweets. Third, much modern-day political communication in the Western liberal democracies plays out in the mass news media. This means that two things happen: the news media report political issues as they happen, and reporters are always looking for politicians to comment on the issues. This is, of course, part of what is known as the 24-hour news cycle. Debates about issues that concern politicians occur in the non-market environment, which is why organisational strategic communicators need to be aware of developments in local, state and national—and sometimes international—politics.

Salient prominent, conspicuous or pertinent; important or significant. Salience in strategic communication refers to how target publics process information; whether that information is significant to them; whether goals, objectives, message delivery pathways and tools are pertinent.

This daily political battle results from what Robert Heath and Michael Palenchar (2009) describe as the competition between politicians, activists and the mass news media to define, prime and support issues and make them **salient** for voters. Heath and Palenchar say the battle is about owning an issue in the news media and in other communication venues. They argue that the resolution of an issue, and the communication context in which that is done, depends on how the issue survives in society itself, and that debates about issues are never separate from how they survive in popular discussion. This is because people use the mass news media to decide what and how to think about the information they acquire. Max McCombs and colleagues (cited in Heath and Palenchar, 2009) argue that issue agendas are formed by:

- The issues that are discussed in the news media
- The media discussing them
- The coverage the news media gives to debates about issues.

These points drive political communication.

First, decisions journalists take about the issues they'll report on are based on age-old traditions that help them decide what is news. These "news frames" vary, but in politics they are usually about conflict—two or more opposing views on an issue. Second, politicians are generally more concerned about issues covered in the daily mass news media than they are about coverage on a small, specialist blog. They are also more concerned if respected reporters, commentators or "shock-jock" radio talkback hosts with large readerships or audiences are covering an issue. Third, continuing page-1 coverage and first-story coverage on the nightly television news, together with commentary from experts, means the news media are treating the issue as important. The issue may not always be salient to readers or viewers, but it is to journalists when this kind of coverage occurs—and if it continues, voters will become interested.

IN THEORY: SALIENCE AND EXPECTANCY

The notion of *salience* is vital to strategic communication. In a strategic communication planning sense, salience applies to whether an issue being addressed is significant to target publics.

Expectancy theory was proposed by Victor Vroom as a way of predicting or explaining the effort a person uses to deal with tasks. Expectancy theory deals with work motivation and it is applied in communication as a way of assessing people's willingness to buy a product or accept an idea. This is an important theoretical concept in public policy discourses in the non-market environment. For people (we'll call them target publics), expectancy theory centres on three key terms:

- *Expectancy*: the probability that target publics will make an effort to understand the organisation's point of view on an issue, or consider buying its products. Is it salient to them?
- *Instrumentality*: the probability that the target public will do something about the message, or buy the product
- *Valence*: the value that a target public will put on the message or the product. For example, do they see it as desirable or undesirable?

An example of how this can impact the political environment comes from Australia. In 2011, the Australian Prime Minister, Julia Gillard, faced extremely low personal approval ratings and rock-bottom nationwide support for her political party. Despite a widespread view in the bureaucracy and among political observers that her minority government had achieved a lot and had made the parliament work against the odds (given that she did not control a majority in her own right), opinion poll results remained dismal for Gillard and her party. The Prime Minister and the government had not managed to improve their position by explaining clearly how it had insulated Australia from the global financial crisis (recognised internationally as a major economic success, unmatched by almost every other nation). Instead, the mass news media frames were her poll ratings, the leadership challenge she would inevitably face if the polls did not improve (in 2012, she was challenged for the leadership and won), the government's inability to resolve several serious policy challenges, and predictions that the next election would be a disaster for the government. And politicians in the Opposition parties attempted to frame her as a liar by continually pointing out that she had promised no government she led would introduce a carbon pollution tax, which she was in the process of doing. At one point in 2011, Gillard explained the predicament this way: "I've tended to allow decisions to speak for themselves." That simple sentence illustrates the tactical nature of political communication: announce a decision and move on to the next issue or photo opportunity without a strategic communication plan to make the decision salient for voters.

ALIGNING POLITICAL ISSUES, HORIZONS AND STRATEGIC COMMUNICATION

Perhaps more than any other profession, politicians need to build, maintain and enhance their credibility with their "stakeholders"—voters. Credibility involves a complex construct that includes perceptions of values, reputations, the impact of change and leadership. This is, for politics, the "perceptual construct" that Joep Cornelissen (2005) describes for business. As is the case in business, building and maintaining credibility for politicians requires open, honest and planned communication that rises above the day-to-day tactical commentary that is often buffeted by media framing of issues.

An exploratory research study in Australia in 2010 suggested that politicians' tendency to utilise tactical communication causes them to avoid effective long-term communication about issues that directly affect people and thus voters' perceptions of their credibility (Mahoney, 2010). The study showed that the issues that consumed Australian politicians and the mass news media during the 2010 election campaign were not dominant issues for those electors who attended a series of community cabinet meetings prior to the election.

In a business environment, the task of linking communication and business strategy includes identifying important mid- to long-term issues and developing programs to address them. Political communicators need to make similar links if politicians are to make the issues they deal with salient for electors. That process includes the constant strategic use of communication (Ströh, 2006), rather than the normative tactical approach, which ignores the complexity of relationships between politicians and voters because it assumes messages will generate linear and connected effects, an assumption that is the major reason so many communication campaigns fail to produce anticipated results (Gregory, 2000).

Given that political communication operates in the non-market environment, adapting the "horizons" approach to strategic communication may assist political communicators to develop programs to build credibility, and to build support for policy. This adaptation would classify issues in, and align communication activities to, the appropriate time horizons:

As *Horizon 1* has a focus on immediate concerns, the horizons approach to political communication would designate this as the arena for the day-to-day tactical chess game of politics, played out through the so-called 24/7 news cycle focusing on immediate political issues.

Horizon 2 would be used strategically to enhance reputations, and to manage relationships with voters in the context of mid-term change. Attempts to resolve issues around climate change are an example. It would be in this horizon that politicians also work towards re-election.

Horizon 3 would provide a focus for long-term public issues identification, such as forward defence postures, and policies related to changing population characteristics, and the associated strategic communication program planning.

FURTHER READING

Heath, R.L. and Palenchar, M.J. (2009), *Strategic Issues Management: Organisations and Public Policy Challenges*, 2nd edn, SAGE, Los Angeles, pp. 210–29.

Mahoney, J. (2010), Strategic Communication: Making Sense of Issues Management, Communication Policy Research Forum, Sydney, November, pp. 174–85, at www.networkinsight.org/verve/_resources/CPRF_2010_papers.pdf

CHAPTER EXERCISE

Analysing news media coverage of issues

In this chapter, we've seen how the strategic communication framework can apply in organisations and in politics. It also applies in not-for-profit organisations, which, like business and politics, deal with issues.

For this exercise, select a national not-for-profit organisation. Research the organisation and identify an issue with which it is concerned. You might, for example, select a health organisation that deals with the issue of obesity.

The exercise is designed to illustrate how communication strategies need to take account of the dynamics of issues, especially in a political context.

Using the research tools available through your library, track how the issue has been reported in one news media outlet (a television station, a news website or a major newspaper) in the last month, by answering these questions:

1. How many times has the news outlet reported the issue in the last month?
2. Has this coverage always been in a news story format; have comments from experts and/or people who oppose the organisation been included?
3. How many times have the organisation's views been the first point in the news coverage?
4. If the organisation's views on the issue have not always been the first point reported by journalists, why do you think that happened?
5. Have politicians, and other people and organisations contributed to the news about this issue? Have their views on this issue been given greater prominence than those of your not-for-profit organisation? Why do you think that is the case?

LINKING PLANNING TO EVALUATION

Planning strategic communication in an orderly way has a significant advantage: evaluation will be more effective. This is especially important for senior practice leaders who need to ensure all the communication needs of an organisation are met. It also helps demonstrate that the whole strategic communication department has achieved its goals and objectives. Sometimes this can be done by preparing a matrix of the various communication functions that shows how they relate to the overall strategic communication program. This approach is sometimes used in organisations where specific functional areas, like the production department, are described as "programs." An example of how such a matrix would work in the context of strategic communication is shown in Table 4.3.

The components will be programs instituted to pursue strategic goals and objectives, while activities will be the tactical elements of the strategy. Yet, if each component has its own goals and correctly written objectives, which are consistent with the overall strategic goals and objectives, there will be clear links between all parts of the matrix. That means that the success of the corporate *Program*, the Strategic Communication Department in Table 4.3, will be an outcome of the success of the *Components*. The success of each component depends on the success of its *Activities*. So, a successful Program outcome (sPo) is the sum

Table 4.3 Functional matrix for strategic communication

Program	Corporate strategic communication					
Components	Special events	Community relations	Media relations	Social media	Publications	Public affairs

Activities	○ Annual Open Day
	○ Annual shareholder meeting
	○ Quarterly financial briefing
	○ Product launches
	○ Corporate stand at industry exhibitions
		○ Annual Open Day
		○ Community consultations
		○ Displays
		○ Visits to schools
		○ Career exhibitions
			○ Media releases
			○ Liaise with journalists
			○ Media conferences
			○ Media monitoring
			○ Write
			  ○ Factsheets
			  ○ Backgrounders
				○ Website management
				○ Social media applications
				○ Post to website and social media
				○ Monitor social media
					○ Design/produce the annual report
					○ Quarterly financial briefs
					○ Produce hard copy communication tools for the program
						○ Government relations
						○ Lobbying
						○ Speechwriting
						○ Draft the annual report
						○ Represent the organisation

of successful Component outcomes (sCo), which in turn are the sum of its successful Activity outcomes (sAo). That's a bit like a maths formula:

$$sPo = sum(sCo_1 + sCo_2 + sCo_3),$$

where $sCo = sum(sAo_1 + sAo_2 + sAo_3)$

In practice what looks like a complicated formula works like the following example. At the end of each year, the Director, Strategic Communication at Ideal Widgets Pty Ltd needs to report on how the corporate program performed. The director will ask questions like, "Did we achieve the goals and objectives written for everything we did?," "Did each activity end the year within budget?" and "What stopped us from achieving our goals and objectives?" The director will know that the success of the public affairs team (a "Component" in Table 4.3) can be determined by weighing up the positive and perhaps negative assessments of the outcomes for goals and objectives, just as the assessments made for the other components can also be weighed up to measure their level of success. In this way, the director can measure the success of Ideal Widgets" strategic communication program in a meaningful way. Remember that this example is for a functional evaluation, or to decide how successful the communication department has been; there are many ways to measure the success of communication goals and objectives, but more about that in Chapter 12.

The next chapter, on identifying organisation communication needs, or situation analysis, begins the detailed examination of the elements of a strategic communication plan.

CHAPTER EVALUATION

This chapter has dealt with the framework that communication strategists use to plan what they need to do for clients. It has illustrated the practical implementation of principles that explain how communication works. Answer these questions about the chapter:

1. Do I understand the framework used to write a strategic communication plan?
2. Am I familiar with the terminology that describes the various strategy elements?
3. Do I understand the similarities and differences between advertising, marketing communication and public relations strategic plans?
4. What else do I need to explore to fill in the gaps in my knowledge about the strategic communication framework?

Chapter 5
Analysing organisational communication needs

Goal: To understand the essential role of a situation analysis in a strategic communication plan.

Objectives: This chapter will help you to:

1. Identify the communication needs of an organisation
2. Appreciate the role of formative research in communication planning
3. Understand the importance of analysis in communication planning
4. Recognise that the success of a communication strategy depends on the correct analysis of issues facing an organisation.

Principle: Formative research underpins effective analysis of the communication needs of an organisation.

Practice: A situation analysis is used to determine the other elements of a communication plan.

STARTING THE PLANNING PROCESS

We've explored why it is important that strategic communication plans link to, and support, an organisation's overall business strategy, and we've looked at the broad structure of a communication strategy. This chapter starts the process of learning how, and why, the formal elements of a strategic plan are written, and how they work together to generate effective communication with an organisation's target publics.

Context "the circumstances relevant to something under consideration," so that something that is *out of context* is "without the surrounding words or circumstances and so not fully understandable" (*Australian Concise Oxford Dictionary*, 2004).

Practitioners need to make sure that a strategic plan is based on the best possible information. They normally do that through formal and informal research, which

DOI: 10.4324/9781003317579-6

enables them to understand the context in which their client or employer operates. The same research enables a practitioner to identify, and to analyse, communication issues to assess what they mean for the client. The outcomes of this research set the directions for a variety of tasks: setting goals and objectives; identifying target publics; preparing messages; deciding how those messages will be delivered to target publics; determining what tools, or activities, will be used; deciding how the plan will be implemented; and, finally, agreeing on how success will be evaluated.

The written summary of the situation you are working on—the analysis of research results, which will give an indication of the direction of the rest of the plan—is the first step in preparing a communication strategy and is known as a situation analysis.

What is an issue?

An issue can be defined in many ways. One definition is "a point in question" (*Australian Concise Oxford Dictionary*, 2004). Communication scholars have built on this. For example, Kirk Hallahan suggests issues are about disputes between two or more parties over the allocation of resources and that the "origins of issues can be traced to the moment an individual identifies a situation as problematic" (2001, p. 28). James Grunig and Todd Hunt (1984) define issues as the topics around which publics are formed. Robert Heath and Michael Palenchar argue that an issue is not what *all* people believe, but what *some* people strongly believe, so that they exert pressure to bring their views into public policy debates. They say that an issue is worthy of attention when it can have an impact on an organisation (2009, p. 55).

Practitioners need to keep these points about issues top of mind when they are researching and writing a communication strategy: issues are disputes, involve two or more people, define the topics around which target publics are formed, and are not what everyone believes. Here is the point about working in an organisation's non-market environment to deal with issues. Important strategic issues occur in this environment.

The success of a communication strategy depends on how well a practitioner analyses and explains research findings. An effective situation analysis helps a practitioner to understand the organisation and its previous communication activities, to maximise the ways in which it can engage with target publics, to reduce uncertainty and to have confidence the plan will work. A poorly prepared situation analysis means a likely failure to meet goals and objectives because the resulting strategy will not deal with all issues the organisation faces in specific situation.

Understanding context

Writing on the Public Relations Society of America's website in 2007, experienced American practitioners Roy Vaughn and Steve Cody discussed the importance of environmental scanning. Their context was public relations, which they described as a kind of barometer that measures external and internal pressures on organisations and that translates the impacts of cultural, societal, generational and political shifts on those organisations. That is precisely the role of strategic communication practice. To be effective, Vaughn and Cody say, practitioners, especially senior people who advise and counsel organisational leaders, need to spend more time pursuing information on these trends and objectively analysing what they mean. Vaughn and Cody say that it is impossible for practitioners to identify every element of global change. Nevertheless, they argue that practitioners will be able to lead more of the discussions in their organisations and with clients if they are measuring these shifts in society.

Analyse systematically examine something's constituent parts. An analysis is the result of this examination. Things are analysed to explain why they are the way they are. For strategic communication, analysing issues means working what they are about, how they might impact on an organisation, and explaining why they are important.

Environmental scanning is part of boundary spanning: interpreting the outside world to the organisation, and the organisation to its external and internal stakeholders. This activity is an essential part of the research needed to write a situation analysis. It is a key task that leads to an understanding of the context in which the client's organisation operates and the importance of the issues it faces in specific situations.

Chapter 2 explained that context includes an organisation's market and non-market environments. Many of the issues that organisations need to deal with in a strategic way relate to public policy and occur especially in the non-market environment. That is, they are issues that relate to how "points in question" in society—about, say, climate change, or transport or health policy—are debated and resolved. Heath and Palenchar observe that "Such debates can positively or negatively affect how organisations are managed and the missions that guide effective organisation planning. These debates are more than relationship management, although the ability of relationships can affect how issues are contested and translated in sound business and public policy" (2009, p. 5).

What happens in the market and non-market environments is complex. One way of understanding this complexity is to imagine that you are approaching our world from space. Once you identify Earth, you can recognise the environment in which it exists. The closer you come to Earth, the more you can see that nothing much is ever still. People are going about their lives; transport and communication systems link them; sport is being played; products are made and sold; wars are fought; some parts of the globe are calm; and the weather is doing, well, what the weather does. Modern technology has facilitated almost instantaneous connections between people, making business easier, faster and more

IN THEORY: YOU CAN'T GOOGLE CONTEXT

Imagine this: in 2012, *TIME* reported that the average American spent about 12 hours a day consuming information involving more than 100,000 words and totalling 34 gigabytes of data. This was part of a special feature about ten ideas that are changing our world. In one article, columnist Annie Paul reported on US research that suggests we are so inundated by information that we can't possibly retain that we are increasingly using search engines and smartphones to remember things for us.

Research exercise: Use your online research resources to find out what the latest figures are for how many hours people in your country consume information and how much data is involved. Take note of where they retrieve that information from—and whether there are any demographic differences between who retrieves what from where. That will all be useful data when you come to decide on communication pathways and tools for your strategy.

Psychologist Betsy Sparrow of Columbia University (*Columbia News*, 2011) found three new realities in relation to how people process information in the internet age:

- First, when we don't know the answer to a question, we think about where we can find the nearest web connection instead of the subject of the question.
- Second, when we expect to be able to find information again later on, we don't remember it as well as when we think it might become unavailable.
- Third, if we expect to locate information later, we don't memorise the information itself but where it can be found.

This may be an efficient way of finding out about things, but Paul reported that this "symbiosis" with digital devices is just an extension of transactive memory—an unspoken arrangement in which groups of people give memory tasks to each individual in the group to be shared when it is needed. In other words, we're increasingly using computers to do this.

Paul points out that this reliance on technology doesn't help with critical analysis: you might be able to access lots of facts, but you can't Google context.

These are important points for strategic communicators. More than at any other time, they and target publics have access to vast amounts of information. But communication needs more than information; it needs analysis of what the information means and why and a context for using it.

cost-effective; giving us access to more and more information in formats that would amaze our grandparents; and generally improving our lifestyles, health and access to entertainment choices. Technology has changed transport; the way we study; how we build and maintain relationships; our decision-making processes; the mechanisms by which we communicate with friends, family and colleagues; our leisure choices; and how our health is managed.

FURTHER READING

Paul, A.M. (2012), Your Head Is in the Cloud, *TIME*, 12 March, pp. 42–3.

CONTEXT AND ENVIRONMENTAL SCANNING

The task of identifying and interpreting the complex and changing world for clients—their business contexts—is part of strategic issues management. It identifies changes in the environment in which an organisation operates and how they will affect the organisation and its activities (Cornelissen, 2005). Grunig and colleagues found in their research that the "most excellent" public relations departments participated in organisational strategic management by scanning social, political and institutional environments to bring an external perspective to strategic decision-making (Grunig, 2006). Chief executives want practitioners who can help them project what the future marketplace will look like from consumer, regulatory, political, cultural and social perspectives (Dilenschneider, 1989). Those perspectives are our contexts, and the issues that surround them are most likely to occur in the non-market environment.

Identifying and analysing issues

Hallahan writes about what he describes as "the dynamics of issues" and how organisations respond to them. Issues dynamics (how issues arise and are responded to) are a central concern of strategic communication (Hallahan, 2001).

Environmental scanning and the analysis that follows it are as important as the work of financial experts who advise companies about how they will be affected by changes in oil prices; the cost of raw materials, labour or electricity; or taxes. In strategic communication, the role of a practitioner is to interpret issues, events and changes in politics, society and culture and to explain what these mean for organisations.

Practitioners who understand the internal and external environments in which their clients operate develop strategic communication plans that work; those who do not are less successful. The eminent Australian practitioners Candy Tymson and Peter and Richard Lazar (2006) observe that the strategic role of identifying, responding to and creating trends means that strategic communication functions as a "communication driver" that creates awareness, educates and influences public opinion, promotes and protects reputations, guides organisations to communicate change and helps them to re-examine the values and ethics of their operations. That's a serious responsibility and reflects the importance of communication strategy.

FURTHER READING

Hallahan, K. (2001), The Dynamics of Issues Activation and Response: An Issues Process Model, *Journal of Public Relations Research*, 13(1), pp. 27–59.

Heath, R.L. and Palenchar, M.J. (2009), *Strategic Issues Management: Organisations and Public Policy Challenges*, 2nd edn, Sage, Los Angeles, CA, esp. pp. 90–122.

Steyn, B. and Niemann, L. (2010), Enterprise Strategy: A Concept that Explicates Corporate Communication's Strategic Contribution at the Macro-Organisational Level, *Journal of Communication Management*, 14(2), pp. 106–26.

AN APPROACH TO IDENTIFYING ISSUES

Practitioners do not always have the necessary budget to engage commercial public opinion researchers to help identify issues that are likely to concern an organisation and the actors who promote them. However, whether you use research consultants to conduct formal, primary research, or rely on secondary sources and informal **desk research**, one way to set parameters for examining an organisation and its environment is to adapt the $(IA)^3$ framework that David Bach and David Allen (2010) proposed for planning business strategies (see Figure 5.1). The $(IA)^3$ framework uses three pairs of questions—thus the cube of (IA)—to inform strategic planning.

....

Desk research informal research that involves using secondary sources from the internet or books and reports that are directly available.

....

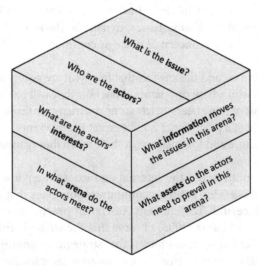

Source: Adapted from Bach and Allen (2010), p. 42.

Figure 5.1 The $(IA)^3$ framework

Table 5.1 Adapting the (IA)^3 framework for strategic communication

(IA)^3 questions	Adapted for strategic communication
What is the issue?	What is the issue? What is the context in which the issue impacts on the organisation?
Who are the actors?	What publics are interested in this issue?
What are the actors' interests?	Do publics support the organisation? What knowledge do publics have about this issue?
In what arena do the actors meet?	How do publics normally prefer to receive information?
What information moves the issue in this arena?	What informative and/or persuasive messages should the organisation provide to publics to help them understand the issue?
What assets do the actors need to prevail in this arena?	What tactics might be used to give publics the information they need?

The questions in the (IA)^3 framework are similar to those that practitioners need to ask in issues identification and analysis to set directions for strategic communication research that will inform a situation analysis. Table 5.1 shows how the framework can be adapted.

Answers to questions like these, which help to define an issue and explain who is interested in it, and why, provide valuable data that can be used to explain what those issues mean for organisations.

You could, of course, use a simpler approach: the 5Ws and H one-word questions you'll likely use to plan a media release. Asking and answering the What, Who, When, Where, Why and How questions about an organisation's situation also helps to identify issues, the people promoting them, and why they are important.

Both approaches are also good mechanisms for beginning an evaluation of how well the strategy worked.

Questions about target publics, how they prefer to receive information, and writing messages will be explored in later chapters.

USING RESEARCH IN STRATEGIC COMMUNICATION

Perhaps more than any other group, politicians try to identify the issues that the community believes are important. Sometimes, because of the way politicians frame an issue, they are able to generate sufficient media interest to make it a matter of community concern. Politicians opposed to the government try to do this all the time, which is why in election years, especially, Opposition parties raise questions about "law and order," failures in the health system, border security, public transport or education. All this is done to suggest that the current administration is not doing its job properly. The topics they choose to pursue are often determined by what opinion polls tell them electors are concerned about. Politicians also keep a watchful eye on opinion polls that measure voting intentions. Most of the polling companies include questions about voting intention in all their regular surveying, and the results are published by major media outlets, often becoming news stories. Political parties, of course, do their own private opinion polling on a wide range of issues, often in significant depth, including what electors think of party leaders. These opinion poll results are important to politicians as they develop, or modify, policies to attract our votes.

Practitioners should also be aware of the information that regular opinion polls provide because it is useful in the desk research that is part of environmental scanning. Where they have a budget for it, practitioners also engage polling companies to research community attitudes to issues that are important to their organisations or clients. From time to time, the polling companies themselves ask people about issues that concern them. For example, once or twice a year, Newspoll in Australia publishes the results of its survey of community attitudes to a wide range of issues, and this data often indicates which are of most importance to Australians. Research findings like this can often be accessed from the polling companies' websites free of charge. More detailed reports that include in-depth analyses are also commercially available from the polling companies. All this data, whether we pay for detailed reports or just scan the publicly available material, can be used as part of environmental scanning.

External consultants sometimes need to find out a client's view on a specific issue—or what a client's competitors are saying about the issue, especially when they are preparing the situation analysis for a strategic communication plan. That can usually be done by exploring the organisation's website; good sites hold a lot of useful information. For example, a consultant may need to know about what a commercial company is doing about the environment, what its policies are and how it reports its achievements. Many companies have sections of their websites that deal with policies on environmental protection and sustainable development. One of the world's biggest companies, BHP Billiton, publishes its approach to these topics so that shareholders, potential investors and the community can access its policies (see https://www.bhp.com/sustainability/approach). That companies publish information like this on their websites reflects acceptance of community concerns about the importance of these issues.

Research exercise: To understand how organisations might differ in their views on issues of diversity, inclusion, equity, and environmental sustainability, visit the websites of six companies in your State and explore the site menus for information about these issues. Jot down some notes about what you discover. Do the same thing for six government agencies, six community groups, and six trade unions. Compare your notes—do the organisations have similar ideas about these issues; what are the differences; why might they differ?

IN THEORY: HELPING PROFESSIONAL PRACTICE

Students studying professional communication subjects at university spend time reading about and understanding the theoretical background to what they'll do in practice. When they start out in the workforce, however, they're unlikely to be asked which theory they'll draw on for a particular project. Nevertheless, by understanding how people access and process information, for example, practitioners can work out how to write and deliver effective messages to the target publics that are important to their clients. This is especially useful when you need to select the most appropriate communication pathways for reaching publics and the tools that match them.

Dan Lattimore and colleagues (2004) make a vital point that theory explains or predicts the way things work or happen. Joep Cornelissen (2000) takes a stronger view: that practitioners should inform their work with theory and research. Those who do this (professionals Cornelissen describes as "reflective practitioners") are better able to work out how to adapt to changing circumstances rather than rely on intuition and on trial and error. For Cornelissen, theory is a resource to help practitioners continuously question and revise their views and make sense of their situation and experiences. He says practitioners who use this critical and reflective ability are not only proficient in the technical aspects of their jobs, but also more sophisticated in interpreting the broader economic, social and political contexts of their practice, and in understanding the kind of society their work is reproducing or changing.

Cornelissen (2000) discusses three models for translating theories and concepts into practice. He describes the *instrumental* use of theory as a traditional, problem-solving approach, whereby academic theory and research provide rational solutions to managerial problems in a direct and instrumental way. In the *conceptual* model, abstract academic knowledge is applied to practical cases by means of generalisations, concepts and ideas. The third model, the *translation* model, treats theory and practice as "intertwined mutually influential entities in the generation of knowledge." Cornelissen explains that the *translation* model recognises that scientific knowledge is hardly ever used unchanged in a practical setting. In other words, practitioners "transform" and interpret research outcomes within the context of professional understanding.

Cornelissen argues that as pragmatic professionals, public relations practitioners will adopt ideas from the "rich pool of academic theory," where these are relevant to their practice. Almost every journal article and textbook that you will read will have examples of theories that are relevant to public relations. This is because understanding theory makes professional practice more effective. Many researchers use theoretical approaches from other disciplines, such as management, sociology, psychology, and the "hard" sciences, to explain how communication works. Many of the theories you study at university are based on these explanations.

Lattimore and colleagues suggest that practitioners should build a set of theories to help their professional practice. Sometimes consultancies base their professional practice on aspects of communication theories and explain proposed strategies to clients in these theoretical frameworks. If you sign on for one or two of the many free newsletters about public relations and strategic communication practice and try to read some of the many research journals regularly publish (you can access these through your library), you'll be able to build your own set of useful theories. Remember, though, the theoretical approaches you learn at university will continue to be as important as new ideas you discover in your professional career.

See also "Time out: On the importance of theory" at p. 60?

FURTHER READING

The literature on corporate communication, public affairs and public relations is rich with material dealing with how theoretical concepts can assist practitioners. The importance of this literature is that it helps us understand how people receive and process information, and what sort of people, or target publics, our organisations need to engage in dialogue. The following suggested readings deal with the role of theory in practice.

Cornelissen, J. (2005), *Corporate Communication: Theory and Practice*, Sage, London, esp. ch. 1 and ch. 4.

Cornelissen, J. (2000), Toward an Understanding of the Use of Academic Theories in Public Relations Practice, *Public Relations Review*, 26(3), pp. 315–26.

Lattimore, D., Baskin, O., Heiman, S., Toth, E. and van Leuven, J. (2004), *Public Relations: The Profession and the Practice*, McGraw Hill, Boston, MA, esp. ch. 3.

KEEPING ON TRACK

Trying to understand the issues happening in the world outside your organisation and what they mean, is not something that you should do only once or twice a year. It is a continuing task and an important professional responsibility. It involves knowing about the political system and its key players, having some understanding of how the economy works, and showing some interest in the news of the day. It does not mean you have to be an expert in management theory and finance, but you do need to develop a working knowledge of how organisations are structured and operate. This is why senior practitioners keep abreast of the daily news.

Of course, the more senior you become in your career, the more you'll need to understand how to manage staff and budgets, so take every opportunity to learn about these skills.

In every job you do in your communication career, you'll need to understand what your organisation does, and how it does it. For example, how might you react if you were asked to prepare a programme for a newly appointed managing director to visit the key officials in the state government agency for your industry if you did not know about the role of public servants in advising politicians? If you were not aware that the media were reporting expectations of a larger than normal crowd at a major footy match, how could you advise your client, a private bus company that runs services to the football stadium, about how to use that news as a way of publicising the company's plans for the game? Knowing about these things is part of understanding context.

The importance of context has been stressed by Anne Gregory who notes that organisations do not exist in isolation and that history is "littered" with examples of companies that failed to spot changing industry trends quickly enough and adapt to them. Those companies suffered a loss of market share, financial collapse or bad publicity because of the way they treated their workforce. Gregory says that given the critical role of communication in building goodwill between organisations and their publics, practitioners should carefully consider both the external and internal contexts in which that communication operates.

RESEARCH FOR STRATEGIC COMMUNICATION

Formal research helps practitioners to determine awareness and acceptance of their clients' businesses and products. Survey questions can be written to test for these. Statistics from a quantitative survey can reveal information, say, that unemployed women aged 20–25 in regional cities do not know about a new online job-search service. A lack of awareness of a company, product or an aspect of a public issue among a specific demographic category should cause a practitioner to investigate more deeply, especially if the demographic group is a vital target public. Qualitative surveying, perhaps using focus groups, can help to explain why people hold certain views. It may be that young females in regional cities don't know about your organisation's new online job-search service because women don't use those services anyway. Or it may have been that none of the women in the group were exposed to your company's messages about the service because the organisation didn't understand the **demographics** correctly. In the latter case, the practitioner would have identified a communication issue—lack of awareness about the job-search service among people in a specific target public—and could write a strategic communication plan to address this.

Demographics statistical data about groups in the general population

Information generated by formal research is important in identifying gaps in awareness and acceptance among target publics that may prevent them from taking positive action that supports an organisation's goals and objectives.

What do we know? What do we need to find out? How might we do it?

Finding out about the organisation, what it does, its business environment, its plans, how its internal systems work, and the communication issues it faces is *formative research*. The research you conduct at the end of a campaign to work out whether you achieved its goals and objectives is *summative research*.

Formative research is what informs a situation analysis. It will help you to identify goals, objectives, messages and target publics. It will be important for determining communication pathways and tools, and it will set a benchmark against which you can measure your success.

Effective strategic communicators are continually researching, even if they are not engaged in a formal process. Their continuing environmental scanning involves daily reading and listening to and consulting with others inside and outside their organisations about current or emerging issues and communication opportunities.

Formal research

Formal quantitative or qualitative research enables a practitioner to identify levels of awareness and acceptance of a client's organisation, or its products, or the issues it faces in the non-market environment that need to be addressed by a communication strategy. If you have an appropriate budget, research of this kind can be commissioned through a commercial market research company. The information it provides contributes to the data you'll use in your situation analysis. Formal research assists practitioners to work out communication pathways and tools because it can identify how specific publics prefer to receive information and how. Most importantly, formative research can be used to set a benchmark against which you can later measure the success of your programme. To do that, a practitioner would repeat the research—now summative research—after the programme has been implemented and thus be able to measure changes in awareness and acceptance.

It is not always possible for a client to allocate money for formative and summative research because it can be expensive. However, if the costs can be included in the project budget, the research will contribute significantly to the plan's strategic effectiveness. Often, especially in large companies, research for communication purposes is funded as part of a broader marketing budget.

Desk research

Not all research need be expensive. Effective research is still possible if you do not have a budget to engage a market research company. In many cases, "desk research" that you, or other members of your team, can do from existing material, official reports, historical data, the media and the organisation's files will produce valuable information for planning and evaluation. Searches of websites relevant to the organisation, or of organisations that study public issues, can also yield important useful information for a situation analysis.

Using libraries

Libraries, among the first institutions to recognise the importance of electronic storage and management of information, are a primary resource of research data. The catalogues of national, state and local libraries can generally be accessed electronically. From an electronic catalogue search, you could, for example, find out what experts have written about the contribution solar power could make to future energy generation. Your state library will hold electronic copies of most newspaper and that will enable you to search back copies of to find out how the media covered the development of solar energy.

The libraries of most national and state parliaments can also be accessed electronically. These libraries provide important public information derived from research reports commissioned by congressional and parliamentary committees, and sometimes research by library staff on issues of the day. For example, in most countries that are concerned about how renewable energy might replace oil, coal and natural gas, politicians have set up committees to investigate aspects of this. Their detailed reports, which usually include research data and opinions from experts, are available through their parliamentary libraries. This material is free of charge, so for a practitioner working for a company producing solar panels, this research would be a valuable resource for elements of a situation analysis.

So, too, is the information available from government statisticians. Data published by government statisticians usually comes from the regular national census and is important in helping you to understanding changing demographics. For example, if you worked for an aged-care organisation, you could identify data on age groups in your state and work out how many people would qualify for care in the next five years.

Annual reports as a research source

A good first step in formative research is to review the organisation's latest annual report. Annual reports deal with the organisation's performance for the latest financial year. For most organisations, the financial year runs from 1 July of one year until 30 June in the following year. Other organisations use the calendar year as their financial reporting year.

Annual reports are also an opportunity for companies to provide more information about their activities than can be covered in the formal, legally required financial statements. That is why most annual reports include information from the board of directors and the chief executive officer that review performance during the past year, set out future plans and comment on issues that the organisation has faced in the last year, or could confront in the coming year. Many also include information about staff, the company's research and development achievements, new operational facilities and other initiatives taken during the year. Publishing information about how the organisation has performed on social and community issues, equity, diversity and inclusion and on environmental concerns, as well as providing financial data, is generally mandatory. When they report performance in this way, organisations are attempting to show that they are not just interested in financial outcomes.

Reading an annual report will reveal important and detailed information about the organisation's financial position, its operations and business interests, its past performance and its plans—all vital to helping a practitioner understand a client's business and its communication needs.

Access to market and political research

All major market research companies conduct regular surveys—called omnibus surveys—that ask questions for their clients on a range of consumer-related trends and social issues. Most also regularly research voting trends to find out which political party is likely to win an election, who is favoured as the national leader and how voters feel about current issues. The results of these opinion polls are published in major newspapers and magazines.

All these surveys generate important demographic information about respondents that the market research companies' clients analyse to help them understand community attitudes towards their products, or opinions on social and political issues, or voting intentions. Your organisation can pay for questions that relate to it to be included in omnibus surveys and for the results to include important demographic, voting intention and other data so that you can make a meaningful analysis of your particular results.

Media monitoring

The strategic communication departments of most private enterprise and government organisations usually pay an external media-monitoring agency to provide a daily electronic summary of how the news media have reported their business. This commercial service includes access to a full copy of a newspaper or blogger's story, social media posts or transcript of a radio or television report. The summary also provides demographic information about readers of the blogs, other websites and/or newspapers in which a story has appeared or about the listeners and viewers of radio and television programs.

Daily media monitoring is not just important for finding out whether your media release was published or broadcast. It is also vital for tracking issues that affect your organisation and monitoring who might be reading or listening to the public debates about them. It also helps you to work out how and when you might participate in those debates and where you might target a media release.

Other important media sources are public affairs programs on radio and television, and web-based services like *The Conversation* (theconversation.edu.au) in Australia. These sources provide expert comment and opinion on issues of the day. Programs and websites like these cover the arts, science, business, religion, history, the law, health, social commentary, politics and philosophy; many programs can be downloaded as podcasts or vodcasts.

University academics as research resources

Another valuable research resource is university academics. Many academics are available to the media for expert comment about issues of the day. Universities list these experts in the "for media" sections of their websites, and commercial organisations offer online services to help people locate academic and other experts. Journalists regularly use academic experts from universities and other research institutions in this way, but they are also often also available to help organisations. Sometimes academics will provide advice free of charge, and they are often willing to address conferences and seminars on the areas of their expertise. Universities also offer regular seminars by academics across their spectrum of disciplines and public lectures from local or visiting experts. These are usually free, almost always interesting and you are likely to find many useful for your strategic communication planning or general understanding of the world.

Think tanks

Privately funded institutions that employ specialists to research and comment on important public issues are colloquially known as policy "think tanks" because their specialists ponder problems and propose solutions to them. Some of these institutions are set up to investigate and comment on issues from a particular political standpoint, while others are unfailingly independent. Some of the people who contribute to the work of think tanks, many of them eminent academics, are regular commentators in the news media. The think tanks publish reports, newsletters and journals and conduct seminars about their work that can include information that practitioners might need to consider in their strategic planning.

The internet

The massive and continual growth of the internet as a communication tool has provided the world with a wonderful research resource. The internet's search engines can connect us to such a diverse range of resources that it sometimes seems to be an overwhelming task to select those that are most relevant to what we need. Nevertheless, the "net" can connect strategic communication practitioners to research and opinions that are important to their work. The resources sections and search facilities on websites designed to support practitioners, like those for the Public Relations Society of America (at www.prsa.org), the World Advertising Research Centre (www.warc.com) and the Public

CHAPTER EXERCISE

How many centenarians are there?

Try this exercise as a way of bringing together some of the research resources discussed in this chapter. Assume you work for the national association of not-for-profit organisations in the aged-care field. Your task is to prepare a communication strategy for a public affairs project conducted by your association to seek government funds for member organisations who provide special care for people aged more than 100. You first need to work out how many people in your country are over 100 (the answer might surprise you). This task fascinates you, so you decide to go further than simply chasing the numbers.

Using the resources identified above, you should be able to locate enough data to answer the following questions:

1. How many people in your country are aged over 100?
2. Do the majority of them live in the major cities, or in rural areas?
3. Which nationalities have the greatest number of centenarians?
4. Are there more centenarians now than there were, say, 25 years ago? If so, why might that have occurred?
5. Do centenarians need more, less, or just different, health care than others?
6. Have demographers explained the impact of people living to be more than 100 on the economy, especially the aged-care system?
7. What experts might you need to contact to further understand this situation?
8. Is there published research material that could help you? What is it? Why would it help?

Relations Institute of Australia (www.pria.com.au) provide valuable practical professional information and links to relevant academic journals and research outcomes.

WRITING A SITUATION ANALYSIS

Once you've identified issues that are important to your organisation, your task is to analyse what the data you've collected means and to decide the directions your communication strategy will take.

A situation analysis is a narrative that tells the story of what your research found, what it means for your client, the specific target publics involved in the situation you face, how you can reach them and what messages are need. All this cannot be adequately conveyed to a client in one or two sentences. A well-researched and written analytical situation analysis is a major key to ensuring your strategic communication plan is successful.

A situation analysis should be long enough to at least include:

- A summary of the organisation, its business and the industry in which it operates (including something about its competitors, especially if you are working in the market environment). You should cover points like the kind of organisation (commercial business, not-for-profit, government agency); its core business (what it does); its formal structure and ownership; the kind of employees it has (manual labour, highly skilled professionals); who its customers, suppliers and regulators are; and perhaps something about publics who enable it to do its business and those who might be limiters. All this can be written concisely in about one page
- An analysis of issues identified in research about the organisation's business context and its non-market environment that explains what they mean, why they are important and how they impact on the organisation. The length of the analysis depends on how many issues you identify as important, but you do not need to over-write as people don't have time to read long narratives. The best approach is to identify an issue and say why it is important to the organisation in a few sentences.
- Include a brief discussion about the people and groups who are important to the organisation. These will become the target publics for the strategy, so including a few sentences in the situation analysis about them is important. Link this to the issues you 've identified and what the target publics need to know about them—there's more about the importance of this in Chapter 6
- A summary of the message themes you will recommend in the strategy. A paragraph explaining that the strategy is designed to deliver messages about specific themes will suffice
- Some brief information that indicates the total budget for implementing the strategy and how long it will take to implement it

A **SWOT chart** (see Figure 5.2), a simple diagram showing how you assess the organisation's strengths, weaknesses, opportunities and threats, is a useful tool for issues analysis. Another simple, but useful, analytical tool is an *issues management matrix* that shows how you assess them in the context of the *impact* they might have on the organisation and the *probability* that they will occur (see Figure 5.3).

SWOT chart a simple analytical tool whereby an organisation or program is assessed in terms of its strengths, weaknesses, opportunities and threats.

Writing a situation analysis in this way gives those who read it an indication of the directions you are recommending for the strategic plan. The analysis you have undertaken provides the reasons.

If you work for a consultancy, your client will almost certainly provide a written brief that sets out what they want you to do. A brief is a primary source for a situation analysis because of the organisational information it includes, especially information on the problem or issue the client faces, and any outline of current or past communication activities. (If you work in an in-house role, then your knowledge of the organisation and the situation, together with the task given to you by your manager, will most likely be your brief.) If the client does not give you a formal brief, then ask for one in the format your consultancy uses for this. This should address the issues the client believes to be important, so you need to understand the brief before you start work so that you are clear about your assignment. You will need to exercise your professional judgement about the material in the brief, including any suggestions the client might make about tools and additional research that might be required. Give logical reasons for any variations to what the client has proposed.

Using a SWOT analysis

A SWOT analysis is a simple analytical tool that helps you to review formative research and write a situation analysis.

> **Strengths** are characteristics of the organisation that can help achieve its goals.
> **Weaknesses** are characteristics of the organisation that might harm its ability to achieve its goals.
> **Opportunities** are *external* conditions that will assist the organisation to achieve its goals.
> **Threats** are *external* conditions that could prevent the organisation from achieving its goals.

By setting out a SWOT analysis in a table format (see Figure 5.2), you can compare your assessments in each of the quadrants and work out, for example, which strengths you might use to overcome a possible threat.

Strengths	Weaknesses
Opportunities	**Threats**

Figure 5.2 SWOT analysis chart

To use this tool, think about how your organisation's perceived *strengths*, including from an internal perspective, might counteract its *weaknesses*. Make an assessment about how *opportunities* to contribute to discourses about public policy in the non-market environment might balance potential *threats* to public policy outcomes from publics who are promoting different views.

Ask realistic questions (maybe by using the [IA³] approach, or 5Ws and H) that will help you to set out the strengths, or good points, of your organisation (or its point of view on an issue) as well as the areas in which it could improve— its weaknesses. Do the same thing when you identify opportunities (perhaps an emerging market) and the threats—the things that may prevent your organisation doing what you plan.

Write the answers down concisely in the relevant quadrants of the SWOT chart. You can then write goals and objectives that build on strengths, minimise threats, pursue opportunities or deal with weaknesses.

ASSESSING ISSUES

As we have seen earlier, the ancient practice of analysing issues is vital to producing an effective situation analysis. An issues matrix (see Figure 5.3) shows the importance of issues to an organisation and identifies those that should be prioritised. The matrix provides a simple way of listing issues by the *impact* that they would have on an organisation, and by the *probability* that they will happen.

Generally, these classifications work in the following way.

Probability

A *high-probability* issue is one that is happening now or could happen in the next six months.

A *medium-probability* issue is one that could happen between six months and a year from now.

A *low-probability* issue is one that could happen in 12 months' time or later.

Impact

A *high-impact* issue is one that is already having, or would have if it were to occur, a major effect on the organisation's operations or policies. That is, a high-impact issue is one that will disrupt operations, cause the organisation to make a major change to its policies or result in some kind of crisis.

A *medium-impact* issue is one that may have a significant effect on the organisation's operations or policies.

		PROBABILITY		
		High	Medium	Low
IMPACT	High			
	Medium			
	Low			

Figure 5.3 Issues management matrix

A *low-impact* issue is one that will not have a significant impact on what the organisation does, but about which the organisation nevertheless needs to be aware.

To identify the issues for your matrix, use the outcomes of your formal and informal research to make a list of, say, up to 30 issues that your organisation either faces or could face in the next two years (there may not, of course, be that many, or there may be more). Work with your team and other people in the organisation to classify them by impact and probability. Record the issues in the sections of the matrix that match your impact and probability classifications. Your strategy will give the highest priority to issues that fall in the shaded area of the matrix.

For most organisations, an explosion in a manufacturing facility would be a high-impact and low-probability issue, but one that they should at least consider. The national body of a professional sporting code might classify "players caught taking recreational drugs" as a high-impact, medium-probability issue. That classification would mean the code believes it is likely a player will be caught in the next six months, and that this would cause embarrassment. Immediately after an election, a change of government would be a low-probability, low-impact issue. Closer to the next election, your environmental scanning might indicate the need for a change in that classification because opinion polls suggest a change of government is likely and that a new government's policies will adversely affect the organisation.

It is a good idea to write a briefing note, or issue a statement, about each issue you include in the matrix so that you have the background facts you might need, notes about the impact the issue might have on your organisation, contact details for internal and external experts on the issue, and information (like email addresses, phone numbers, news organisation, position) about journalists who may have contacted your organisation about the issue before. You could add details of specialist journalists who write about particular issues in the statement even if they have not contacted you—their contact numbers would be there for when you need to contact them.

By regularly reviewing the issues in your matrix and their classifications, and your issue statements—plan to do this, say, every six months—you can make up-to-date assessments about the issues you need to address now, think about for possible future action, and be aware of over the longer term. You should be flexible, changing impact and probability classifications if needed so that you always have an up-to-date assessment of the issues you face.

Most often, a SWOT, issues matrix and briefing notes will be kept on your computer system as separate documents. Make sure they are stored in a consistent way so that you can easily and regularly access, review and update them—and back them up.

TIME OUT: AN ELECTRONIC ISSUES MANAGEMENT DATABASE

If you have time and you are familiar with using an electronic database, you could develop one to hold information about the issues facing your organisation. Each issue would be a single *record* in the database, and the information related to it would comprise the *fields* in each record. An electronic database gives you the ability to include, by using pre-set value lists, your categorisations of the impact and probability axes of the matrix by using the drop-down box options. Value lists enable you to select pre-determined "values" for each field: for example, "high," "medium" and "low" categories for impact and probability, so you do not need to manually enter them each time. Your database can include fields that record who is responsible for managing the issue, other organisations facing the same issue, government agencies associated with it, the journalists who have previously contacted you about it, and hyperlinks to policies, research data and media coverage. Most databases that you can use on your desktop computer will allow you to attach issue statements (written in ordinary word processing applications) to individual records. A database of this kind will store data you need to write a situation analysis. A simple example of some of the fields that *each* record in your database might include are set out in Table 5.2.

Over time, you will end up with a lot of issue records in your database but, when you use the "sort" function, you will be able to identify commonalities: all those that have a High/Medium Impact/Probability categorisation, or the media coverage in online news sites, for example. Using a database in this way will give you efficient access to information that can be regularly updated and sorted, especially the impact and probability fields, and cross-referenced with other records. If you think carefully about the data you need about issues, and the database design, it will become a powerful tool for your strategic issues communication and an extremely valuable resource that can also inform the evaluation of your plan. As you get more comfortable with building and managing your database, you'll find new ways of expanding the information it contains.

Table 5.2 Record fields for an electronic issues management database

Record: Name the issue (for example, Union demand for 5% pay rise).

Fields	Value list	Comment
Probability	High Medium Low	For this field, set up a value list that gives you the option of selecting High, Medium or Low for **Probability**
Impact	High Medium Low	For this field, set up a value list that gives you the option of selecting High, Medium or Low for **Impact**
Responsible	–	Enter the name of the organisation's person managing the policy on this issue
Email	–	Enter the policy person's email address
Phone	–	Enter the policy person's email office phone number
Policy URL	–	Add a link to the policy document about this issue. You could create another text field, Briefing Note, and paste the briefing note in it
Other organisations	–	In this text field record the other organisations and industry associations associated with this issue. Include URLs to the appropriate sections of their websites
Govt agency	–	List the relevant government agencies in a text field. Add agency contacts and their email and phone details
Media coverage	–	Use a text field to hold the URLs for any media coverage your organisation gets on this issue
Journalists	You could add the names of journalists with whom you are in regular contact, and "Other" for new names.	In this text field, add the names, media type, and contact details of journalists who seek information about this issue from your organisation, and dates on which you talked with them. Over time, when you sort this database by the individual names in this field, you will find out what issues each journalist has been interested in. This can help you plan future contacts with them about those issues
Last updated	–	Add a date field to indicate the last time this record was updated

Issues analysis and the three-horizons approach

It would also be useful to classify the issues you've identified in terms of the three time horizons discussed in Chapter 2. This is especially important given the nature of strategic communication as a process that helps organisations with mid- to long-term business planning.

Horizon 1 deals with current business. In a situation analysis, that means identifying issues in the market and non-market environments that have the potential to impact on the organisation's current business performance. These are likely to be issues related to the supply of resources, price, customer expectations, what competitors are doing, the current economic situation and how public policy has a contemporary effect on what the organisation does.

Horizon 2 deals with emerging business—or where the organisation believes it will be in, say, five years' time. That means identifying issues in the non-market environment that will need to be addressed in strategic communication activity between now and when emerging business starts.

Horizon 3 deals with future business directions, or where the organisation will be, or how it will change, beyond five years from now. For most organisations, that will mean identifying public policy issues in the non-market environment to enable those directions to be pursued. For communicators that will mean preparing strategies that help the organisation to engage in policy debates about those issues.

You might use Table 5.3 to help plot issues in the three-horizons framework. (This will work best if you re-design it in landscape format so that you can increase the column widths to give you more space to enter issues information.) In the columns next to the Issues subheading, list the market and non-market issues that are likely to occur in the relevant planning horizon. For example, a current Horizon 1, market environment issue might be increased interest rates; a Horizon 2 issue might be the planned introduction of a rival company's new version of its mobile phone in 18 months and its impact on your organisation's ability to sell its phone; a Horizon 3, non-market environment issue might be planned new legislation to mandate more explicit safety warnings on electrical goods.

Table 5.3 Planning horizons and issues

	Horizon 1 *Now*	**Horizon 2** *Mid-term*[a]	**Horizon 3** *Long-term*[b]
Focus	*Current business*	*Emerging business*	*Future business*
Issues			

Source: Adapted from Baghai et al. (2000), p. 130.

[a]Mid-term = Up to five years from now.

[b]Long-term = more than five years from now.

Strategic Plan Checklist: Your analysis

Write a situation analysis for your strategic plan project

This exercise involves writing a situation analysis for the strategic plan project you chose in Chapter 1. To do this, follow the approach discussed in this chapter, and:

- Use the results of the other exercises you have completed so far in relation to this project
- Identify the issues your plan will address, and explain why they are important and what they mean
- Explain the most important issues
- Identify the publics who are important to your organisation.

Write your analysis as a narrative. Use headings for each section of the analysis if this will help you to organise what you write. Your situation analysis should be no more than about 2,000 words less if you can write the analysis clearly, precisely and succinctly.

The next chapter will discuss the role of target publics in communication strategies, how they can be identified and why it is important to understand what they know and believe about organisations.

CHAPTER EVALUATION

Test your understanding of the role of a situation analysis in a strategic communication plan by answering these questions:

1. Can I use the information in this chapter to identify the communication needs of an organisation, especially the organisation I chose for my strategic plan project?
2. What is the role of *formative* research in communication planning?
3. Why is *analysis* of research outcomes important for communication planning?
4. How does a successful communication strategy depend on the correct analysis of issues facing an organisation?
5. Why is it necessary for strategic communication practitioners to prepare a situation analysis before they decide the other elements of a communication plan?

Chapter 6
Why target publics matter

Goal: To recognise the importance of target publics to organisational communication

Objectives: This chapter will help you to:

1. Recognise the central role of target publics in communication strategies
2. Understand the need to accurately segment target publics
3. Recognise the roles that different categories of target publics play in strategic communication.

Principle: Target publics have vital relationships with organisations

Practice: Communication strategies are designed to meet the information needs of the organisation and its target publics

Let's go back in time and review one of the world's most significant environmental disasters to see what we can learn from a communication perspective. In April 2010, the *Deepwater Horizon* oil rig in the Gulf of Mexico exploded. Eleven people died in this incident, and others were injured; hydrocarbons leaked into the Gulf, wildlife died and the water was polluted; people's jobs, especially in fishing, were seriously affected; and whole communities around the Gulf coast suffered. It took 87 days to control this environmental disaster, and much longer to clean it up. This was a major crisis—perhaps the biggest environmental crisis ever in the Gulf—and one that involved a significant communications effort from the company to explain what happened, how and why it happened, and what it was doing to fix the problems caused by the explosion. The crisis had environmental, economic and political dimensions, and caused significant economic and social disruption for Gulf communities. The reputation of the company that owned the rig, BP, suffered, and people outside and inside the organisation focused on what it should do to resolve the technical and socio-economic disaster. More than at any other time in the company's history, BP was subjected to intense scrutiny and pressure from workers, the local community, politicians, bureaucrats and the international news media.

The crisis played out in BP's non-market environment because of the social, environmental, political, regulatory and public policy aspects of what had occurred. It also had a major impact on the company's market environment, as the public policy issues affected its suppliers, customers and competitors.

In the hectic hours and months that followed the explosion, rescue crews and technicians battled the fire and the after-effects of the explosion. The BP communication team would have concentrated on the people with whom the company needed to deal as it communicated actions, information, advice and opinions. Among those people were the families of those who died or were injured; activists; community groups; technical specialists; emergency services; the military; fishermen and their families; coastal municipal councils; environmentalists; local, state and federal politicians; regulators; the news and specialist media; and lawyers. That's quite a list, and not a complete one. Practitioners would describe them as **target publics**.

Target public the people who receive messages to raise awareness, generate acceptance and promote action. They are specific to the situation you face and can be precisely defined. Formative research for a public relations plan will help you to identify your client's target publics.

This chapter comes earlier in the book than it would if the text was following the formal structure of a written communication strategy. That is because in learning about researching and planning a strategy, it is important to know about identifying target publics before considering goals and objectives, messages, communication pathways for reaching target publics and communication tools for delivering messages. Some important theories can help us decide how to reach target publics and to write messages. These include those that deal with how people process information, about dialogic communication and demographic considerations.

CREATIVE TENSION

In scholarly literature and in professional practice, there's a creative tension about the use of the terms *target publics* and *target audiences*. The former is more likely to be used by people practising and researching public relations; the latter by those whose focus is on marketing communication, especially advertising. Some scholars find the notion of "targeting" anyone with anything difficult to accept, especially if the goal of communication is to generate a dialogue about issues. How can someone who is "targeted" be regarded as an equal in a discussion? Terms like *target public* and *target audience* are professional jargon, just as *patient* is a way of referring to people who go to a doctor, or *client* is a name for someone who consults an accountant. Professional communication terms like *target public* or *audience* generally mean the same thing: people with whom the organisation already has, or wants to establish, a relationship, and with whom it exchanges messages or points of view. Which term you use will depend on your specific professional practice. Here, *target publics* will most often be the term used.

WHO ARE TARGET PUBLICS?

Target publics are people.

However, target publics are defined, segmented, researched and addressed, and no matter what you read about the theoretical principles and arguments behind this concept, it is important not to lose sight of the point that they are people. People take decisions, participate in discussion and debate, become activists; employees, customers, regulators and journalists are all people. Some are highly knowledgeable about an organisation; some are just aware that it makes something; others know nothing about it and care even less.

People's views about an organisation determine its reputation; their views about the quality of the products it sells determine whether they'll be repeat buyers or buy somewhere else. People in organisations build relationships with other people inside and outside the organisation. The way people talk and work with others determines the strength and quality of organisational relationships.

Fraser Seitel (2011) says that target publics are strategic constituencies with whom organisations develop and maintain relationships, and that they are related to issues. Robert Heath and Michael Palenchar (2009) make an important point about publics when they argue, in an issues-management context, that publics have a different sense of the importance of an issue, and of the priority of values by which it should be judged and solved. Erica Austin and Bruce Pinkleton (2006) note that organisations must prioritise the publics on whom they focus, just as they prioritise the things they do. A higher priority is thus given to the public whose opposition or support can hinder or help an organisation's ability to achieve its goals.

QUESTIONS ABOUT TARGET PUBLICS THAT NEED PRECISE ANSWERS

When working out who target publics are in a given situation, we need to answer some specific planning questions:

- Who are they, specifically?
  What do they know and believe about the situation or issue?
- Do they have any views about the issue—positive or negative?
  Do they need to have opinions about the situation or issue, and if they were to have an opinion, would it likely be supportive or negative?
- What do they know about the organisation?
  What is their opinion, or likely to be their opinion, about the organisation's reputation?

A properly researched situation analysis will help to answer these questions.

Sometimes, research will help a practitioner to make an informed judgment about a potential target public's likely opinion on an issue. For example, if a bank was considering raising its account fees, it would need to know how its customers would react. It is a fair assumption that customers would not like the decision. Researching how customers—target publics—reacted last time the bank, or one of its competitors, made a change like that would give a practitioner a sense of how the proposed move would be received. It would identify who were the most vocal publics (individual customers, business customers, consumer groups, shareholders, politicians) and whether they had positive or negative views about the change. Knowing that is valuable information that would assist in deciding the direction of a communication strategy designed to inform publics about the change; it would help a practitioner to work out how to reach various publics and to design messages and to select communication pathways and tools to do it.

It is axiomatic that senior people in organisations see value in making others aware of what the company, government agency, charity, or community group does, how well it does it, and that people understand and accept the organisation's values and opinions.

Target publics are so important that defining who they are, and how they behave, is a "foundational task" and a necessary "key step" in strategic communication management (Kim and Ni, 2010).

Target publics are specific people for specific situations. It is important to define them as clearly as possible because they are the people who will receive messages designed to raise their awareness and understanding of an issue, and to convince them to take action—perhaps to buy a product, if you are working in the public relations aspects of marketing communication, or to engage in a dialogue, if you are a specialist in public affairs. Anne Gregory (2005) points out that a great deal of effort and resources could be wasted if it is not clear who an organisation's target publics are, and that the segmentation of audiences (publics) is at the heart of successful, strong strategies that define people in terms of real segments: groups with similar needs who respond similarly to a core proposition.

THE KID BROTHER

Target publics are those people who are important to an organisation and with whom it needs to establish relationships to build *awareness*, generate *acceptance* and promote *action*. Organisations and their target publics share common interests and interact with each other on issues.

Jim Macnamara (2012) notes that publics are individuals who form associations around common interests, concerns, needs and circumstances. He cites John Dewey's (1927) definition of a public as a group of people who recognise an issue or problem, engage in discussion about that issue or problem and sometimes attempt to do something about it. David Guth and Charles Marsh (2006, p. 93) take this a step further by defining a public as a group of people who share common interests or values in a particular situation, especially interests and values they might be prepared to act upon. This notion of recognising, discussing and sometimes doing something about an issue or problem has led scholars to explore the nature of target publics and their relationships with organisations.

Publics can be internal (like employees) or external.

Irrespective of the theoretical paradigm you explore, Ronald Smith (2005), a US academic who writes about strategic communication planning, makes a simple, but valid, point: target publics are like family: you don't choose them; they choose you, and like a kid brother, they might be helpful or annoying.

Of course, not everyone has a direct link with every organisation. And not everyone with a link has that link permanently. That's why it is important for strategic communicators to work out who is important to an organisation and why, and who ought to be aware of what it does and why—and when they need to become aware.

FURTHER READING

Guth, D.W. and Marsh, C. (2006), *Public Relations: A Values-Driven Approach*, 3rd edn, Pearson, Boston, esp. ch. 4. Kim, J-N. and Ni, L. (2010), Seeing the Forest through the Trees: The Behavioural, Strategic Management Paradigm in Public Relations and its Future, in R.L. Heath (ed.), *The SAGE Handbook of Public Relations*, 2nd edn, SAGE, Los Angeles, CA, pp. 35–58.

Macnamara, J. (2012), *Public Relations: Theories, Practices, Critiques*, Pearson, Sydney, esp. chs 2 and 4.

FROM STAKEHOLDERS TO PUBLICS

The principle being explored here is that target publics have vital, situation-specific relationships with organisations. A relationship involves interaction, and for an organisation and its publics this happens because publics are affected by the organisation in some way. Sometimes relationships are permanent; sometimes they are temporary. Employees have a permanent relationship with the organisation for which they work; students with the schools, colleges and universities they attend; sports fans with the football or hockey teams they support; and people of faith with their local congregation. A temporary relationship would be established when an organisation interacted with people in unusual circumstances. In a physical crisis, for example—say, a fire at a factory—an organisation would need to work with the emergency services, something it doesn't do every day. Similarly, a new access road being built for a manufacturing plant means relationships are developed for the duration of road building but may not be needed after that, just as people need to work with lawyers when they buy a new home, but that relationship ends when the legal matters are resolved. Sometimes relationships are established with publics with whom the organisation has never previously needed to interact (Cia and Synott, 2009; Sison, 2009a).

In these contexts, relationships are *situational*—that is, they occur because of a particular, or extraordinary, situation. Chapters 3–5 dealt with the importance of understanding situations, and analysing what they mean for organisations.

Target publics can be identified by analysing which people are important to an organisation in a specific situation. All organisations have stakeholders, people who have an interest in the organisation. Often, the term *stakeholders* is used as a synonym for *target publics*, but this is an insufficient description of the people who matter to an organisation in a specific situation, and the two terms are not interchangeable. Strategic communication practitioners need to be more precise about the people with whom they need to build relationships, especially when planning for each of the three business horizons discussed in Chapter 2. Nevertheless, understanding an organisation's stakeholders is the first step in identifying and segmenting its target publics for a particular situation.

IN THEORY: STAKEHOLDERS AND RELATIONSHIPS

The traditional, primary meaning of the term *stakeholder* is the person with whom people making a bet deposit the money being wagered. But a stakeholder is also defined as "someone with an interest or concern in something" (*Australian Concise Oxford Dictionary*, 4th edn). That's the definition of stakeholder used in professional communication. Stakeholders are those who help an organisation to go about its business or have an interest in (or receive a benefit from) what it produces, or regulate it, or have some impact on its market and non-market environments.

Stakeholder theory involves thinking about how things should be in relation to groups of people external to an organisation (say, customers) or inside it (employees). The theory suggests that these groups can exert positive or negative influences on the organisation. For example, activists advancing their point of view in the non-market environment would be an external group attempting to influence a public policy decision that may have a negative effect on the organisation.

Stakeholders can be people who support, or are opposed to, an organisation. For strategic communication, it is preferable to further segment stakeholders into target public classifications because that allows a practitioner to build a more accurate understanding of specific groups' interests.

Relationship-management theory is often used to explain the different ways in which organisations and their publics relate to each other. Identifying the relationships that target publics have with an organisation provides important information for a situation analysis. It is also important in deciding how to reach target publics, what kinds of messages need to be sent to them and, of course, how to manage relationships. Relationship-management theory can help you to decide:

■ The nature of relationships: are they positive, negative, or neutral; individual, professional or group (activists, regulators)?
what information publics already, or need to, know about the organisation, and what the organisation needs to know about the views and attitudes of its publics
■ The benefits of maintaining and improving relationships.

Figure 6.1 shows an organisation's general stakeholder groups in a classification that divides them into four basic categories: those who provide *inputs*, receive *outputs*, *govern* the organisation and *service* it. Sometimes in this approach to classifying stakeholders, some groups, like employees and governments, appear in more than one sector of the chart. That is because these groups have more than one relationship with organisations. For example, governments establish regulatory environments and receive tax income; employees provide their labour skills as input for the organisation's process but they also receive outputs in the form of wages and conditions.

For different situations, an organisation might need to communicate with stakeholders for different reasons and in different ways. Guth and

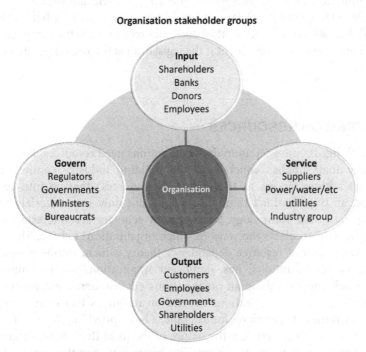

Figure 6.1 Organisational stakeholder groups

Marsh (2006) suggest why this might be so. To do what they do (achieve their goals and objectives), organisations need resources—for example, money, people, technology, raw materials—which they don't always control. To acquire resources, organisations must build relationships with those who supply them. Building relationships in this context (the theoretical principle of resource dependency theory) involves publics and organisations exchanging information about each other. In other words, they establish a dialogic relationship. So, in a given situation, the "regulators" in Figure 6.1 could be segmented into bureaucrats who implement rules about tax, manufacturing, industrial safety, health, exports, company registration, transport and the environment. A strategic communication practitioner working in Australia, the United Kingdom, Canada or the United States would need to further segment these bureaucrats into those who work for the national or federal government and those who work for regional, state or provincial governments. In some situations, they'd also need to identify regulators in local government. This is because each level of government has different regulatory responsibilities. For example, if an industry association was planning a public affairs campaign to lobby for a change in tax legislation affecting its members, it would need to identify which level of government was responsible for that legislation. That is, which government, state, national or regional, levies the tax cuts members are concerned about? Equally important would be the selection and timing of communication tools with which to engage the relevant regulators, and later the appropriate politicians. It would be an example of what Gregory (2009) describes as a waste of effort and resources to focus the campaign on a state or provincial government if the legislation is the responsibility of the national government.

DEPENDING ON RESOURCES

To do the things they are set up to do, organisations need resources. For example, a company that supplies concrete to the building industry cannot produce its product without access to the materials (resources) that go into concrete. Of course, an organisation's resources include not only raw materials but also finance, people and technology. Management scholars are interested in how acquiring resources affects the ways in which organisations behave. This has led to the development of resource dependency theory, which, among a number of management considerations, has significant implications for communication because it helps in describing an organisation's environments and relationships. For example, because organisations depend on resources that come from their external environments (think of, for example, a bank providing finance for a new project), it is vital to understand the nature of the links that result. Sometimes a resource dependency means that a supplier has power over the organisation. In this sense, resource dependency theory is situational.

In many ways, resource dependency theory intersects with Michael Porter's (2008) five forces that influence industry competition. Porter argues that within an industry (say, the concrete industry), there are five factors that influence the ways in which companies (concrete manufacturers) compete:

- The bargaining power of suppliers: who set the price for raw materials, and therefore determine what the producers have to pay for them
  the threat of new entrants—who would aim to take market share from existing producers
- Rivalry between competitors: which might lead to different prices for cements as producers compete for market share
  the bargaining power of buyers—who might argue that a competitor is providing the same product at a lower price
- The threat of substitute products or services: which might mean that steel building products could capture traditional markets for concrete.

Both Porter's five forces and resource dependency theory suggest a framework for analysing who is important to an organisation and the strengths and weaknesses of relationships with target publics.

FURTHER READING

Porter, M.E. (2008), The Five Competitive Forces that Shape Strategy, *Harvard Business Review*, January, pp. 79–93.

Thinking about stakeholders in this way, and the specific situations in which they need to be engaged, should drive communication practitioners to be more precise in their planning. After analysing the situation, or the issue, they are addressing, and which people are important in that situation, practitioners need to **segment** stakeholders into specific target publics.

Segment to divide something into several parts. Think of the structure of a peeled orange; each segment is a part of the whole. For communicators, target publics are the segments of a stakeholder group.

TARGET PUBLIC SEGMENTATION

James Grunig and Fred Repper (1992) point out that the basic idea of segmentation is simple: divide a population into groups whose members are more like each other than members of other segments of the population. To do that, practitioners utilise demographic, **psychographic** and geographic variables and theories that explain how people think, behave and communicate.

Psychographics the study of people's attitudes and aspirations.

Segmenting stakeholder groups is important because it enables communication strategists to identify specifically who they need to engage on specific issues. Segmentation enables communicators to work out how they can reach publics and with what. In Australia, enrolling (registering) to vote, and voting, in state and federal parliamentary elections is compulsory for all citizens aged 18 years and over. All people living in Australia, citizens, migrants, temporary residents—the general public—are stakeholders in the electoral process because that's what determines the state or federal government. But only a quite carefully defined segment of the general public can and must vote. For electoral communication purposes—messages about when, where and how to enrol and to vote, and why voting is important—citizens are the target public. Even "citizens" can be further segmented into specific target publics of first-time voters, people living in remote areas, people who will be overseas at the time of an election, elderly voters in nursing homes, voters in hospital, people for whom English is a second language, all of whom have special electoral information needs about requirements, rights and services for their specific situations, and for whom effective communication pathways and tools are required. This example is an important illustration of why "the general public" is not a useful nor an effective target public. It is too broad for most strategic communication purposes and, when you think about it, may only be a relevant target public in a time of disaster that affects everyone in a geographic area. There's more on this point later in the chapter.

SOME PEOPLE LIKE FOOTY; OTHERS DETEST IT

Even within their own categories, stakeholders have different world views, personal opinions, likes and dislikes, and vary in their demographic make-up and the ways in which they prefer to receive and process information. Refugee activists are a target public in specific situations for national governments because they share the same issue but from different perspectives. National governments want a border security approach that prevents unauthorised refugees entering the country until there is certainty that individuals are genuine refugees. Refugee activists argue that the detention regimes that governments put in place to control the flow of refugees across national borders are inhumane and unnecessary. This results in a public policy debate. But the term *refugee activists* includes women and men of different ages, occupations, income levels, religious beliefs, geographic locations, political voting intentions and methods of accessing information. And more. While refugee activists are a cohesive public when they engage in dialogue about that public policy issue, their individual demographic characteristics illustrate the complications involved in identifying target publics. People in older age groups, for example, generally access information in different ways from those in younger age groups, and this difference has significant implications for relationship building, message delivery and the creation of dialogue.

IN THEORY: WHO ARE THEY AND HOW DO THEY BEHAVE?

Demographics refers to statistical data about groups in the general population. This data relates to factors like age, gender, employment (in work, out of work), marital status (single or married), family (kids or no kids), income and educational levels, where people live (in the city or in the country), professional status, faith beliefs, and how they say they will vote at the next election. Regular opinion surveys collect this data and aggregate it. It is then possible to know, for example, how many people in your state are: aged 25–30, married females with one child, living in a regional town, tertiary educated, working full-time as pharmacists, earning US$95,000 a year and intending to vote for the government at the next election. This would be important data for a strategic communication plan to reach young professional women in regional areas.

Psychographics uses surveys and focus groups to study and explore people's attitudes and aspirations. This helps communicators to understand, say, purchasing habits, the reasons they will vote in a certain way at the coming election, or whether they think the organisation is ethical. Knowing this kind of information will help communicators to design messages and other parts of a strategy.

Consider this. The former English football coach Bill Shankly is credited with saying, "Football is not a matter of life and death; it is more important than that." To those who like football, Shankly's saying resonates deeply. To those who detest football, that saying would illustrate over-the-top support for a silly pastime. These different responses are a useful illustration of how we might understand and identify target publics. The large crowds that attend important football matches present communication opportunities to reach fans. They share a common interest in football, but does that necessarily mean they are an appropriate public for your campaign? Might those who detest football be more appropriate? Is a common love of football, or a shared hatred of it, the characteristic that defines your target public?

Strategic Plan Checklist: Publics

Segmenting stakeholders to identify target publics

In Chapter 2, you produced two tables for your strategic plan project—one for your organisation's market environment and one for its non-market environment.

The exercises in this chapter are designed to help you develop specific target publics for your strategic plan project.

For this first exercise, use the table you set up for your organisation's non-market environment. Start by using the information you compiled in the "Element" and "Relationships" columns of the table to categorise your stakeholders in four lists headed: "Input," "Output," "Service" and "Govern" (see Figure 6.1). Some stakeholders will appear in more than one list (employees, for example, provide *inputs* through their labour and skills, and receive *outputs* in the form of wages and benefits).

Now you need to revise these lists to make them specific to the situation, or issue, your strategic plan will address. Revise the lists to *segment* the stakeholders into those groups who have a specific interest in the situation or issue.

It is likely that you have listed "government." Be more specific. For example, which government: the local town council, the regional or state government, the national or federal government? If you have listed "regulators," be more specific: which regulators have specific roles in relation to your organisation's involvement in this particular issue? Which politicians do you mean: local members or ministers? Which "media" are important in this situation? Do you mean current customers, potential customers or lost customers? If you have listed suppliers, do you mean every supplier the organisation has, or just one or two? Which ones?

You should have four detailed lists of specific target publics from this segmentation. You'll use these again in the next exercise.

FURTHER READING

Chia, J. and Synnott, G. (2009), *An Introduction to Public Relations: From Theory to Practice*, Oxford University Press, Melbourne, esp. ch. 1.

CATEGORIES OF TARGET PUBLICS

Working out who the specific target publics are for your organisation in a specific situation is a crucial step in preparing a strategic communication plan. Identifying how each specific target public is involved in, or affected by, the issue or situation is an equally important step in planning, because not every public is directly impacted. Understanding this makes it easier to decide about goals and objectives, about the kinds of information you need to include in messages, and about what communication pathways and tools should be used. All this has implications for the plan's budget, the timing of its implementation and how you will evaluate it.

If you review the list you compiled in the exercise above by asking who is directly affected by, or involved in, the issue addressed by your project, it should become clear that some people are directly affected, others are indirectly affected but may have some influence in the situation, and some are not affected in any way but have a real ability to influence others.

Communication strategists use this idea to categorise target publics in three ways:

■ *Primary target publics* are the people who are *directly* affected by the situation or issues and with whom the organisation needs to engage in a dialogue. They are regarded as *primary* (the first in a series) target publics because in each situation, they are the most important. It might be that they are public policy decision-makers, or potential customers for a new model of car, or potential university students. Most strategic plan objectives, messages, communication pathways and tools will be devised to reach these publics and to establish a dialogue with them.

   Secondary target publics are the people who are *indirectly* affected by the situation but who may be an information source for, or *influence* on, the primary public. While they are categorised as a secondary public, they are still important. Identifying and understanding their influential role with primary publics helps practitioners to plan how they can reach them. For example, mums and dads are secondary publics when universities try to convince high school graduates (primary publics) to study at their institutions. This is because mums and dads have an influence on the study choices their kids make, especially in relation to finances. A practitioner who knows why it is important to reach the parents of potential university students, how to do that and what to say to them is more likely to be successful than one who does not.

■ *Tertiary* or *intervening target publics* are not at all affected by the situation, but they can influence or inform primary and secondary publics. That's why they are also described as *intervening* publics. Someone who intervenes in something can interfere, but also has an influence that can prevent or modify a course of events. In a communication context, that could mean a positive or negative influence, or simply an agenda-setting role. Take, for example, journalists. When they write about a current issue, they are usually not directly nor even indirectly affected by it. Journalists might not convince people to accept a particular point of view, but what they write about, and what is broadcast, posted, or published, does set an agenda that influences what people might think about. For this reason, practitioners provide journalists with information as one of their public relations tools because journalists, and the organisations they work for, are communication channels to reach primary and secondary publics. (There is more about this idea in Chapter 9.)

WHY "GENERAL PUBLIC" DOESN'T WORK

Think about it: the term *general public* really means everyone in the community from the newest baby to the oldest person. Everyone. Rarely is everyone in the community affected by a situation. Perhaps natural disasters and wars are the only times in which referring to "the general public" works. Even paying tax only involves those people who must do so because they earn an income above a certain level. It is much more effective to segment the "general public" into meaningful specific publics, depending on the situation you are addressing—for example, taxpayers, accountants, financial advisers, small business owners and corporate tax-payers, when the taxation department needs to advise deadlines for tax returns.

JOURNALISTS AS TARGET PUBLICS

David Conley and Stephen Lamble (2006) describe journalists as "the consummate outsiders," partly because their craft does not rate highly in public opinion. But journalists are also "outsiders" because of their role as independent observers of all forms of society. They make a virtue of their independence, of their designation as the so-called "Fourth Estate" and of their privileged position, which derives from the freedom society grants the media to report and comment on events and issues, no matter how uncomfortable that freedom might be for others. Yet despite their role and their power to set the agenda for discourses about public affairs, journalists are not the most important target public in strategic communication. Nor is that collective noun, "the media" but you wouldn't know it if you looked at how many times practitioners use this term in their strategies.

Journalists are important, and they provide a unique communication channel for reaching target publics, but journalists are rarely directly or indirectly affected by a situation. If they are directly or indirectly affected—probably for reasons other than their involvement in journalism—then they are a primary or secondary target public. Journalists certainly influence what the rest of us think about and, sometimes, if they have a specific role as a commentator, maybe what we think.

Communications strategists need to share journalists' legendary cynicism and ask why specific categories of journalists (never "the media," because that term is too general) should almost always be tertiary or intervening publics. From time to time, specific categories of journalists might become primary publics, perhaps in a public policy debate when an organisation needs specialist writers and commentators to understand a particular point. In that case, it is likely an interpersonal communication pathway would be used with a meeting, email, or telephone call as a tool for briefing journalists on the organisation's views. This is common practice and if pursued with openness and honesty is an ethical approach. Sometimes, especially in politics, senior people meet editors, often over dinner, for this.

One of the frequent complaints journalists make about communicators is that too often they send them material in which they have no interest—for example court reporters being sent media releases about domestic sport. This happens because communicators are too quick to use distribution lists of journalists that are not segmented into topic areas. This is wasteful and annoying and demonstrates that many communicators have little clear knowledge of how the news media works. Take the time to learn about who is responsible for what topics and tasks in the news media, especially those who report and comment on your industry, and be more effective in how you target information to journalists. So, like the general public, the broad term "journalists" needs to be segmented into meaningful categories—their "rounds," or the topics they report on—depending on the situation you are dealing with: sports writers (football, cricket, netball, baseball, basketball, hockey), economics editors, finance reporters, health reporters, police reporters, political correspondents, environmental writers, foreign correspondents and so on. Is it necessary, for example, to identify the whole group known as "journalists" or "the media" or just specifically "finance reporters" as an intervening public for a media release on a bank's new credit card? Could you be more specific? And by doing that, could you be more efficient and effective with your communication? Of course you could.

FURTHER READING

Conley, D. and Lamble, S. (2006), *The Daily Miracle: An Introduction to Journalism*, 3rd edn, Oxford University Press, Melbourne.

TRADITIONAL AND NON-TRADITIONAL PUBLICS

In most situations, organisations will know who their *traditional* publics are. These are the groups with whom they have their regular interactions: employees, share-holders, customers and a range of suppliers. At other times, perhaps in a crisis, they need to interact with people with whom they rarely, if ever, come into contact. These groups—perhaps categories of journalists, emergency services, government agencies or community groups—are known as *non-traditional* publics.

Knowing and understanding traditional and non-traditional publics is important for deciding how much information is needed in specific situations. A non-traditional public, for example, would need more information about the organisation than a traditional public.

CHAPTER EXERCISE

Identifying categories of target publics

Using the information you collated in the last exercise, categorise the target publics into two lists, one for *primary publics* and one for *secondary publics*. Do not include journalists in either list.

Ask questions about the people who are directly or indirectly affected by the issue your project will address. Make the tough choices about who goes in what category.

Now list the specific categories of journalists who would be *tertiary* or *intervening* target publics for your strategic communication plan. Think about your organisation's business and the industry it is in. Do news websites, newspapers, and radio and television stations have spe-cialist journalists who report on your kind of business and industry? Most news outlets use bylines on news stories and commentary to identify who wrote the story and their specialisation. For example: Sam Simpson,

Medical Correspondent; Ivy Bate, Environment Reporter; Janine Hitchens, Transport Correspondent; Peter Thompson, Chief Political Reporter; Ivor Fortune, Finance Editor.

If you are writing a strategy about a transport issue, it is likely that the reporters who cover that industry will be interested in what your organisation is doing and has to say. You'd be interested in them because you'd know that the primary and secondary publics read what they write to keep up to date with transport news.

Who else from your original list should be categorised as an intervening public? Add people who are neither directly nor indirectly affected by the situation or issue but can influence those who are.

You should now have three categories of target publics—primary, secondary, and tertiary—for your strategic plan project.

WHAT DO TARGET PUBLICS ALREADY KNOW ABOUT YOUR ORGANISATION?

When practitioners identify target publics for a strategic communication plan, they are recognising the people who are important to an organisation. Some, like employees or shareholders, are easily identified. Others become apparent from research on a specific issue facing an organisation.

So, you must discover what a target public already knows about the organisation and whether they have specific positive or negative opinions about it. This includes knowing what target publics expect from the organisation, how they obtain information about it and the best, most cost-effective ways of reaching specific categories of publics.

This information will come mainly from secondary research—it won't normally be necessary to pay for specific opinion research. A great deal of professional judgment is also needed in this process. For example, environmental groups would likely have concerns about a new factory proposed for a rural town. They will also be knowledgeable about the impact the factory might have on the local river system, and native flora and fauna. Residents living near the land on which the factory would be built might be in favour of it, or they might oppose the plan. Administrators in the local municipal council will have views about the proposal, as will businesspeople and community groups. In each case, a professional judgment could be made about the level of knowledge each of these publics has about the proposal. Nevertheless, target publics will need information about the proposal and about the organisation planning to build the factory.

The organisation will need information about target publics' knowledge of the proposal, attitudes towards it and possible actions.

Target publics' attitudes towards an issue are determined based on their knowledge, life experiences and demographic, psychographic and geographic characteristics:

- *Demographic*: variables like age, gender, education, cultural background, marital status and socio-economic background help determine what the messages might be and how they might be written and delivered.
  Psychographic variables like opinions, values, perceptions and concerns determine the tone of messages.
- *Geographic*: variables like whether people live in a city or in a rural area, or whether a campaign is to be national or limited to one state or region, are important for working out how messages will be delivered. That is, by which communication pathways and communication tools.

This helps practitioners understand the specific common traits of target publics, like interests and expectations, age, gender and culture, occupations (skilled or unskilled) and their socio-economic status—all important in planning. Ronald Smith (2005, pp. 40–1) says this information helps practitioners understand whether a target public group is:

- Distinguishable
  homogeneous
- Important to the organisation and the issue it faces
  large enough to be important enough to matter
- Reachable.

The work of the scholar Kirk Hallahan (2000, 2001) is helpful in categorising target publics and working out their information needs. Hallahan explores the concept of issues dynamics or how disputes arise and how organisations respond to them. He argues that because many communication programs involve building positive relationships, differences between organisations and their publics might be minimal—or might not even exist. His view is based on research that shows that a person's behaviour towards an organisation (or issue) is determined by what they know about it as well as their involvement in it. In his view, issues are complex and dynamic, and involve people with direct stakes in a dispute but also others who are merely aroused, or who are aware but not motivated to act, and who are neither knowledgeable nor concerned about the problem (2001). Hallahan suggests that people are selective about the issues that they think are important and that because of this, some people simply have low levels of knowledge about an organisation and low levels of involvement in its operations. He calls these people *inactive publics* and argues that they are the "forgotten publics."

Table 6.1 shows Hallahan's five classifications of target publics—active, aware, aroused, inactive and non-publics—and includes their characteristics.

Table 6.1 Hallahan's typology of target publics

	Low involvement	High involvement
High knowledge	**Aware publics** Potentially vocal and aggressive	**Active publics** Potentially influential
Low knowledge	**Inactive publics** Potentially volatile	**Aroused publics** Potentially inert
No knowledge No involvement	**Non-publics** Potentially aggressive	

This way of thinking about publics is an important tool for assessing their likely involvement in an issue and for planning how they might be engaged. That is, if strategic communication is planned in the three-horizons paradigm explored in Chapter 2, decisions about when and how to engage publics on an issue can be managed appropriately.

For example, identifying an organisation's *active* and *inactive* publics helps a practitioner to decide how and when they need to be engaged. *Non-publics* represent a potential source of support, or a potential threat, if they become aware and aroused and actively engaged in discourses about an issue, so trying to identify who they are is important in strategic communication planning.

Hallahan (2001) says that strategies for dealing with publics should vary in line with their level of knowledge and involvement in an issue. He suggests that:

CHAPTER EXERCISE

Who is really interested in this issue?

Use the discussion of Hallahan's typology to further categorise the lists of primary, secondary and tertiary publics that you have made for the strategic plan project you selected from the examples in Chapter 1.

Who in your lists are already actively engaged in the issue, and who are not even aware of it? Who would be positive supporters if they became aware and active, and who might become opponents? Who knows something about the issue (are aroused) but are not actively involved? How might all these groups react if they knew more about the issue you are addressing in your plan? Would they become opponents or supporters?

Keep the results of all the work you have done in this chapter's exercises for later chapters.

- *Active* publics could be engaged through negotiation by acknowledging them, bargaining with them and making concessions to their point of view
  aware publics could be engaged through education involving alliance building, lobbying and media advocacy
- *Aroused* publics could be engaged through activities like monitoring their views, outreach and handling enquiries from them
  inactive publics could be engaged through reputation enhancement, organisation performance, poll-taking and market monitoring.

The implementation of these strategies can be planned in the three-horizons paradigm. For example, for an emerging issue, building knowledge for all categories would be a mid-term, Horizon 2 activity.

ON INCLUSIVENESS

One scholarly criticism of the term *target public* is that it is not inclusive, that it objectifies people. This view holds that practitioners classify publics according to the way an organisation regards them, rather than the way they choose for themselves (Macnamara, 2012). It is important to be aware of critical analysis of communication practice, and how scholars argue about the implications, including the ethical considerations, that are involved in the notions of strategy and targets. This chapter has taken an issues-based approach to identifying target publics. In this way, it recognises that individual groups do have points of view, which they have chosen, and that are specific to a situation being addressed, and that the organisation needs to hear these views if it is to give more than lip service to the notion of dialogic communication. Macnamara (2012, p. 169) puts it this way: "The notion of publics gives expression and emphasis to the plurality of groups of people with specific interests and concerns with which organisations in democratic societies may need to interact... at various times." That suggests the term *target public* need not mean classifying people in some artificial way. Whatever view one takes about the term, identifying target publics is an important step in planning how an organisation needs to respond to an issue.

FURTHER READING

Hallahan, K. (2000), Inactive Publics: The Forgotten Publics in Public Relations, *Public Relations Review*, 26(4), pp. 499–515.

Hallahan, K. (2001), The Dynamics of Issues Activation and Response: An Issues Processes Model, *Journal of Public Relations Research*, 13(1), pp. 27–59.

Kent, M.L. and Taylor, M. (2002), Toward a Dialogic Theory of Public Relations, *Public Relations Review*, 28(1), pp. 21–37.

Chapter 7 will examine *goal* and *objective* setting—the elements of a communication strategy that set its direction.

CHAPTER EVALUATION

This chapter introduced you to the importance of target publics by exploring their central role in communication strategy.

Evaluate your understanding of the topic by answering these questions:

1. How can the people with whom the organisation needs to build, or maintain, a dialogic relationship be identified?
2. Who are the most important people, and how would you categorise them?
3. Why is it important to specifically segment target publics?
4. What role do primary, secondary and intervening publics play in a communication strategy?
5. Why would specific journalists be regarded as tertiary or intervening target publics?

Chapter 7
Setting the compass

Communication goals and objectives

Goal: To understand how effective goals and objectives provide direction for a communication strategy.

Objectives: This chapter will help you to:

- Understand the specific roles of goals and objectives in a communication strategy
  Recognise how goals and objectives connect to later elements of a strategy
- Be aware of the need for correctly written objectives to enable a proper evaluation
  Write effective goals and objectives.

Principle: Goals and objectives deal with the changes a communication strategy is designed to achieve.

Practice: Goals and objectives need to be realistic.

Ancient mariners and the early travellers in the Arabian desert used the stars to navigate for their journeys. The stars guided them because the ancients understood that particular stars and constellations would be in the sky at different times of the year. The stars were reference points they could use to work out where they were. Later, mariners developed a device called an astrolabe for navigation. In more modern times, sailors used the compass and the sextant to plot their courses and work out where they were. Now, satellite navigation systems help sailors, aircraft pilots and astronauts to navigate; car drivers to find their way in unfamiliar cities; and smartphone users to identify their position, and to find their way to friends' homes. Before they start their journeys, sailors and pilots "set the compass"—that is, adjust their navigation tools—so that their readings are accurate.

Compass readings give direction, and that is also the role of **goals** and **objectives** in strategic communication. Goals and objectives are the reference points that "set the compass" for a communication strategy so that its course can be plotted,

DOI: 10.4324/9781003317579-8

and its success can be evaluated. They give directions on resolving a situation or issue by providing specific information about what must be achieved, and when it needs to be achieved. Once these directions are set, the specific actions needed to implement the goals and objectives—the communication pathways and tools that are needed to reach publics and to deliver messages—can be worked out. Goals and objectives lock the elements of a strategy together, much like pieces in a jigsaw puzzle.

Goals broad statements that deal with what must be done. Goals are about building *reputation*, about *relationships* and about *tasks*. Laurie Wilson and Joseph Ogden (2008) describe goals as statements of the end to be achieved to resolve the core problem. In their view, goals are a positive restatement of that core problem.

Objectives precise, measurable statements that indicate the steps needed to achieve goals. Objectives deal with change, such as increasing awareness, acceptance or understanding; or generating action. They are mostly *outcome* specific. Objectives back up a goal and they are the steps needed to achieve the goal.

The directions that goals and objectives give to a communication strategy mostly deal with change. Changes can be about, for example, improving a public's understanding of a situation, or building acceptance of a point of view about an issue, or about generating action, like convincing you to buy a particular smartphone because it will do all the things you need to keep in contact with friends.

EFFECTIVE GOALS AND OBJECTIVES

When communication strategists write *effective* goals and objectives, they focus on:

- Desired results: positive outcomes about an issue or situation they are addressing and the changes they seek
  realistic outcomes—changes that can be achieved
- Efficient outcomes: changes that can be achieved within budget, and in the time required.

Each of these points has consequences, not only for setting effective goals and objectives but also for accurate target public segmentation and the selection of communication pathways and tools.

Defining communication goals and objectives

Communication goals and objectives are not the same. They have different roles, but they are in a symbiotic relationship: they interact in a way that is mutually advantageous; one doesn't work without the other.

The Harvard Business School's guide on *The Essentials of Corporate Communications and Public Relations* (2006) says communication goals and objectives should be aligned with the strategic goals of the organisation and the people (target publics) who need to be informed and influenced to meet those strategic goals. Communication goals and objectives, the guide says, will be developed from all the information a practitioner compiles in the research phase of planning (see Chapters 3–5). That means a research phase leads to a situation analysis.

Communication goals, objectives and corporate strategy

Corporate business strategies begin with statements about the organisation's vision or mission. These are broad declarations about purpose and values and relate to how an organisation wants to position itself. They are not outcome-oriented but are abstract, altruistic and philosophical. They provide valuable clues for strategic communication goal and objective setting because they deal with what the organisation stands for, values that can guide advertising, public relations and sales programs.

Corporate vision and mission statements lead to goals by outlining what the organisation wants to do, and to specific objectives related to one outcome that will help achieve a particular goal.

The following extract shows how Coca-Cola's mission, vision and values statements provide direction for the business.

Case: Mission, vision and values statements

Most companies publish information about their mission, vision, values statements and their links to the community, on their websites, and include them in their annual reports to shareholders. It is worth reading examples of what they say about these issues because as a practitioner, you will write about your internal and external clients' approaches to them in a range of communication contexts.

BHP-Billiton

https://www.bhp.com/about/operating-ethically

BP

https://www.bp.com/en/global/corporate/sustainability.html

Coles

https://www.coles.com.au/about-coles/community

Meta (Facebook)

https://about.meta.com/actions/

Twitter

https://about.twitter.com/en/who-we-are/our-company

Volkswagen

https://www.volkswagenag.com/en/group/compliance-and-risk-management/whistleblowersystem.html

Walmart

https://corporate.walmart.com/purpose

Aligning goals and objectives to those of the organisation means they will deal with the communication aspects of what the business is trying to achieve. This is a major reason why communication strategists need to understand the organisation and its market and non-market environments, and why a properly researched situation analysis is so important in planning a strategy. When communication goals and objectives clearly make and reflect the links between an analysis of a situation or issue and why it is important to the organisation and its overall goals and objectives, the strategy will have a strong prospect of success. Fraser Seitel (2011) says tying communication goals and objectives to those of the organisation, and managing progress towards achieving them, is the key to a successful plan.

Communication departments have responsibility for a number of activities, many of which occur regularly. For example, most are likely to have an activity that deals with public affairs, or relationships with governments about public policy, and many will also have programs that build community relationships; manage sponsorships; work with the mass news media (media relations); implement employee communication; manage the corporate website and social media applications; deal with financial, investor and shareholder relations; oversee marketing communication; and manage events. Each of these programs will have ongoing communication strategies so that the people working in them will know what their projects have to achieve. Specific strategies will be written for one-off projects—for example, the launch of a new model of car, or the need to engage in community consultation in a new area. The organisation will also have a communication strategy that sets the broad direction for all these activities and that explains what the department seeks to achieve. Chapter 11 explores how all this works together as a communication system. For now, it is important to note the vital "genetic link" between the organisation's business strategy, and the goals and objectives of the communication department and its various regular and one-off, functions. The goals and objectives of these strategies won't be exactly the same, but they will be consistent, support each other and be recognisable as part of the whole organisation's direction. Just as the top-level communication strategy reflects the corporate business plan, so do the goals and objectives of specific projects.

FURTHER READING

Gibson, J.L., Ivancevich, J.M., Donnelly, J.H. and Konopaske, R. (2003), *Organizations: Behaviour, Structure, Processes*, 11th edn, McGraw-Hill Irwin, Boston, ch. 6, pp. 164–72.

Hodge, B.J., Anthony, W.P. and Gales, L.M. (2003), *Organization Theory: A Strategic Approach*, 6th edn, Prentice Hall, Upper Saddle River, NJ, ch. 3, pp. 51–80.

IN THEORY: BORROWING A CONCEPT

The principles behind the concept of communication goals and objectives reflect those in business management theory. And that's a relevant link for strategic communication, given its role in advancing organisational interests.

Business management theorist Billy Hodge and colleagues (2003, pp. 54–78, esp. p. 75) describe the setting of goals and objectives as an important assignment for managers. This assignment involves setting goals and objectives that meet the desires of what they describe as a complex set of internal and external constituents to set the desired future state that the organisation wants to achieve. Goals then create legitimacy through the rationalisation they provide for its existence, guide managers' and employees' actions and set standards by which performance can be measured. They suggest three categories of organisational goals:

- *Official goals* (or mission): which set guiding principles by focusing on a broad strategy
  operative goals that guide organisational business units or sections by specifying actions that will implement the strategy
- *Operative goals*: that guide people's behaviours by focusing on individual jobs or tasks.

Management theorists are often concerned about how people behave in organisational contexts and how managers can motivate employees to do their jobs effectively. This has included research based on goal-setting theory. James Gibson and others (2003, pp. 164–72) noted that, in this context, "intent" plays a significant role in goal-setting theory—that is, once a person starts something, they work until a goal is achieved. That's an important concept for setting strategic communication goals because it's the goals that define the intent of a strategy (that is, what it aims to achieve).

WRITING MEANINGFUL GOALS

Goals deal with reputation, relationships or tasks.

A strategic communication plan usually has more than one goal. Goals define the broad parameters of what the plan is trying to do about a situation or issue and should reflect an organisation's business strategy. Practitioners identify goals after talking with clients and conducting research, which will start with reviews of the corporate business plan and latest annual report. This is the information-gathering process that leads to a situation analysis.

Strategies may have more than one goal in which case they need to work together.

If a goal deals with *reputation*, a practitioner will have considered what makes the organisation distinct from others, what target publics think about its personality, and what the organisation claims to be. The goal will be related to the organisation's purpose, values and performance.

A *relationship* goal will be a statement about how the organisation interacts with its publics.

Reputation and relationship goals are about outcomes. That means they are concerned with changing, or strengthening, reputations and relationships.

A *task* goal will be about process, what needs to be done to make sure communication, say to strengthen relationships, occurs. Task goals are sometimes referred to as output goals.

Reputation and relationship goals build trust and respect, for example, for a charity, planning a new program to raise money for research into cystic fibrosis:

- A *relationship* goal might be "to build and maintain positive relationships with potential sponsors and supporters"
  a *reputation* goal might be "to gain recognition among target publics for our positive work"
- In fundraising for cystic fibrosis research
  a *task* goal might be "to distribute materials that shows people how to contribute."

FURTHER READING

Seitel, F.P. (2011), *The Practice of Public Relations*, 11th edn, Pearson, Upper Saddle River, NJ, esp. ch. 5.

Wilson, L.J. and Ogden, J.D. (2008), *Strategic Communication Planning for Effective Public Relations and Marketing*, 5th edn, Kendall Hunt, Dubuque, IA.

> **Strategic Plan Checklist: Goals**
>
> **Write strategic communication goals**
>
> From the work you've done so far on your strategic communication project, write three broad goals. One should deal with reputation and one with relationships, and one should be a task goal. Consider these questions:
>
> ■ What reputation do you want to build, or reinforce, or maintain, for your organisation?
> ■ With whom does your organisation need relationships in order to do what it does?
> ■ How will you go about reinforcing the current reputation?
>
> Remember that goals are broad statements; objectives deal with the steps needed to achieve goals. Remember also Wilson and Ogden's point that goals are positive restatements of a core problem, so reflect that thought in each of the goals you write for this exercise.

MEASURABLE OBJECTIVES

Objectives are steps along the way towards meeting a goal. Each goal should have specific objectives outlining the steps needed to make sure the goal is achieved. Practitioners must be able to measure how successful each of these steps has been.

Objectives demonstrate the effect the campaign is designed to bring about. They are about action—for example, generating change, reinforcing an existing attitude, or accepting an opinion on a public policy issue. That is, objectives are written so that target publics:

■ Understand an idea, or become aware of a new product
  agree with the idea, or that it is a good product, and then
■ Take action to support the idea or buy the product.
  If a public is not aware of a product, it won't be able to decide whether it is a good product, and therefore won't buy the product.

SMART objectives are **Specific, Measurable, Achievable, Relevant, and Time-Bound**. Defining these parameters as they relate to a goal helps ensure that that objectives are attainable within a certain time frame.

Clear, precise and measurable objectives are about achieving *outcomes*. Task goals are supported by *process* objectives that give the steps, or outputs, required to complete the task.

Process objectives are generally about doing the tasks that support the objectives that have been set to bring about change.

An objective's **outcome** will be something more important than producing a media release, installing a display at the local shopping mall, publishing an online newsletter, or engaging in social media listening and tweeting. Those actions are about **process** and **outputs**. Outcomes result when an understanding, attitude or belief changes, or when a public takes a supportive action. That is why objectives are expressed in terms of building *awareness*, generating *acceptance* and persuading target publics to take *action*. Awareness objectives are designed to build knowledge of a topic; acceptance objectives are written to generate acceptance of, say, a point of view; and action objectives seek a response from publics, hopefully positive. Objectives to generate awareness or acceptance or action are not mutually exclusive: you can write objectives directed at each of these in one plan.

Why measuring change is important

To measure something means to work out the extent or quantity of something by comparing it with something that is fixed or of a known. So, a change in a public's understanding of an organisation's position on an issue after a strategic communication plan is implemented can be measured by comparing the outcome with the level of understanding about that issue identified in the initial situation analysis.

Politicians spend a lot of time reading and worrying about opinion polls. When the polls move up or down, politicians look for the reasons why the change occurred. Obviously, politicians from opposing political parties will often have different views about what the poll results mean, but the new numbers indicate something has changed in voters' attitudes towards an issue or a political party. The difference between the last poll result and the new one is a *measurement* of the level of change. Communication practitioners need objectives that help them generate the same kind of data for their campaigns.

Communication objectives are designed to influence target publics, to bring about change in a public's awareness and attitudes. It is useful, then, to relate objectives to target publics. Figure 7.1 illustrates what objectives do.

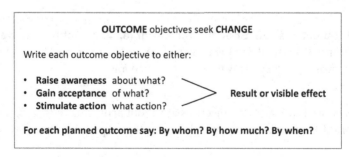

Figure 7.1 Objectives and change

IN THEORY: CONCEPTS FROM PSYCHOLOGY

Some key concepts from psychology can help us understand how to write objectives:

- Raising awareness is about *cognitive* processes—that is, provoking publics to think about a product or an issue. Maybe target publics haven't heard of an issue, or known about a new product, until they have seen the organisation's communication for the first time.
  Gaining acceptance is about *affective* processes—that is, generating an emotional response to a product or an issue. Perhaps the emotional response is that people like the new model of car because of its modern shape, or because film stars are buying it. Perhaps they'll support an organisation's attitude towards an issue.
- Stimulating action is about creating behavioural responses—that is, *conative* processes, or building a desire to act.

These terms are important not only in setting objectives but also in making decisions about messages. The theories they deal with are foundations for the concepts of informative and persuasive messages, and how they will be delivered to target publics.

WRITING OBJECTIVES

Objectives do not include information about how they will be achieved. That is, an objective should not say that a change in awareness will be achieved by using Facebook or YouTube, or the company's website, or via regular tweeting. Planning how you will reach a target public, and what you'll produce, in order to achieve an objective is the job of communication pathways and the tools associated with them.

Setting an objective means writing down what you need to change, by how much (usually a percentage) and by when. Writing objectives in this way provides direction—the reference points—and ensures that they can be evaluated. Figure 7.2 shows a formula for writing outcome objectives.

It is best to include a specific target public in an objective. For example, a practitioner writing a city council communication plan about new roadworks might write an objective like this:

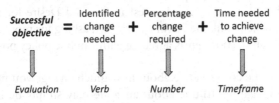

Figure 7.2 A formula for writing objectives

To increase local shopkeepers' awareness of the new road building program by 50 per cent in the next three months.

That makes it quite clear to whom the communication will be addressed and what needs to be achieved.

A second objective might be:

To convince 75 per cent of local shopkeepers to support the road works plan by the end of the campaign.

The key is to know what needs to change, by how much and in what time frame—and what target publics are involved.

Process objectives are written in a similar way but deal with tasks, not changes. Because they deal with outputs, they are in a sense easier to write. Here are some examples:

▪ To write and distribute ten media releases about our views during the campaign.
To redevelop the corporate website within the next four months.
▪ To participate in the industry's trade exhibition to be held in six months.

Process objectives indicate what needs to be done and by when—and are still measurable. You could, for example, evaluate whether you did write and distribute ten media releases during a campaign (and if only seven were produced, you could explain why), or whether the website redevelopment was completed at the end of four months. That evaluation would indicate whether the identified outputs during the campaign helped to achieve outcome objectives.

Dennis Wilcox and Glen Cameron (2012), American academics who write about strategic public relations, suggest that a test of whether an objective is appropriate is whether you can answer "yes" to questions like:

▪ Does it really address the situation?
Is it realistic and achievable?
▪ Can success be measured in meaningful terms?

For each broad goal, realistic objectives will build awareness, then acceptance and then generate action. This step approach to objective setting reflects the so-called AIDA hierarchy of effects, or persuasive communication model, used in marketing communication. That model proposes that brand messages should seek customers' Attention to a brand; garner their Interest in it; build Desire for the brand; and generate Action, which could be buying a product, asking for more information or, in a strategic communication sense, agreeing with a public policy position.

It is a good idea to be conservative about how much change you need to achieve: a 100 per cent change in attitude about an issue may simply be impossible, but 65 per cent might be achievable. The same principle applies to setting process

Case: Ten big ideas

The Business Chamber in the Australian state of New South Wales (NSW) won a 2011 Golden Target Award from the Public Relations Institute of Australia for a campaign designed to promote ten major policy solutions that would support a more competitive business environment in the state. The chamber (NSWBC), the state's largest and most representative business group, had identified a policy void that was causing NSW to lose its economic competitiveness. The goals and objectives for the campaign were:

Goal 1: Establish NSWBC as a thought leader and leading business advocate in NSW.
Objectives

- Produce an easily accessible policy blueprint, 10 Big Ideas to Grow NSW, to demonstrate thought leadership and research.
  To have at least five of the 10 Big Ideas adopted by the NSW Government either pre or post–2011 State Election.

Goal 2: Strengthen the relationship between NSWBC and key political figures.
Objectives

- Secure the Premier and Opposition Leader to speak at the 10 Big Ideas at the campaign launch.
  Attendance of key candidates and parliamentarians at supporting local events.

Goal 3: Demonstrate the advocacy value of membership of NSWBC to members and prospective members.
Objectives

- Work with local chambers of commerce to develop localised versions of the 10 Big Ideas campaign to demonstrate the value of a close relationship with NSWBC.
  Support the membership strategy of NSWBC in converting the 300 local chambers of commerce to alliance partners and accessing their membership for service and product opportunities as well as strengthening NSWBC's advocacy with Government.

The *goals* reflect the guidelines set out in this chapter. The *objectives* are a mix of outcome-oriented and output-based objectives, and all provide enough information to enable an evaluation of how successful the campaign was.

objectives. Realistically, do you need to issue two media releases a day during a six-month campaign? How many would be appropriate?

Deciding what is a realistic objective will come from your understanding of what objectives do, from your knowledge of the organisation for which you are

---

Strategic Plan Checklist: Objectives

Write objectives to implement your goals

Remember that objectives are action steps to implement a goal. Objectives seek an identified change, by how much, and how long it will take to achieve the change. Each goal can have more than one objective.

Using the three goals you wrote earlier in this chapter, think about the steps that will be needed to achieve each of them. Using the formula in Figure 7.2 (p. 135), write awareness, acceptance and action objectives for the first two goals. Use the three Wilcox and Cameron tests above to help you to assess whether your objectives are appropriate.

For the task goal, write the process, or output, objectives that will be needed to ensure it is achieved.

Revise what you have written to ensure the goals and objectives reflect (1) your organisation's business strategy, and its top-level goals and objectives and (2) the issue or problem you identified in your situation analysis that needs to be changed.

Ask these questions about the objectives: Are they consistent with the organisation's overall business goals and objectives? Do they demonstrate progress towards achieving those overall goals and objectives? Are they realistic—can they be achieved? Can they be measured? How?

---

working, from a properly researched situation analysis, and from your professional skills and experience.

FURTHER READING

Gregory, A. (2006), 'Public Relations as Planned Communication', in R. Tench and L. Yeomans (eds.), *Exploring Public Relations*, Pearson Education, Harlow, Essex, pp. 174–221.

Smith, R.D. (2005), *Strategic Planning for Public Relations*, 2nd edn, Lawrence Erlbaum Associates, Mahwah, NJ.

Wilcox, D.L. and Cameron, G.T. (2006), *Public Relations Strategies and Tactics*, 8th edn, Pearson Education, Boston, MA.

GOALS, OBJECTIVES AND PLANNING HORIZONS

Strategic communication deals with how organisations respond to issues that concern them. That means identifying and analysing not only those issues that impact on the current day-to-day operations of the organisation, but also those that are highly likely to occur in the mid- and long term—perhaps over the next 5–10 years.

For strategic communicators, both the market and non-market environments are important because the time horizons in which they work can vary from a few days (sometimes hours, as in a crisis) to many years for an intractable issue.

Senior practice leaders who are responsible for strategy must, then, have an eye on the future while they also manage day-to-day communication. And they must set goals and objectives that reflect this dual reality of communication practice.

The goals and objectives that are set for market-environment communication plans are about achieving results in what Chapter 2 described as Horizon 1. While most deal with immediate bottom-line concerns like product promotion and marketing support, they should also address responses to current public policy issues that have an immediate impact, such as activism, social changes and attitudes, current politics, the economic situation or changes to legislation that will in some way affect business.

In Horizons 2 and 3, goals and objectives should reflect what needs to be done to promote the organisation's position on emerging public policy issues. An organisation has only a faint hope of influencing public policy debates if it does not engage as a social actor. To do that, it needs to engage in constant environmental scanning and analysis to identify issues likely to emerge, and to set organisational policy responses. Heath and Palenchar (2009) described this as "surveillance" that may result in awareness that:

- A new issue is emerging
  something that has been a concern is maturing into an issue or
- An issue has taken a new turn.

Strategic Plan Checklist: Reputation

Write a reputation goal and objectives

The organisation for which you are planning your strategic communication project will face public policy issues, and some of them are likely to influence its reputation. That's a reality of business.

Revise your research findings for the public affairs and managing issues exercise in Chapter 3 (pp. XX). Select one of the issues that you identified in that exercise and the organisation's policy response to it. You need to be sure your communication strategy will advance the organisation's position on that issue. For this checklist, write:

> One *reputation goal* that would help advance the organisation's views in the mid-term (say, up to two years)
> Four *outcome objectives* that will help achieve the reputation goal.

Remember that you are working on an emerging public policy issue and on the contribution, your organisation should make in public debate about that issue. What can it realistically expect to achieve?

The next chapter deals with the role of messages in a communication strategy. That is, what does the organisation need to tell target publics so that it can achieve communication strategy goals and objectives?

Being aware of potential and emerging issues enables the organisation to consider a variety of responses, which means effective communication goals and objectives can be set to address them in the time provided by Horizon 2 and 3 planning.

CHAPTER EVALUATION

This chapter has explored how goals and objectives provide direction for a communication strategy. While goals are broad statements about what needs to be done to address a situation or issue, and objectives are precise and measurable steps that help achieve the goal, both need to be effective. That is, they should be based on research that leads to a correctly written situation analysis.

Test what you now understand about goals and objectives by answering the following:

1. Why do goals and objectives in a communication strategy differ?
2. What are the specific roles of goals and objectives in a communication strategy?
3. How do goals and objectives set the direction for the other elements of a strategy?
4. Why is it important for communication goals and objectives to reflect the organisation's business goals and objectives?
5. What are the three important elements of a communication objective?
6. Why is it necessary for goals and objectives to be realistic?

TIME OUT: ON INTERCULTURAL COMMUNICATION

If we agree with the theoretical approaches that ground strategic communication in a rational decision-making process—especially those that guide the selection of target publics, messages, communication pathways and tools—then it is axiomatic that the practice of strategic communication deals with "difference." No two target publics share the same demographics, nor do they access information in the same way or need the same level of information. Often the differences relate to generations. For example, while many seniors use smartphones and social media applications, it is a fairly safe assumption (we could test it with research) that most do not access information with these tools with the same enthusiasm, speed and dexterity that younger people do. The two generations share the same citizenship, but they don't necessarily share the same interests; political views; hobbies; lifestyles; and ways of communicating with friends, families, employers and the agencies and community organisations that support them. It could be argued, then, that seniors and younger people belong to different **cultures**—and understanding that difference, and what it means for communication strategy, is another example of the importance of context in decisions about how an organisation should communicate with target publics.

Culture "the customs, civilisation and achievements of a particular time or people" (*Australian Concise Oxford Dictionary*, 2004). Some people, perhaps migrants, suffer "culture shock" when they experience an unfamiliar culture or way of life. *Multiculturalism* means the existence of many culturally distinct groups in a society.

Gyorgy Szondi (2009) argues that culture and communication influence each other, especially if the latter is about symmetry. Szondi is writing about national cultures and how practitioners deal with differences when they work in an international context. In other words, practitioners need to be aware that the messages, communication pathways and tools that might work in middle-class Britain will not automatically be successful in Thailand. Cultural differences explain why. For example, Australian businesspeople often feel frustrated with Japanese approaches to business, especially the way that Japanese businesspeople negotiate trade contracts. What might be described as a pragmatic, let's-get-the-job-done style by some Australians doesn't always fit with the more considered and subtle style of Japanese decision-making.

The point is also true in domestic communication practice. Almost every Western nation has experienced positive changes to its culture from great waves of international migration. The United States prides itself on its cohesive mix of people from different ethnic backgrounds, drawn from the many immigrant groups that have been arriving almost from the nation's inception. Australia had a similar experience after the Second World War. Displaced people and immigrants from Greece, Italy and former Yugoslavia saw Australia as a country of opportunity where they could rebuild their lives. The same thing happened after the Vietnam War and the more recent wars in Iraq and Afghanistan. Each wave of immigration—either organised through official channels or embarked upon by people fleeing war and famine as refugees—has changed not only on the national make-up but on the way in which Australia sees its place in the world.

Just as Szondi (2009) points to the need for practitioners to consider cultural differences in international public relations practice, so, too, must they factor these differences into strategic communication planning. Krishnamurthy Sriramesh (2007) argues that issues such as cultural diversity and multiculturalism must be dealt with in texts dealing with public relations writing, planning and campaigns. Ignoring the significance of culture in human communication and relationship-building, and not integrating it in pedagogy and practice, would be, Sriramesh argues, at the discipline's peril.

Marianne Sison (2009b) has raised important questions that can help in planning for culturally sensitive communication. Sison notes that global public relations audiences include people of multicultural backgrounds. That means practitioners should ask some serious questions about multicultural publics in strategy development:

> How do existing target public-segmentation models account for cultural variability?
> Whose cultural values predominate among multicultural audiences?

Sison's questions reflect Sriramesh's (2007) argument that communication planning all too often means imposing Western strategic communication principles and decisions on other cultural environments, usually in a global communication context. Many government agencies, for example, do this at a quite basic level, failing to address Sison's questions. They translate existing material into a series of ethnic languages that reflect the make-up of their broad categories of target publics. This is important because not everyone is fluent in, say, English. While some people may be able to understand spoken English, they may not have the literary skills to understand written English. Yet citizens from all ethnic backgrounds have rights and responsibilities, so there is an equity requirement to make sure they are properly advised about these. A common solution to this communication challenge is to provide translations of messages for printed material and for radio, television and press advertising; to select appropriate communication channels to deliver these messages; and to employ people fluent in other languages to work in the relevant enquiry offices. Unfortunately, this simplistic response often becomes a last-minute activity, factored into the program because a policy requires it to be done. But is it effective, and is there another way?

Different cultures use words in different ways; react differently to authority, gender and social circumstances; support family members in different ways; and differ in the ways in which they go about business. Multiculturalism is not just about allowing people to speak their native languages, and to live and worship in culturally appropriate ways. Nor is it only about the impact of African, Asian and Arabic cooking on the traditional local diet. It involves respecting that diversity, and for strategic communicators, it also means planning in an appropriate way.

In a discussion about culture and global public relations, Robert Wakefield (2010) raises two important points that apply equally to decisions about intercultural communication planning. He argues that practitioners should build strategies that do not lose sight of local publics and potential local issues, and that they should seek intercultural understanding. While these points are made in an international practice context, they recognise that publics in different cultures are concerned about different issues and that practitioners need to understand this.

Sison's (2009b) research found that cultural factors in 12 award-winning Australian public relations strategies designed to change behaviour were limited to representations of race and language. While these factors were important in making sure messages were understood, Sison argues that strategic decisions should first be based on research into the community's cultural perspectives. Only one of the strategies (to promote the health benefits of a new cycle path) acknowledged cultural diversity, but the research component did not investigate how the diverse ethnic communities in the relevant community thought about bicycles as alternative means of public transport. The evaluation of this communication project (which was generally highly successful) did not provide comparisons between the overall outcome and those for ethnic communities. On a strategy designed to convince 18–26-year-old women to ask their doctors about a free cervical cancer immunisation (also generally rated as successful), Sison argues that the research should have sought answers to questions like: How do different ethnic communities view vaccinations for women? What would be the religious and ethical considerations among young women from different communities, or second-generation families, regarding vaccination? How might these issues be addressed in the campaign? What are the cultural implications of using "influencers" for health-related issues? The importance of Sison's research is that it shows how cultural diversity should be a significant factor in all aspects of strategic communication planning.

Based on their research, Arlette Bouzon and Joëlle Devillard (2009) argue that cultural communication is an essential business function. To plan and implement intercultural communication, practitioners need to, as Sison (2009b) puts it, acknowledge cultural variables beyond the descriptive factors of race, religion, language and values. From a professional practice perspective, this isn't easy, but it is an extension of the need for situation analysis to adequately deal with cultural differences, for stakeholder segmentation to mean the selection of relevant target public groups, for appropriate messages and for delivery strategies to recognise cultural difference. May be effective intercultural communication needs separate and specific strategic planning. More than anything, intercultural communication involves an understanding of diversity, and it needs clarity to generate equitable and ethical outcomes.

FURTHER READING

Bouzon, A. and Devillard, J. (2009), Changes in Contemporary Organisations and Interculturality: From Orchestrated Communication to Confidence, *PRism*, 6(2), at www.prismjournal.org/fileadmin/Praxis/Files/globalPR/BOUZON_DEVILLARD.pdf

Sison, M.D. (2009b), Whose Cultural Values? Exploring Public Relations' Approaches to Understanding Audiences, *PRism*, 6(2), at www.prismjournal.org/fileadmin/Praxis/Files/globalPR/SISON.pdf

Sriramesh, K. (2007), The Relationship Between Culture and Public Relations, in E.L. Toth (ed.), *The Future of Excellence in Public Relations and Communication Management: Challenges for the Next Generation*, Lawrence Erlbaum Associates, Mahwah, NJ, pp. 507–26.

Szondi, G. (2009), International Context of Public Relations, in R. Tench and L. Yeomans (eds.), *Exploring Public Relations*, Prentice Hall, Harlow, pp. 117–46.

Wakefield, R.I. (2010), Why Culture Is Still Essential in Discussions about Global Public Relations, in R.L. Heath (ed.), *The Sage Handbook of Public Relations*, 2nd edn, Sage, Los Angeles, CA, pp. 659–170.

Chapter 8
Planning effective messages

Goal: To explore the role of messages in a communication strategy.

Objectives: This chapter will help you to:

- Recognise the important role that messages have in a communication strategy
  Understand how informative and persuasive messages help to achieve objectives
- Use ethical practice when writing messages.

Principle: An ethical approach is required for writing informative and persuasive messages.

Practice: Messages are chosen to meet target public needs for information or to convince them to act in some way.

Politicians always seem to be in hot water for something. Whenever they break election promises, accept a pay rise, introduce unpopular measures, or sometimes just act as politicians to defend their views, they are criticised. The biggest criticism of politicians happens when they use language that communicates a positive perspective on their position, especially when they are dealing with criticism, or are in political strife. They are then accused of trying to manipulate public opinion. Promoting a positive interpretation of something in this way is known as "spinning," a term also applied to the practice of releasing bad news at a time when media coverage of it will be swamped by positive coverage of more important things. Alistair Campbell, who was Director of Communications and Strategy for former British prime minister Tony Blair, was accused of spinning when he edited two documents in 2002 and 2003 about weapons of mass destruction in Iraq to strengthen the British government's reasons for joining the Iraq war. Critics claimed that Campbell's edited versions of these dossiers overplayed actual intelligence findings about the presence of weapons of mass destruction in Iraq.

Most believe spin is propaganda, and those accused of practising it are labelled "spin doctors," whether they are involved in politics, industry or communication consultancies. Spin has become a clichéd pejorative term, often directed at the entire practice of public relations. Journalists—trained to question any information and to use simple, direct language—mistrust material not written in a

DOI: 10.4324/9781003317579-9

straightforward way and accuse communication practitioners of spinning regularly, and of ignoring the theoretical underpinnings of modern ethical professional communication practice. It is an irony of modern news reporting that the term *spin doctor* is so widely and pejoratively used by hard news reporters and commentators, despite them using "angles" to frame their stories. An angle is the news lead, the first paragraph that sets the tone and direction for what and how news is reported.

Spin veers close to unethical practice, so why start a chapter on writing effective messages with a reference to spin? First, discussing spin and the criticism it generates highlights the need for communication specialists to work ethically. Ethics are paramount in every aspect of strategic communication but become even more significant when practitioners craft messages. Ethical practitioners do not resort to spin. Second, the concept of "messaging" in strategic communication plans is contentious, especially in the context of practice that involves the use of social media applications. Ethical communication practice must involve decisions on what needs to be said, to whom messages should be relevant and how they will be delivered. It is sound practice to make these decisions all the while knowing that critical analysts challenge the concept of messaging. Planning messages—some informative, some persuasive—about an issue or situation is legitimate and good preparation. It is not spin. But this does lead to considerations about the role of informative and persuasive messages in strategic communication planning, topics covered in this chapter.

THE IMPORTANCE OF MESSAGES

Messages should be planned and written to inform, build understanding or persuade people to act. The idea that messages can be about persuasion prompts critical analysis. A list of messages needed to achieve goals and objectives is an element of a strategic communication plan. Poorly planned, written and delivered messages will likely mean all the effort that goes into preparing a strategic communication plan will be ineffective because publics will not receive or understand them.

Professional communicators need the ability to write clearly, fluently and with meaning; indeed, this is an essential skill for all public relations practitioners. Everyone in all the professional communication disciplines, whether a practitioner is working in advertising, writing a major speech for the chief executive, preparing a submission for a parliamentary committee, writing a blog post, or preparing a media release, needs high-level writing skills. Knowing how to craft messages with clear and concise language is crucial if those messages are to stand out from the thousands of others that people receive every day through email, websites, advertising, newspapers, conversations, telephone calls and meetings.

Your writing ability

It is tough to hear, but one of the harshest criticisms levelled at communication graduates by senior practitioners is that they "don't know how to write." This criticism is persistent and harsh but not always precisely defined. It is rarely clear that it means they can't write a sensible sentence, or write to the house style, or write news leads for media releases, or can't adapt their skills to features, news-letters, web sites, social media posts, formal business reports or emails, all of which relay messages. And journalists are equally savage in their criticism of media releases not providing news, or being misdirected to the wrong specialist, or simply being exercises in useless spin. Good writing is as vital for producing a communication strategy as it is for communication tools. Being able to write clearly, accurately, professionally and with flair is a key to successful practice—and to getting a job. It is that important.

Large corporations, politicians, welfare agencies and local community environ-mental groups need to plan exactly what to tell their target publics about their views on public policy issues, debates about the things that affect the organisation and its industry and their achievements and concerns. Those messages can be applied in all levels of professional communication practice, from a simple phone call to a journalist about an upcoming event, to a major community consultation project. A strategic plan is the place to identify key messages; to show how they link to target publics, strategic goals and objectives; and to explain how and when they will be delivered.

WHAT ARE MESSAGES?

At their simplest, **messages** are the information that organisations want target publics to know. Messages may be about the benefits of a complementary medi-cine product, or an organisation's views on a specific public policy issue playing out in the non-market environment, or a government agency's information about changes to speeding fines. Research for a situation analysis will identify what needs to be said about the issue or situation. In public policy discourses in the non-market environment—where Robert Heath's (2001) view that communica-tion practice is rhetorical applies—knowing what needs to be said, how it should be said and when and where it will be said is important for strategic planning.

Messages the key themes that guide the content of communication tools like websites, brochures, meetings, displays, media releases, speeches and podcasts. **Informative** messages provide facts objectively. **Persuasive** messages seek to influence publics by presenting an argument to bring about change. Messages can be re-crafted into summary briefing notes for people from the organisation when they are interviewed by journalists or when they represent the organisation at meetings.

Messages are included in a communication strategy because they are:

■ Linked to an objective
  for a designated target public

147

■ Informative, or
   persuasive.

Messages provide the information needed to help change a situation—the information that people process in their decision-making, and that is used to alert publics to their rights and responsibilities in civil society. A client may need to improve their reputation among key publics after a crisis. A communication practitioner would decide what information would help to achieve an enhanced reputation and how that information should be delivered to the appropriate publics. It may be that a simple apology for the disruption caused by the crisis would suffice. More likely, the practitioner would recommend objectives that build awareness and understanding among key publics based on a series of messages. Earlier, we saw how BP attempted this approach after the 2010 Gulf of Mexico oil spill.

The website www.care2.com provides resources to help people initiate, or join, petitions against what it describes as "bigots, racists, bullies, science deniers, misogynists, gun lobbyists, xenophobes, the willfully ignorant, animal abusers, frackers, and other mean people." Petitions like these are another way of thinking about sending messages on important social and political issues.

RELEVANCE AND TRUTH

Messages must be relevant to target publics. Relevance means messages provide information, or arguments, that publics need to make decisions. In speeches and podcasts, and on websites, YouTube posts, brochures, media releases, displays, letters and submissions, messages must be expressed in a way that target publics understand. If they are not written clearly, the information an organisation wants its publics to know is likely to be misunderstood or worse, ignored. David Guth and Charles Marsh (2006) say that successful messages must respect publics' needs and preferences by addressing their values and interests. That means clear, concise and meaningful messages are vital in all aspects of strategic communication practice. The Almond Board of Australia's website (www.australianalmonds.com.au) reflects this precision with the message "…almonds are nature's energy snack for people on the go," which sends a lot of information about almonds in a few concise words.

Some scholars are critical of communicators who focus their professional practice too heavily on message design and delivery. They argue that this sometimes happens because of the practitioners' backgrounds in mass communication or journalism and suggest that this approach to public relations is simply press agentry, the first level of practice identified by James Grunig and colleagues (see p. 137, and J. Grunig, for example, in Heath, 2001, pp. 11–30). This focus limits communication to an interest in message design and delivery to achieve awareness, to inform, to persuade or even to manipulate target publics, and it indicates one-way communication; preparing messages for participation in a dialogue requires a more complex approach. Scholars sometimes point out that messages reduce important, often complex matters to simple statements. The

English academic Kevin Moloney (2006) believes that in its use of messages, public relations is just "soft propaganda" and he writes about what that means for democracy. His colleague Johanna Fawkes (2006) has written about the ethics of persuasive messages. In an issues-management context, Moloney writes that messages may or may not have "full, partial (or any) truth statements in them" (2006, p. 40) and that truths are most easily identified after public wrangling among competing messages. Brian Sollis and Deirdre Breakenridge (2009) say that the use of myriad social media applications in public relations means practitioners need to "lose" the word *message*. This is because audiences are immune to general, mass-targeted, impersonal messages and because web communities evolve and thrive when people share thoughts and opinions with others. In the context of her critical analysis of messaging, Anne Gregory (2009a) argues that messages and the dialogue they are designed to create are often undervalued or reduced to simple statements but are more important than that because they provide points of contact and meaning between organisations and their publics.

Awareness of these critical comments is important, but in communication planning, messages are:

- Key points publics need to know about organisations and issues. They stimulate awareness, understanding and action contribute to dialogic relationships, because they are the points that are made in conversations, public debates, meetings, correspondence and publications
- Not just brief sentences. Key points can be expanded, enhanced, explained and supported in different ways and through written, visual and oral communication tools

Messages also:

- Establish the essentials of a discourse by focusing management on what needs to be said in a situation, thus avoiding woolly thinking
- Demonstrate that corporate communication strategies are appropriate
- Are essential in evaluation.

A communication paradox

When he opened the Public Relations Institute of Australia national conference in 2010, Dan Tisch, a Canadian consultant and then chair-elect of the Global Alliance for Public Relations and Communication Management, noted some of the paradoxes of professional communication. One paradox was about messages. Tisch argued that for practitioners and their clients, controlling a message is essential, yet the paradox is that controlling a message is impossible. Tisch's paradox is grounded in communication theories that deal with how target publics receive and interpret information. For example, the most basic communication model illustrates how a sender transmits a message to a receiver through a channel. Yet this simple linear model does not explain how the message is interpreted by the receiver. More complex information-processing theories deal with the reality that the receiver has total control over the meanings given to messages. Those meanings are influenced by factors like the receiver's own knowledge of the situation, education, life experiences, socio-cultural demographic, age, gender and marital and work status. Reception of the message is usually clouded by whatever else is happening in the receiver's general environment, just like static in a dodgy radio or television transmission. This is the point of Tisch's paradox. No matter how well a communication strategy is planned and implemented, its success depends on messages that cut through the "noise"—all that information and all those events that compete with what organisations want to say. Writing messages in ways that ensure publics will understand them and react to them is a skill. For a public to understand a message, what practitioners write must relate to that public's interests, concerns, expectations, aspirations, knowledge, attitudes and beliefs. Knowledge about all that comes from effective formative research summarised in a situation analysis.

FURTHER READING

Gregory, A. (2009a), Public Relations as Planned Communication, in R. Tench and L. Yeomans (eds.), *Exploring Public Relations*, 2nd edn, Prentice Hall, Harlow.

Moloney, K. (2006), *Rethinking Public Relations: PR Propaganda and Democracy*, 2nd edn, Routledge, Milton Park, Oxon.

MESSAGES, PATHWAYS AND TOOLS

Identifying what needs to be said in discourses about public policy, or in product promotion, is an essential step in deciding how to reach target publics. They are the fulcrum on which a communication strategy is balanced. Once a practitioner knows what needs to be done to deal with a situation, then decisions about what messages to use will drive the selection of communication pathways and tools, the allocation of resources and the choice of evaluation methodologies. Chapter 7 dealt with how objectives seek to raise awareness (a *cognitive* or thought-provoking step), gain acceptance (an *affective* step that leads to an emotional response) and stimulate action (a *conative* or behavioural response). Messages provide the information

IN THEORY: WORRYING ABOUT MESSAGES

Planned professional communication includes efforts to persuade people to act or to change their beliefs and behaviours. At its most basic level, this involves exercising power that derives from using organisational resources to implement communication strategies. Many scholars are concerned about this aspect of professional practice and warn of the need for communicators to act ethically. Practising ethically involves ensuring that messages are based on facts that can be tested; it does not mean inventing material or lying. And it is definitely not spin, no matter how much journalists like to frame it that way. It is, however, legitimate and ethical practice to use persuasive language to advance an organisation's point of view.

Many theories deal with messaging.

Framing theory refers to how information is presented to make it salient to target publics. Practitioners decide the ways in which information is presented, in the same way that journalists use news frames to decide what is news. Messages to provide informative or persuasive communication can be framed in the context of issues, action and choices sought from target publics, situations or responsibilities.

Two-step and multi-step flow theory suggests that opinion leaders are important in influencing how members of their groups process informa-tion. The concept is that opinion leaders can be people like parents, teachers, politicians, leaders of community groups, elders in indigenous and cultural communities, even talk-back radio hosts. It is these people who pass information on to groups, often with opinions, hence the notion of "two-step" or "multi-step" flow. This is an important concept that helps to classify target publics as secondary or tertiary.

Co-orientation theory suggests that people (groups) will have different views about an issue. They might understand some of the views of others and can achieve a consensus if they discover they share the same ideas. The extent to which they can do that depends on:

- *Accuracy*: or the extent to which they share each others' ideas or cognitions
- *Understanding*: or whether they have a common definition of the issue irrespective of how they evaluate it
- *Agreement*: or the extent to which they evaluate an issue or situation in the same way
- *Congruence*: or how similar their views on the issue are to those of the other person.

Co-orientation theory provides a frame for deciding how messages should be written to build acceptance, understanding and action, and suggests some principles for implementing the concept of symmetrical communication.

to generate those responses. Chapter 9 will deal with how communication path-ways are used to reach publics with messages, and Chapter 10 with tools, the actual "packaging" that carries the messages, such as social media applications, displays, annual reports, speeches, media releases, meetings and podcasts.

HOW MANY MESSAGES?

Most strategic communication plans include more than one message. Some messages provide information; others try to persuade publics to take some action. A strategic plan can include both types of messages. Formative research will help in making decisions about how many messages are needed, and what kind they should be: informative or persuasive. Research that identifies what target publics already know, or don't know, about the situation or issue will provide a reference for how much information is needed in messages. Often clients have a clear idea of what they want to say, and this will help to define the key messages. Sometimes there may be one main message for a plan: the most important point that the organisation needs to express. This key message will be the foundation for additional information that expands the discourse. An example: during his 2008 election campaign, US President Barack Obama used the key message 'Yes we can.' It was a campaign slogan, but it was used as a positive message that answered questions about issues facing the United States and whether change could resolve them.

One way of working out what messages you need to write is to use a "message map," a planning tool that uses a hub-and-spokes framework to help you write simple, concise key messages about a topic. A message map produces a visual representation of key messages that makes the interrelationships between them easily understood and remembered. Use your research skills to find examples of message maps on the web.

Another tool that can help identify potential messages is an analysis of the organisation's communication strengths, weaknesses, opportunities and threats (a SWOT analysis). This helps to sort out what people already know about the organisation and what they might need to know. For example, the organisation's strengths are positive points that can be emphasised in messages, maybe to balance perceived weaknesses and negative attitudes. By identifying opportunities, a practitioner will begin to understand the situations in which messages can be delivered effectively. You can find examples of SWOT analyses on the web.

The number of messages needed for a strategic communication plan is not limitless. One of the skills a practitioner needs is the ability to define the key messages as simply as possible. It may be that four message points are all that is needed; rarely would 20 be appropriate, because that may lead to confusion.

Strategic Plan Checklist: Writing

Try writing concisely

When they argued the need for concise, fluent language in professional communication, Sollis and Breakenridge (2009) proposed that most practitioners would fail the test of writing one sentence that explains why others should write about their client, organisation or issue and why their social media followers or readers should care.

Apply the test to your strategic planning project. In 25 words, write one sentence explaining why one issue you are addressing is important.

Test how clear and fluent your explanation is by asking a friend to read it and tell you what it says to them.

THEORETICAL PARADIGMS THAT HELP MESSAGE DESIGN

Many of the theoretical paradigms used to explain how people communicate, form attitudes or behave are derived from other disciplines but are helpful when planning messages and deciding how to deliver them. These disciplines include psychology, sociology, philosophy, management studies and the physical sciences. For example, *complexity theory*—which suggests that all systems, natural and human-made, are continually changing, often in small ways—comes from the physical sciences. Some scholars use complexity theory to study interactions and relationships in organisations.

Social exchange theory suggests that people make a kind of "what's-in-it-for-me" economic judgment on the benefits and costs of them behaving in a certain way. They want to maximise the benefit of what they are being asked to do but keep the costs of doing it low.

Diffusion theory proposes that people go through a five-step process before they decide whether they will adopt an idea or buy a product. The steps are:

- Awareness (they know about the idea)
  interest (they are aroused by the idea)
- Evaluation (they decide whether the idea is useful to them personally)
  trial (they try the idea out on friends or family)
- Adoption (they accept the idea and take it up or act on it).

In the 1980s, Petty and Cacioppo proposed the *elaboration likelihood model* (ELM), which dealt with how people process, or elaborate, information (Petty, Cacioppo and Schumann, 1983; Cacioppo and Petty, 1984). They argued that people process information in two ways—via "central route" and "peripheral route" processing. *Central route processing* involves careful, rational thinking about information (or "elaborating"), leading to considered decisions. This is important for persuasive communication because it means people who elaborate in this way need sufficient information to balance possibilities. A simple example of central route processing is a decision about buying clothes: do you buy an expensive brand name because it is fashionable, or do you buy a lesser brand because the quality is the same but the price lower? For someone with low disposable income, a rational, central route decision would be to buy the lesser brand. *Peripheral route processing* occurs when people are less motivated to elaborate and instead take decisions based on peripheral clues, perhaps the perceived credibility of an information source. In the simple example above, a peripheral route decision would involve buying the expensive brand because the person wants to be regarded as fashionable. This would not involve a rational choice about whether they could afford the purchase.

In proposing four models to explain public relations practice (press agentry; public information; two-way asymmetrical communication; and two-way symmetrical communication), James Grunig and Todd Hunt use *systems theory*, which is regarded as a way of thinking about relationships. It is an important approach in professional communication because the theory regards organisations as systems that adapt to their environments; changes in the economic, social or political environments in which an organisation operates impact on that organisation. Grunig and Hunt use this concept to suggest that ethical and effective public relations practice means building relationships in which an organisation interacts equally, or symmetrically, with its publics. The implication is that organisations change their policies and behaviours because of this symmetrical interaction. Their three other models of practice are simply one-way communication of information from the organisation to its target publics.

It is important to consider all four Grunig and Hunt models when deciding how messages might be delivered. Many strategic communication plans involve more than one of the four models, especially in politics and government. For example, most government agencies use informative messages to advise appropriate publics of their rights and responsibilities. The Grunig and Hunt press agentry and public information models are most likely to be used for this: register to, and vote, in the election; pay taxes now; the highway is closed for repairs in the next two weeks; clean your gutters before the wildfire season. But government agencies also need dialogic relationships with their clients, perhaps for feedback and discussion about the efficiency of services, so two-way models are used for this, although critical scholars question whether symmetrical communication is ever truly possible, given the power imbalances in relationships between organisations and individuals.

Organisations with "open" systems allow a flow of information to and from their environments. Those with "closed" systems find it difficult to build relationships with publics inside and outside the organisation.

The *situational theory* of public relations, also proposed by Grunig and his colleagues, can predict when publics will actively seek information and how they will process it. The theory suggests that publics can be identified by the context in which they are aware of a problem and the extent to which they do something about the problem. The theory suggests there are three independent variables in relation to how they do this and two dependent variables. The **independent** variables are:

- *Problem recognition* (the extent to which people recognise the problem) *constraint recognition* (how people see factors beyond their control limiting their behaviour)
- *Level of involvement* (the personal and emotional relevance of the problem for an individual).

The **dependent** variables are *information seeking* (when active publics seek information about a situation) and *information processing* (when a passive or inactive public does not seek information but processes it when it comes to them randomly).

Situational theory helps to explain why some people become activists on an issue while others do not and may even be apathetic towards the issue.

Kirk Hallahan's *typology of publics*, discussed in Chapter 6, provides important clues for message design. For example, having identified aroused publics, a practitioner can decide what information is needed to engage them in a dialogue. Similarly, it may be that an organisation decides to engage inactive publics and thus needs to prepare messages that provide them with basic information so that they become aware publics.

FURTHER READING

Gabbot, M. and Clulow, V. (1999), The Elaboration Likelihood Model of Persuasive Communication, in P. J. Kitchen (ed.), *Marketing Communications: Principles and Practice*, Thomson, London, pp. 172–88.

Macnamara, J. (2012), *Public Relations: Theories, Practices, Critiques*, Pearson, Sydney, pp. 10–86.

Sison, M.D. (2009a), Theoretical Contexts, in J. Chia and G. Synnott (eds.), *An Introduction to Public Relations: From Theory to Practice*, Oxford University Press, Melbourne, pp. 54–89.

Propaganda

Most communication practitioners object to criticism that characterises their persuasive messages as "propaganda." The term *propaganda*, which has its roots in ancient Latin, was once simply used to describe information. Since the seventeenth century, for example, the Roman Catholic Church has used the word in the name of the group that is responsible for propagating, or disseminating, the faith. In modern times, though, it is used to describe persuasive practices—especially in support of an ideology or in politics—that intentionally set out to mislead publics, and that are deceitful, false, duplicitous or based on lies.

INFORMATIVE MESSAGES

Writing informative messages is often an uncomplicated task. That is because clients already know what they want to say, or research has identified a lack of knowledge among target publics that can be met by straightforward information.

To write informative messages:

- Decide exactly what target publics need to know in the situation you are addressing
- Summarise that information into simple, brief sentences
- Limit each message to one information point.

Remember that informative messages will guide material written for a range of communication tools. They'll be the key points for a speech; headings for a display; explained in more detail in a brochure; or used as a set of reminders when the chief executive is interviewed on television.

> ## Strategic Plan Checklist: Informative messages
>
> ### Write an informative message
>
> Try writing an informative message for your strategic planning project.
>
> Using the sentence you wrote for the previous exercise about why a particular issue is important, and one of the primary target publics you identified in Chapter 6, write an informative message conveying something that the target public would need to know about that issue. Then apply the idea behind the two-step and multi-step flow theory (outlined above) to recraft your message for a secondary public in your project. Align the definition of a secondary public to the principle behind the two-step and multi-step flow theory to help in this.
>
> Is there a difference between the two messages? Should there be a difference? Why?

PERSUASIVE MESSAGES

The ancient philosopher Aristotle defined rhetoric as the ability to use the available means of persuasion—that is, using language to communicate effectively.

Writing persuasive messages involves rhetoric and is a more challenging task than writing informative messages. Sometimes persuasive messages are criticised as propaganda; often they labelled as "spin." That happens because persuasive messages attempt to convince publics to accept a point of view or to take some action. Persuasive messages are designed to bring about changes in behaviour or attitudes and doing that is always hard. To write persuasive messages, practitioners need to know about the ways in which people process information, and how they make decisions. And that's why the communication theories outlined earlier are important.

To think theoretically is to use a set of assumptions about how the world works to help us predict what will happen (Mackey, 2004). That's an important point, because planning a communication strategy involves working out how messages might persuade a public to act. If a communication theory suggests how a specific public is likely to react to information, or a point of view, then messages to generate that reaction can be planned. This point is reflected in Joep Cornelissen's (2000) observation that practitioners need to inform their work with theory so that they have a better chance of being successful than they would if they only relied on intuition, and in Dan Lattimore and colleagues' (2004) suggestion that practitioners need to build a set of theories to help in professional practice.

Ethics and communication practice

Planning a communication strategy to convince people to take some action requires careful reflection about the ethical implications of what is proposed.

This is a special consideration for practitioners who work for large, powerful organisations that have relationships with publics who do not have equal economic or political power. Asking questions like, "Is the information we are using factual?," "Are we asking people to do something that is against the law?," "Might our plan harm people in some way?" and "Am I involved in something that goes against my personal and professional ethical standards?" can help you resolve a potential ethical dilemma.

The code of ethics of a professional association (for example, the Chartered Institute of Public Relations, United Kingdom; the Public Relations Institute of Australia; the Public Relations Society of America; or the International Association of Business Communicators) can help answer these and other questions. So, too, can the codes of practice that employers produce to guide the way staff interact with each other at work and with clients. It is useful also to know what an organisation says about its values and its views on corporate social responsibility, because these are the principles on which it bases its business practices. Several laws govern how businesses operate, covering libel and defamation, copyright, contracts and the ownership and protection of ideas, as well as formal financial reporting. If in doubt about any of these, and what they mean for ethical communication practice, seek advice.

Persuasive messages use language that is designed to motivate people to take some kind of action. Depending on the situation and target public, they might be written as *emotional* appeals or *rational* appeals. The so-called "rhetorical triangle" (see Figure 8.1), which uses Aristotle's three appeals—the concepts of ethos, pathos and logos—helps us understand this. *Ethos* means that publics need to believe the sender of a message is credible and trustworthy (in our context, an ethical source of information); *pathos* means that a message appeals to a public's emotions by, for example, providing incentives to change; *logos* means that messages must be consistent, rational, factual. Persuasive communication works through the interaction of the points of the triangle.

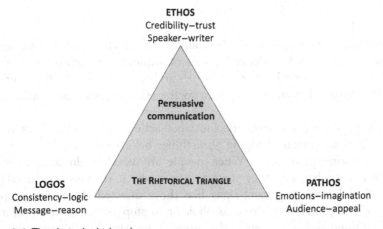

ETHOS
Credibility–trust
Speaker–writer

**Persuasive
communication**

LOGOS
Consistency–logic
Message–reason

THE RHETORICAL TRIANGLE

PATHOS
Emotions–imagination
Audience–appeal

Figure 8.1 The rhetorical triangle

CHAPTER EXERCISE

Climate change and ethical practice

Climate change has for years been a highly, and emotionally, contested issue. While most people believe it is real, many others, including some scientists, argue that it is not. Industry leaders around the world are divided about climate change and its effect on the environment, politicians argue incessantly about it, and environmentalists despair at the lack of action to resolve it. Regular high-powered international meetings discuss what can be done and set targets for countries to reduce greenhouse gases. Communication professionals are hired to work for both sides of the climate change debate, mainly by companies trying to convince people that they are not high polluters or are doing their best to reduce their environmental impacts.

In 2022, Britain's national news service, the BBC, published an online feature article that it called "The audacious PR plot that seeded doubt about climate change."

Follow the link below, read the feature article, then answer the questions for this exercise.

https://www.bbc.com/news/science-environment-62225696

1. Was the plan devised by the PR company ethical communication practice? Why do you believe that?
2. Does the PR company appear to have asked relevant questions about the truth of the Global Climate Coalition's claims?

   1. Is the title "Global Climate Coalition" a transparent description of the organisation's views?
   2. What parts of your country's code of ethics for communicators might the PR company have breached with this project?

Rational (logos) messages should be sourced from facts, research findings, case studies, experts or acknowledged voices of authority and statistics. *Emotional* (pathos) messages appeal to people's beliefs and feelings. *Ethical* (ethos) messages should be delivered by competent, trustworthy, reliable, respected people.

To write persuasive messages, decide what action you want publics to take. Mostly, that will mean changing something: behaviour, attitudes, purchasing habits or voting preferences. When people are asked to do something, they need to know what, and they want to know why it is important to take that action. Social marketing campaigns like those directed at convincing people to stop driving after they drink alcohol, or to stop smoking, or to wear protective clothing and sunscreen in the summer, are based on this principle. They all involve calls to action ("stop smoking") with reasons for doing it ("smoking causes cancer;" "smoking kills").

This formula might help you to write a persuasive message:

persuasive message	=	required change	+	reason to act
		or		because
		call to do something		

To write a persuasive message:

- Identify the change that is required—your objectives will have set this out. You should know from the situation analysis whether publics have all the information they need to make their decision
- Identify target publics and their preferences for receiving information. This is about communication pathways, the topic for Chapter 9, but the situation analysis and target public segmentation will identify this
- Provide a reason for the desired change. This will flow from the situation analysis, from the goals and from precise objectives that identify the change needed
- Summarise this information in a simple, brief sentence. Sometimes you might need to write two sentences. How effectively you do this will be determined by your skill as a writer
- Limit your message to one call for change. Again, this will rely on your skill as a writer.

FURTHER READING

Fawkes, J. (2006), Can Ethics Save Public Relations from the Charge of Propaganda? *Ethical Space, Journal of the Institute of Communication Ethics*, 3(1), pp. 32–42.

Fawkes, J. (2009), Public Relations, Propaganda and the Psychology of Persuasion, in R. Tench and L. Yeomans (eds), *Exploring Public Relations*, 2nd edn, Prentice Hall, Harlow, pp. 252–72.

Strategic Plan Checklist: Persuasive messages

Plan and write persuasive messages

Reflect on the earlier checklists and exercises in this chapter and review the action objectives you wrote for your strategic communication project. Using your segmented target public lists, identify the reasons why primary and secondary publics need to take the action you have identified. Then write:

Two persuasive messages that apply to both primary and secondary publics

One persuasive message that could be delivered to one of the tertiary, or intervening, publics that you have identified.

Use the definitions for primary, secondary and tertiary (or intervening) publics to help in this task. Write your messages in the contexts of your goals and objectives, and the theoretical principles outlined in this chapter.

Review both your informative and persuasive messages to answer the following:

1. Does your situation analysis provide enough information for you to write these messages? If not, why not? What else is needed?
2. Are the messages appropriate for the information needs of each target public?
3. Do the messages provide the reasons for action that each category of target public would need to fulfil its theoretical role?
4. Do the messages reflect the goals and objectives of your communication strategy?

MESSAGE TEAMWORK

It follows that informative and persuasive messages can work as a team. That is, to build awareness, target publics must have information. Generating understanding and action requires a persuasive argument based on reasons that motivate publics. Objectives will set the steps for doing this. Gregory proposes four steps for doing this (see Table 8.1).

Table 8.1 Four steps in writing messages

Step	Source	Theoretical examples
1. Take existing perceptions that encapsulate the issue or problem.	This comes from the research for a situation analysis. Think about the issues, problems, beliefs and target publics; identify what information needs to be provided to generate changes.	Research methods, situational theory; complexity theory; systems theory.
2. Define realistic shifts for those perceptions.		Elaboration likelihood model; co-orientation theory; target public segmentation.
3. Identify elements of persuasion. Work on facts.	This involves applying professional skills based on research. Consider ethos, logos and pathos.	Social exchange and diffusion theories; rhetorical theory; typology of publics.
4. Ensure messages are credible and deliverable.		Ethics; rhetorical theory; principles of writing.

Source: Adapted from Gregory (2009a), p. 187.

The role of messages, and how they are used to achieve objectives, is part of the "genetic code" that determines whether a communication strategy will work. Each element reflects and supports the others in much the same way that genes work to determine our personal characteristics. Chapter 4 extended this analogy by dealing with that part of the code that establishes how messages can be delivered to target publics in a way that reflects goals and objectives.

CHAPTER EVALUATION

In this chapter, we explored the role of messages in a communication strategy.

Assess your understanding of that role by answering the following questions:

1. What principles determine the role of messages in a communication strategy?
2. Why is an ethical approach required for writing informative and persuasive messages?
3. How do messages reflect strategic objectives?
4. Why does message design require high-level writing skills?
5. Why is a segmentation of target publics important for decisions about using messages?

Chapter 9
Reaching target publics

The role of communication pathways

Goal: To learn about the role of communication pathways in a strategic plan are the methods used to reach target publics with messages.

Objectives: This chapter will help you to:

■ Understand how communication pathways help deliver messages to target publics
Identify appropriate communication pathways for specific target publics
■ Appreciate the diversity in the ways in which people access information.

Principle: Communication pathways must reflect the ways in which target publics prefer to access information.

Practice: Communication pathways are channels for achieving objectives.

In every election in every country, politicians go out of their way to demonstrate their links with voters. They continue doing this after they are elected and while they are working as voters' representatives. Their normal tools for this include paid advertising, street walks, letter writing, social media tools, town meetings, telephone calls to voters, press conferences and one-on-one media interviews. They are at it incessantly because their political lives depend on name recognition and on convincing voters that their needs are being met. Politicians, then, provide good examples of strategic communication at work—even if sometimes it is difficult to work out whether they have a strategy, or are just following age-old campaigning tools. A great example of politicians doing, well, what politicians do, comes from the United States way back in 2011, when the Republican Party's nomination to stand for election as US President in 2012 was being contested. Candidates used a variety of methods to convince potential party electors that they would be the best choice to stand against President Obama. Their first test came in the State of Iowa when members of the Republican Party voted in county caucuses for the candidate they preferred. All seven candidates in the Iowa

DOI: 10.4324/9781003317579-10

caucuses used normal electioneering techniques. In the months before the Iowa vote, however, one candidate, Rick Santorum, spent considerable time meeting party members personally in a range of face-to-face settings in addition to the normal political campaigning techniques. Many commentators believed this long-term personal approach paid off for Santorum, who lost by only eight votes. The campaign techniques used by all candidates, especially the interpersonal communication used by Santorum, illustrated the role of **communication pathways** in the distribution of messages to target publics.

Communication pathways *how* a message will be delivered (as opposed to its format or packaging). This is sometimes also called a message delivery strategy or a communication channel.

DEFINING COMMUNICATION PATHWAYS

After setting goals and objectives based on a properly researched situation analysis, and identifying target publics and messages, the next task for a practitioner is to work out how to deliver messages effectively. This is the job of communication pathways. A metaphor for a communication pathway is the role that the postal service plays in delivering a snail-mail letter. You write a letter (a communication tool containing a message) to your grandfather, seal it in an envelope and post it; the postal service delivers the message to your grandfather's house (the communication pathway); he opens the envelope and reads your message. Communication pathways, then, indicate how a message is delivered, not the format of the message. The format (or package) in which messages will be delivered is the job of *tools*, which will be covered in Chapter 10. Each communication pathway can be matched with a number of tools, so it is vital to remember that communication pathways and tools work in tandem, much like the way goals and objectives work together.

Using your grey matter

Communication pathways indicate *how* an organisation can *reach* its target publics to achieve its objectives. Communication pathways deal with the mechanisms by which this will be done. That is, they identify whether messages will be delivered in hard copy format; via social media; via the mass news media; or through the techniques of interpersonal communication, special events, sponsorships or alliances (see Figure 9.1). Often it is appropriate to use more than one communication pathway to reach a target public. Anne Gregory (2009a) warns that planners are often tempted to begin with tools (or tactics) because it is easier to think of ideas for these than it is to think about the rationale behind them. Identifying appropriate communication pathways means exercising your inbuilt hard drive, the grey matter of your brain, to think about how efficiently you can reach your target publics. Communication pathways provide a rationale for communication by identifying how each tool will be delivered and why.

USING COMMUNICATION PATHWAYS

Planning how messages will be delivered, and selecting appropriate communication tools, requires informed thinking about the ways in which target publics normally access information. Different demographic groups do this in different ways, although increasingly people use the internet and social media applications for this. So important are net-based mechanisms in the exchange of information that all news outlets, for example, now enhance their traditional formats with interactive websites and other social media applications to send subscribers breaking news alerts, updates on stories and promotional information. These websites enable news organisations to instantly update their offerings with "breaking news" (sometimes identified from Twitter feeds and mobile phone video), provide online discussion forums, allow readers to comment on the opinions of specialist writers and commentators, and expand what is published or broadcast in the traditional format. Social media applications have had a major impact on how journalists produce what David Conley and Stephen Lamble (2006) describe as the "daily miracle" that our mass news media products are. These applications are as responsible as any other factor for what has become known as the "24-hour news cycle." Not only are social media transforming the news cycle, but these applications provide strategic communicators with a powerful interactive communication pathway.

But not all communication occurs through the internet, social media, email or mobile telephone text messaging. Nor should strategic communication rely on media releases as though coverage of what your organisation has to say on a television station's website, or in the local daily newspaper, will solve the issues it must deal with. Effective communication is more complex than a simple mass news media focus. Kirk Hallahan (2010) notes that the communication revolution generated by technological change gives practitioners access to a full range of tools but that they still need to think broadly and strategically, and to ask what media (used here in its broad sense) would be the most effective for reaching key publics. Not every communication pathway works for everyone all the time, so choosing the best communication pathway for a specific target public to address a situation is a decision practitioners must make based on their professional and theoretical knowledge, and on their research findings. The questions that need answers in this process, then, are:

- Which communication pathway?
- Why that specific pathway?
- How do we decide on a communication pathway?
- Where do we start?

Let's answer the last question first by identifying the seven basic communication pathways. These are listed in Figure 9.1.

Gregory notes that the selection of communication pathways "is dictated by, and springs from, the issues arising from the analysis of the problem" (2009a, p. 188),

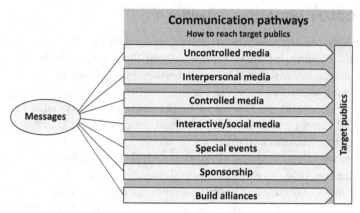

Figure 9.1 Communication pathways

and that these pathways are the foundation on which communication tools are built. An understanding of the specific role each pathway plays helps determine which one should be used, or what combination of pathways will work best, and, later, identify matching tools. An example: William Shakespeare used an *interpersonal communication pathway* (live performances in the Globe Theatre in London) to reach his target publics (his audiences) with messages contained in his tools (plays). One cartoonist has used a play on the words of a famous line from *Hamlet* to suggest that had he been writing in the twenty-first century, Shakespeare would have asked, "To blog or not to blog? That is the question." That's an example of another communication pathway: a blog is a communication tool that uses an interactive (or social media) pathway.

Each pathway has a specific job and using them in combination maximises the chances of success.

About media

Four of the communication pathways in Figure 9.1 include the noun *media* in their titles. *Media* is the plural of *medium*. In our strategic communication context, media are the ways in which information is transmitted to target publics. Thus, *media* in the context of a communication pathway means a group of more than one medium. In only one case, uncontrolled media, does this relate to using the mass news media, or newspapers, radio, television, news websites and their associated digital applications and other platforms.

CONSIDERATIONS FOR CHOOSING COMMUNICATION PATHWAYS

People access and process information in different ways. Petty and Cacioppo's elaboration likelihood model, discussed in Chapter 8, helps us understand how people process information. Younger generations are totally comfortable with using multiple social media platforms, often more than one at a time, to arrange

Table 9.1 Considerations for decisions on communication pathways

Factor	Consider these questions
Reach	How many people need to receive the message?
Richness	How much information—or argument—needs to be included in the message?
Control	Can you control the content of the message, and when and how it will be distributed?
Repetition	How often should you repeat the message?
Effectiveness	Did the message reach the target public, and was it understood?
Efficiency	Will the campaign make the best possible use of the money, people and technology available?

their lives, research and write university assignments, communicate with friends and family, and to access the news, as well as for entertainment. On the other hand, seniors may be less comfortable using social media and rely only on a mobile phone and standard computing and email applications, preferring to have the newspaper thrown on the front lawn each morning, and to watch the nightly television news. Convincing people on a point of view about an issue will almost certainly be more effectively done in a face-to-face meeting if busy schedules allow that. The anti-smoking research discussed earlier found that young women would prefer to receive health messages from medical people in face-to-face meetings, while young men prefer advertising. Strategic communicators should consider differences in publics' preferences when they select specific communication pathways to address situations.

Table 9.1 shows other equally important factors that impact on the selection of communication pathways.

Before exploring how these factors inform the selection of communication pathways, we should look at each in detail.

UNCONTROLLED MEDIA

Using an uncontrolled media communication pathway means trying to communicate with target publics through the mass news media. Messages delivered via this pathway are:

- Non-personal
- One-way
- *Uncontrolled* because messages are *mediated* by gatekeepers—journalists, sub-editors and all those in newsrooms who make decisions about what

IN THEORY: ON FRAMING

To *mediate* means to intervene, usually to resolve a dispute, or to be the medium for conveying something. A journalist may be interested in your media release and decide to write a story based on it, but the way they do that won't necessarily be the way you intended. The journalist will almost always treat your material differently from the way you approached it.

When journalists treat your material in this way, they choose a different news frame. Understanding news frames is important in writing content for communication tools (see Chapter 10), especially media releases: using the appropriate news frame maximises the chances of the release being run.

Successful professional communication doesn't rely on media releases, even though they are an essential tool, especially in discourses about public policy issues in the non-market environment. More important is the ability to deliver messages that are not *mediated*. That's why practitioners need to combine communication pathways.

stories are included in media products, how much is run, whose views are included, what the headlines will be, what the first paragraphs will say and the prominence they are given (where they are placed in a television news bulletin, for instance, or appear in the newspaper).

The realities of the news decision-making process mean that practitioners lose control of message delivery. There are no guarantees here because someone else decides how the message is presented to intended target publics, and even whether it will be published. Journalists are hard-nosed, busy professionals who work to strict deadlines using specialist skills and time-honoured ways of deciding what is news. The 24-hour gathering and dissemination of the news we all consume is based on a tough approach in which journalists are trained not to accept something just because you say it is so; they want to check and to ask for someone else's view. They won't publish your material unless they deem it to be new. In the United States, reporters attempt to triangulate sources for a story—that is, find three people who can verify it. When reporters do use your material, there is no guarantee it will be a word-for-word replica of your media release or that your views won't be buried in a story with a lead paragraph focused on your critics' views. The competition for news covered is enormous and editors often say they receive more "news" than they have room to publish. That's why strategic communicators need to understand the news process: how news stories are written, framed, selected, edited and placed in a radio bulletin, on a website or in the newspaper. And it is why they also need to know how to write clear and professional news copy for media releases.

Nevertheless, professional communication relies heavily on generating news media coverage of opinions, products and events. This is an important, but not the most important, task in professional communication practice. Uncontrolled media communication pathways are used because the mass news media have the potential to reach millions of people who watch the news, listen to it on the radio, access blogs and scan newspapers. It is low cost.

Missing the target

The fact that millions of people can potentially be reached through an uncontrolled media pathway is attractive, and a major reason many campaigns rely on the mass news media. But that reliance begs the questions: did those for whom a message was intended see it or read it in the news media? Did they understand it? Did they take some action as a result? This is another reason for closely segmenting target publics and carefully selecting pathways and tools to reach them. In other words, it's not enough to believe that you'll be successful if your media release gets reported.

Advertising planners utilise sophisticated media-planning computer software to maximise their access to audiences. This software enables them to analyse the demographic characteristics of, say, radio listeners at certain times of the day and by different stations. The software helps them buy television and radio time, or newspaper space, for paid advertisements that their analysis suggests will have the best chance of reaching the most people who are interested in a client's products. The software could answer, for instance, the question of when and where it would be best to advertise a new lipstick designed for women in their twenties. Other communication practitioners, like public relations people, usually don't have access to this software, except perhaps if the marketing department of their organisation helps them out. However, their decisions about using an uncontrolled media communication pathway can be informed by:

- proper segmentation of target publics (who do you really need to reach?)
- an understanding that journalists are tertiary publics (messages are not written just for them)
- identification of appropriate media outlets for the topic of the message (which specific media do specific publics access?)
- awareness of how much information needs to be provided and in what format
- an appreciation of the need to write material in a way that journalists recognise so that the prospects of it being accepted and published are enhanced (professional media release writing, for a start).

Research into readership and into the viewer and listener profiles of mass news media outlets will help in this process. And it will make sure you don't miss your target publics by assuming that a media release included in the main evening television news will reach them.

Practitioners who understand the news process—who write for it in a professional way, treat it with the same professional pragmatism that journalists display, don't guarantee clients will get coverage, and refrain from getting agitated when news stories don't reflect a media release—are more likely to be successful than those who deluge reporters with non-news.

FURTHER READING

Working with journalists and writing material for the mass news media are important functions for professional communication practitioners. The following texts can help you understand these tasks.

Mahoney, J. (2017), *Public Relations Writing*, 3rd edn, Oxford University Press, Melbourne.

Johnston, J. (2007), *Media Relations: Issues and Strategies*, Allen & Unwin, Crows Nest.

Wilcox, D.L. and Cameron, G.T. (2012), *Public Relations Strategies and Tactics*, 10th edn, Pearson, Glenview, IL, esp. ch. 14.

INTERPERSONAL MEDIA

Communicating via an interpersonal media communication pathway is doing precisely what the name suggests: talking to people. Messages delivered via this pathway:

- Are personal, usually face-to-face, and direct
- Support two-way communication or dialogue
- Are chosen by practitioners and target publics.

The pathway works, as telemarketing and personal selling demonstrate, but it is expensive because speaking directly to people means not every member of a target public can be personally engaged. Another of Dan Tisch's paradoxes (see p. 149) dealt with this. He said face-to-face (or interpersonal) communication works, but the paradox is that it is not always possible.

Practitioners working in public affairs and lobbying know the value of interpersonal communication because they are constantly telephoning, meeting, writing to and emailing people they need to contact so they can present their clients' viewpoints on products and public policy issues. They also know that personal contact means there is a better chance of a dialogue about an issue in which information and opinions can be exchanged. Politicians around the world also know the value of interpersonal communication—that's why they engage in what the news media call "walkabouts," in which they visit shopping malls, factories, events, meetings and sports matches to shake hands, talk to potential voters and kiss babies. The regular "town hall" meetings and local coffee mornings held by politicians are an example of interpersonal communication because they provide citizens with opportunities to discuss issues directly with their representatives. Research on topics raised by citizens at these Australian community cabinet meetings (Mahoney, 2010b) found that the most frequently raised issues were those related to Indigenous matters (especially jobs and education), affordable housing, climate change, issues for seniors, education and disability services. Many of these issues were not raised in the grand narratives on these topics covered by the mass news media, but were more personal, immediate, local and community-based perspectives on those issues.

Corporations and government agencies also use interpersonal communication when they hold town meetings for community consultation over development plans. For example, in Australia, the Murray–Darling Basin Authority engages in interpersonal dialogue with irrigators and townspeople living in that region to explain plans for managing the basin, especially water use, and to hear feedback. These are not all supportive dialogues, because the plans often mean significant changes to the way water is allocated and used. Many irrigators become concerned about the changes reducing their access to water; townspeople about the impact the changes would have on local economies and jobs. But the important point is that the meetings provide opportunities for interpersonal dialogue and for people to express their opposition in person to those who make the final decisions. Corporations planning new factories, or expansions to existing facilities, use similar meetings for consultation about their plans, especially when the projects will have an environmental impact.

Communication tools like these, which apply interpersonal media pathways enable true communication. They involve people discussing issues, exchanging views, maybe changing their personal attitudes, hearing more information, providing feedback, and expressing an opinion.

CONTROLLED MEDIA

When an organisation publishes its annual report, posts material to its website, sets up a display at the local shopping mall or distributes a leaflet directly to target publics, it is engaging in a controlled media communication pathway. Sometimes this pathway is termed "own media" because it involves the organisation's own communication tools. Messages delivered by a controlled media pathway are:

- Non-personal
- One-way
- Chosen by practitioners.

This communication pathway is described as "**controlled**" because the tools that will be delivered in this way go directly to target publics. No one mediates message content, format or timing in that delivery process. Using a controlled communication pathway means no journalist decides what should be passed on to target publics, or who else's comments should be added; no one edits the material; no one acts as "noise" between the organisation and the target public. Messages are delivered directly to the intended target public.

Control the power to direct, to command, to restrain or to regulate. When he was Federal Treasurer, former Australian prime minister Paul Keating was fond of saying he had control of the levers that drove the economy. These are the concepts embedded in a controlled media communication pathway: practitioners pull the levers that drive the content, timing and decisions about the communication tools for delivering messages; no one else has that role.

This pathway is an example of what James Grunig and colleagues (see Grunig, 2001, pp. 11–30) might describe as their "public information" model because it is one-way and impersonal, but controlled media communication pathways are standard practice. Every communication plan applies this pathway in some way. When people are thinking about buying a new car, renewing their phone plan, or planning a vacation overseas, they are given brochures that provide a lot of information. These are tools implementing a controlled media communication pathway. The motoring writer of the local newspaper hasn't written about a new car from a personal angle as would happen with a test drive review; the phone company has given potential customers its information unfiltered by a mediator; holiday brochures provide details of accommodation, facilities, flights, costs and things to do, direct to enquirers. Formal communication by government agencies about the services they provide, and about citizens' rights and responsibilities, also utilises this pathway.

Implementing controlled communication is expensive because of the costs involved in producing quality material. For example, laws require companies to produce annual reports for shareholders. Annual reports include a lot more information about the company's achievements and plans than just detailed financial data, so they are used as communication tools to promote the company, particularly in media kits and to answer general enquiries. Most are published first on the company's website, but limited numbers of copies are printed in full-colour hard copy for "hand-out" purposes. There are costs associated with designing and printing a hard copy report, packaging and mailing it, and publishing the electronic version on the company's website.

The need for organisations to have a stock of materials that explain what they do to a wide range of target publics means that researching and writing tools to implement a controlled (or own) media pathway are the day-to-day, "bread and butter" tasks of communication technicians. These materials, online or in hard copy, provide basic information about the organisation, answer questions, report progress, explain points of view, argue for policy changes and put information on the record.

Usually, a controlled media pathway will work in tandem with other communication pathways to achieve goals and objectives.

INTERACTIVE (SOCIAL) MEDIA

Advances in technology have delivered exciting opportunities to communication practitioners. Mobile phones and email have brought flexibility; social media applications have led to new ways of communicating; and continually upgraded computer software has made research, planning, writing and evaluation more efficient. The ability to use the internet to access information about almost anything at any time of the day is no longer a novelty. These ways of communicating for business, for pleasure, and for building and maintaining personal relationships, are so mainstream that describing the applications that empower this kind of communication as "new media" is no longer necessary. All of this is what Hallahan (2010) means when he writes about the full range of tools communicators can access. In many ways this has led to a reinvigorated profession that is excited about the opportunities the technology provides, especially social media. Communicators working in politics, not-for-profits, corporations, government agencies and consulting have discovered the power of social media to deliver messages, obtain feedback and keep in touch with publics. Brian Sollis and Deirdre Breakenridge (2009) caution communicators about how they use social media and warn that the pitching ideas and repeatedly messaging journalists, for example, via these applications is not always appreciated. But they argue that effective use of social media involves a proper understanding of what they enable and how they work, and that they offer the potential to put the "public" back into "public relations."

Interactive means people act reciprocally and can influence each other through a two-way flow of information. This is dialogic communication. Interactivity includes the notion of *feedback*, and it is one of the principles behind Grunig's (2009) argument that social media can enhance his concept of two-way symmetrical communication.

Messages delivered through an **interactive** (or social) media communication strategy are:

- Non-personal
  chosen by target publics: they decide what they read.

Social media applications have transformed the way modern society works, and the way language is used. No organisation can afford not to have an up-to-date website that provides effective links to its own and external information, and that offers interconnectedness through social media applications. We shop; pay bills; do the banking; search the sports results; take lecture notes (and sometimes listen to them); interrogate search engines to find out about restaurants, cars and movies; listen to music; and do a whole lot more via mobile phones, which are now essentially personal computers with a phone application. Modern language has a whole new set of verbs: *to blog, Google, tweet, text* and *click*. Often, *to search* means to look for something on the net, rather than in the cupboard (or, sadly, the library). And then there are *apps, sites, pages* and *tablets*. We are linked like never before through networks based on social media and share personal and professional information we never thought of sharing before. We make friends easily, often with people from the other side of the world, through our social media pages and find those we lost contact with after walking through the high school gates at the end of secondary education. And many of us are so addicted to using these new gadgets that we walk about oblivious to the risks of crossing the road without looking.

Yet all this technology has empowered people. The connected society that social media has created has had far-reaching implications for political, social and economic change. Mobile phone video clips and photographs record world events, natural disasters, atrocities and triumphs; footballers misbehaving; and millions of happy, sad and serious experiences every day. So dominant is digital photography that ordinary people often become "citizen photojournalists" whose work is published on news websites and other applications.

So, using all this technology and the applications it has generated makes sense for communicators.

FURTHER READING

Grunig, J.E. (2009), Paradigms of Global Public Relations in an Age of Digitalisation, *PRism*, 6(2), at www.prismjournal.org/fileadmin/Praxis/Files/globalPR/GRUNIG.pdf

Applying an interactive (or social) media communication pathway means more than simply clicking on an application to publish material, take feedback, email shareholders, post a media release or a comment or update the CEO's personal blog. Sometimes communicators act like the kid given free rein in a lolly shop when they use social media toys: they're available, let's play. It is fine to concentrate your practice solely on delivering communication through social media platforms, and many professional consultancies do just that, and very effectively. These specialists have strategic explanations for their approach and pragmatic business cases for specialising in providing social media counsel and products for clients. Journalism's increasing use of social media (viewers can even follow their favourite television news service via digital services and a range of applications) and electronic products means that media relations specialists in the communication departments of organisations are building new kinds of relationships with reporters that are instant, flexible and efficient. Those new relationships are with reporters who work only on social media as well as with those in the traditional media like television, radio, newspapers and hard copy magazines.

Deciding to use an interactive media communication pathway involves thinking about what needs to be done and why this approach will work for both the messages and the target publics. Social media applications are tools, not pathways, so finding answers to the simple "what" and "why" questions is the first step. Answering the "how" question is about selecting appropriate tools: which application will suit this pathway for this situation given the target publics that need to be reached? The point is that no matter how useful social media is, we need to remember that it is not the only, nor perhaps the most important, game in town.

An interactive media communication pathway is efficient and effective provided practitioners use it appropriately. Doing that involves segmenting target publics accurately into the groups most likely to access the application under consideration as a tool. For example, information intended for young people is more likely to be successfully distributed via a social media platform than if it were published in the national financial newspaper and broadcast on radio and the nightly television news.

Engaging in discourses about public policy issues using social media requires great care. There are sites, like *The Conversation* in Australia (theconversation. edu.au), that are designed for discussion of opinions, but intruding on social media discussions about issues in the robust way you might in a face-to-face debate is likely to work against your organisation. Macnamara notes that online communities prefer dialogue and conversation, not the top-down transmission of viewpoints and monologues of traditional media approaches. He writes that online conversations are often unstructured, and in the vernacular, and that a lack of authenticity is quickly recognised and "earns the ire of online communities" (2010, p. 12).

FURTHER READING

Macnamara, J. (2010), 'Emergent' Media and Public Communication: Understanding the Changing Mediascape, *Public Communication Review*, 1(2), pp. 3–17. at epress.lib.uts.edu. au/journals/index.php/pcr/article/view/1867

SPECIAL EVENTS

Practitioners use events of all kinds to reach target publics. Media conferences, product launches and major international trade fairs are all events. So, too, are shopping mall displays, fun runs, fund raising door knocks, award ceremonies, conferences, building openings, welcome ceremonies, book launches, cocktail parties, state funerals and university graduations.

Using special events as a communication pathway is another stock-in-trade way to promote an organisation's messages, and it is often pursued in tandem with sponsorship and alliance pathways (see the next two sections). The special events that are the actual tools are almost always supported by other tools applied through an uncontrolled media pathway. Messages delivered by a special event pathway are:

- Quasi-two-way personal communication chosen by practitioners.

Special events enable people from the organisation to engage in dialogue with target publics. However, dialogue at a special event is often brief and temporary because it is exhausted at the end of the event, hence the description "quasi-two-way." Messages are chosen by practitioners because they usually become the theme that is used for framing tools. Examples of this are the way in which the national swimming team's sponsors' logos and slogans are positioned in the backdrops for media conferences with race winners, or the way an organisation's corporate theme features in the slides for the CEO's talk to an industry's annual conference.

Sometimes this communication pathway results in zany tools that are known as "media stunts," or in events designed to attract media coverage. The British entrepreneur Sir Richard Branson is adept at using stunts to promote his airline and mobile phone company. Politicians are pretty good at it, too, when they appear, say, at the fish market in rubber aprons and gloves, net hats and rubber boots, and wielding big knives to carve a salmon, all the while making a point about the failure of their opponents to consider the implications of this or that policy on the price of fish. When he was Leader of the Opposition, former Australian Prime Minister Tony Abbott, made a virtue of his superb fitness by using stunts involving cycling and swimming, particularly, to attract media to cover his pronouncements. The Russian leader, Vladimir Putin, took this strategy to new levels when he publicly engaged in stunts showing him, often bare-chested, fishing and hunting and, on one occasion, wrestling a wild animal. And then there was former US President Donald Trump who was masterful at this approach.

When the Australian National University awarded an honorary doctorate to the former South African president Nelson Mandela, it used a special event pathway by holding a one-off degree-conferring ceremony, supported by an uncontrolled media pathway designed to enable worldwide media to cover the event. It earlier utilised the same pathways when it installed a new Chancellor (Emeritus Professor Peter Baume) and awarded an honorary doctorate to Bishop Desmond Tutu, and again when it celebrated its fiftieth anniversary.

Using a special event communication pathway can be financially expensive and requires detailed planning about how the tools will be implemented. Often a one-off event is insufficient, especially if nationwide coverage is needed. A simple example is the launch of a new novel by a renowned author. One function in one city will not be enough, so publishers arrange launches in other cities, requiring the novelist to tour the nation. Sometimes local launches are held in bookstores; at other times they happen because the author is guest speaker at a literary dinner; at others, the author is a guest of a writers' festival. Almost always, a book tour involves radio, television and newspaper interviews, sometimes three or four a day. All this needs to be planned, coordinated with hosts and paid for, as does associated transport and accommodation.

SPONSORSHIP

Using sponsorship as a communication strategy can be valuable, especially if it is used as part of a genuine desire to help, and therefore impacts positively on an organisation's corporate social responsibilities.

Sponsorship takes many forms, from cash grants to sporting teams in return for exposure on their uniforms, to funding for health research to associate the organisation with a good cause, to funding for a pre-school playground, a park bench or programs and events for groups helping kids with cancer. Sometimes, sponsorship does not involve payment but "in-kind" support. Examples of this include when a television station gives free airtime for commercials promoting fundraising appeals or, in a less formal way, when a company provides equipment without charge to help recovery efforts after natural disasters. Messages delivered through a sponsorship pathway:

- Are one-way
- Can involve both personal and non-personal communication
- Are chosen by practitioners.

Sponsorship is a pragmatic pathway designed to generate exposure and goodwill by paying to be associated with another organisation or event. It requires clear thinking about the reasons it is being used. In 2022, a mining company in Australia withdrew a US$15 million sponsorship of the national netball team after players supported a First Nations colleague who had felt uncomfortable wearing the company's name on her uniform. The players' reaction related to seriously negative comments about First Nation's people by the company's founder. The incident demonstrated how important it is for those offering, and those accepting, sponsorship to think through the potential consequences of the alliance (see below) they are about to engage in.

Sponsorship is an expensive pathway, even at a local sporting level, which means a corporation, sometimes a government agency, will not commit money to sponsor something that is not in some way allied to its goals and aspirations. Manufacturers of cricket bats pay national team players to use their equipment because television coverage means people associate a particular brand with success—and buy the sponsor's bats. Major corporations sponsor the opera, ballet, classical music concerts, art galleries, theatres and individual exhibitions because they want to be associated with quality events. The department of health might sponsor an anti-drinking campaign because it leads to better health outcomes and thus lowers costs to the national budget.

On sponsorship and philanthropy

Sponsorship and philanthropy, two ways of providing financial support for other organisations, causes or events, are allied, but they are not synonymous.

Sponsorship seeks a clear, measurable return, usually exposure or an attitude change in which publics come to regard the sponsor as socially responsible. **Philanthropy** seeks no overt return. It is benevolence on a large scale, like the vast funds that Bill Gates and his family donate worldwide to prevent illness and improve living standards in developing nations. Philanthropists expect no return, certainly not financial, and often donate money without public fanfare. The annual Nobel Prizes are the result of philanthropy by the Swedish industrialist Alfred Nobel, who invented dynamite, among other things, and who bequeathed most of his fortune to fund the prizes.

BUILDING ALLIANCES

Alliances between like-minded organisations provide a communication pathway whereby they can cooperate to promote common interests. Political parties do this when they formalise coalitions or work together on a specific public policy issue.

Alliance a union, or an agreement to cooperate; "a relationship resulting from an affinity in nature or qualities" (*Australian Concise Oxford Dictionary*, 2004).

A communication pathway of building alliances delivers messages:

- Through a mixed approach based on other communication pathways
- Chosen by members of the alliance and by target publics.

Alliances require two-way communication between their members.

Industry associations, labour unions and professional associations like national medical practitioner organisations are all examples of alliances. Their members are individuals or companies working in a specific industry who cooperate to maximise their interests, promote industry views and exchange information. They engage in political lobbying on behalf of their members and usually research industry-wide issues. Their research outputs make them important resources for communication practitioners.

One or more organisations often form an alliance on a particular issue because this provides more resources and enables a coordinated approach to dealing with it. Some alliances are built through sporting sponsorships which reflect similar values. This was reflected in a renewed long-term sponsorship by the Oak milk company with the Penrith Panthers rugby league football club. In the renewal announcement, the company's marketing manager, Angela Burr, said "Our part-nership of over a decade has been built upon shared values based on teamwork, innovation, high quality performances and of course, a focus on our community" (Burr, 2022).

Alliance-building pathways, then, mostly work in tandem with the other six pathways.

REACH, IMPACT AND CONTROL

Communication pathways are the mechanisms for reaching target publics. Not all pathways deliver communication tools to target publics in large numbers, nor do they guarantee high impact, and it is difficult to guarantee that elusive message-control factor.

Controlling messages—that is, making sure they reach publics with as little mediation as possible—relies on professional judgments about adopting appropriate communication pathways using the factors identified in Table 9.1, including their potential impact. Figure 9.2 suggests the potential reach and impact of the seven potential communication pathways. Note the caution about the impact of uncontrolled media communication and interactive/social media pathways. That's because while these pathways offer a potentially huge reach and an equally large impact, none of this can be guaranteed. The pathways rely on difficult variables: whether consumers see them, the level of mediation by the news production process, media consumers' awareness and understanding of messages and whether they act on that understanding. The other pathways offer greater potential impact because they are based on accurate public segmentation. The impact of a social media pathway may be low, despite a potentially huge reach. That is because social media usage is phenomenally high but without accurate segmentation of publics and how they access information, and matching tools, using social media doesn't guarantee impact. This is a reminder of an old cartoon in the US magazine *The New Yorker*. Two dogs are talking, and one says, "I used to twitter, but I decided to go back to just pointless, incessant barking." Just because you are tweeting doesn't mean people are listening.

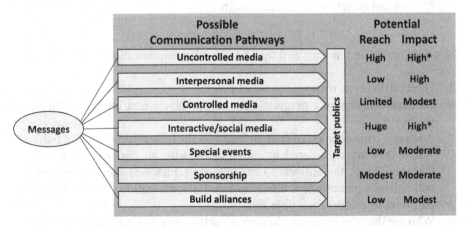

* Remember, if you use these pathways you cannot guarantee that intended target publics will see/read messages, nor that they will accept and act on your messages.

Figure 9.2 Potential reach and impact of communication pathways

CHAPTER EXERCISE

Social media use

Perhaps the most spectacular technological advance in recent history has been the development and growth of computing and the tools and applications that have come with it. Almost all of us use computing everybody, whether through laptops, mainframes, mobile phones, computers that control how cars perform, in elevators, smartwatches, fitness tackers, thermometers for checking BBQ meat temperatures and so on. For practitioners, this "new" technology has provided exciting prospects for faster, better and more efficient ways of contacting target publics when that is the most appropriate approach.

This exercise will help you to understand how pervasive modern social media technology is in all aspects of professional communication.

1. **Use your search engine to find out how many people**:
2. **In the United States say their** purchasing decisions were influenced by social media. If you don't live in the United States, can you find this data for your country?
3. **Read** customer service–related tweets every week
4. Use Facebook—and how has this changed from 10 years ago; how many are estimated to use Facebook in five years?
5. Use at least one social networking service—and has that changed in the last five years?
6. **In the United States (or your country)** watched online video content in May of last year.
7. **Use internet banking services.**
8. **Used** an e-book reader in January last year (think after Christmas!).
9. Had a telehealth conference with their doctor.
10. Booked entertainment tickets online.

Message control and impact, and thus successful communication, is enhanced by:

- Direct delivery of messages to target publics
- Indirect delivery by a pragmatic use of secondary and intervening/tertiary publics
- Adequate consideration of content based on the information needs of publics. When they are considered in combination with an understanding of how pathways work, the answers to the following questions about target publics will enhance practitioners' ability to select a combination of communication pathways to achieve their objectives:
- Who are the target publics? (In answering this question, remember the roles of primary, secondary and tertiary publics. Identifying the primary publics, in the situation you are addressing, is the most important decision. Consider how secondary and tertiary target publics influence or support primary target publics.)

Strategic Plan Checklist: Which pathways?

Selecting communication pathways

Before you do this exercise, you should use the information in this chapter to critically review the work you've done so far on your strategic plan project. Communication pathways provide the rationale for the tools you'll use, and they reflect the goals and objectives you've set. Before you select pathways, then, you need to be sure that other elements of your strategy reflect the problem or issue they are designed to address. So:

- Is your goal a broad statement indicating what has to be done about the issue you identified?
- Do your objectives provide clear and measurable steps towards achieving that goal?
- Are the target publics appropriately identified and segmented?
- Have you written messages that reflect what you need to say about the issue or problem?

Now, using the information in this chapter, identify *two* communication pathways that will show how you will reach *each* of the target publics you have listed.

Assess your communication pathways by answering these questions:

- Do they reflect the methods by which each public normally accesses information? If they do not, why don't they, and what pathways would be more appropriate?
- What potential does each communication pathway offer for reaching each target public? What extra information do you need to make this decision?
- Do the pathways you have selected for the secondary and tertiary publics in your plan match those for primary publics? Should they? Why or why not?
- Can you deliver messages directly by these pathways? Why or why not?
- How much information can be delivered by the pathways you have chosen?
- Is there a different combination of pathways that would enhance your plan's ability to reach publics? If so, what combination?
- Do the combinations of communication pathways you have chosen maximise the chances your plan will be successful?

Prepare a matrix like that set out in Table 9.2 (use a landscape page layout) to match your goals, objectives, target publics and communication pathways. The matrix includes one example of how you should compile it. Extend each table as needed. Save and keep this matrix: you'll complete it in Chapter 10.

What are they interested in?
- What do they know about the organisation?

What does the organisation want them to know?
- How do they access information?

How can they be reached?

Chapter 10 will discuss how communication tools work with communication pathways.

Table 9.2 Matrix for matching goals, objectives, target publics, communication pathways and tools

Goal: *To generate increased enrolments at the university by school leavers*

Objective 1: *To increase target publics' awareness of the university's range of degrees by 50 per cent within 12 months*

Communication pathways	Target publics	Communication tools
Controlled media	Potential students	
	School career advisers	
	High school principals	
	Parents	
Interactive media	Potential students	
	School career advisers	
Uncontrolled media	Parents	
	School career advisers	
	High school principals	
	Education reporters	

Objective 2: [Write the objective here.]

Communication pathways	Target publics	Communication tools

Objective 3: [Write the objective here.]

Communication pathways	Target publics	Communication tools

CHAPTER EVALUATION

This chapter dealt with the role of communication pathways as the mechanism by which target publics can be reached. Communication pathways provide the rationale for using tools.

Evaluate your understanding of the topic by asking yourself how you would explain to a client:

1. The role of communication pathways in delivering messages to target publics.
2. What communication pathways are appropriate for specific target publics.
3. The diversity in the ways in which people access information.
4. Why communication pathways must reflect the ways in which target publics prefer to access information.

Chapter 10
Communication tools—the things we do

Goal: To understand how tools implement communication pathways.

Objectives: This chapter will help you to:

■ Understand how tools implement a communication pathway
Link communication tools to communication pathways.

Principle: Tools describe how a communication pathway will be implemented.

Practice: Tools are what practitioners write and produce. They are the action items that target publics see.

Chess is a game of strategy and tactics. For chess players, a strategy is about winning the game. It is the long-term plan for what they need to do if they are to checkmate their opponents. Tactics are the short-term moves they make with each piece. Chess strategy and tactics are dependent on the moves opponents make, and on each other. Winning at chess means expertly using short-term tactics in the context of a long-term game strategy, countering an opponent and knowing how to change an approach when that is necessary. A player's use of individual chess pieces, which can only move over the board in specific ways, both implements the player's strategy and reacts to moves an opponent has made.

Communication tools for implementing a communication pathway are like chess pieces: players can see the pieces and they know each does special things in specific ways. Just as a knight in chess can only move in an L-shaped pattern, so, too, can a blog, or a website, or a media release only do so much to implement a communication pathway. The task for a professional communicator is to understand how tools work, how they are linked to communication pathways, how they reflect the situation analysis, goals, objectives and target public information needs and how they should be coordinated for a successful outcome. That sounds complicated, but it isn't. It does require a sound knowledge of how and why strategic communication planning works and that means selecting appropriate communication tools for the task at hand, not an automatic use of news media releases or social media applications. That is, as ever in communication planning, ask why a particular tool is needed for what pathway.

DOI: 10.4324/9781003317579-11

For most practitioners, deciding communication tools, and preparing and implementing them, is the fun bit of their jobs. Whether they are planning a campaign for external target publics or working on the regular employee communication activities, this is a time when practitioners can be creative, use tools that are novel, or rely on those that are tried and true, depending on the contexts in which they are working, and the communication situation. This is also the time when the hard work of research, analysis, goal and objective setting, target public segmentation, message writing and decision-making about communication pathways takes a physical shape. At last, there's some definition to what will be done, for tools are the things that target publics see. They implement the overall strategy and selected pathways. Joep Cornelissen (2005) describes them as action items; Ronald Smith (2002, 2005) that they are the visible elements of a communication strategy. Anne Gregory (2009a) says tools should always be linked to, and flow from, pathways (Gregory uses the term "strategies").

PLANNING COMMUNICATION TOOLS

A practitioner's task is to effectively link communication tools to communication pathways. That is, having determined how to reach target publics with communication pathways, practitioner must then ask what tools will efficiently and effectively carry the messages. This may be situation specific.

A properly researched and professionally prepared strategic communication plan should rely on a blend of communication pathways. That means utilising myriad tools. In this way, pathways and tools are situational. They are the mechanisms and action items that deliver messages that:

- Provide information
  build awareness
- Establish a dialogue
  encourage action
- Persuade people to buy a product
  make a point in a debate about an issue
- Respond to a crisis.

All strategic communication projects should reflect all these where appropriate. That is, launching a new smartwatch is not responding to a crisis nor trying to make a point in an issue debate unless that debate is relevant to smartwatches.

WHICH PATHWAYS AND WHAT TOOLS?

So, if tools are the things that implement a strategy, what might they be? And how do they match communication pathways? Perhaps more importantly, which tools match which pathways? Table 10.1 lists a range of pathways and some allied tools.

Table 10.1 Communication pathways and tools

Communication pathway	Examples of possible communication tools
Controlled (or own) media	Websites, brochures, annual reports, point-of-sale material, direct snail mail, email, podcasts
Interpersonal media	Meetings, personal visits, site visits, face-to-face lobbying, snail-mail letters, email, telephone conversations
Interactive (or social) media	Social media applications, podcasts, vodcasts, other internet applications, email, newsgroups, blogs, wikis
Uncontrolled media	Media releases, media conferences, media interviews, factsheets, backgrounders, question and answer sheets
Special events	Exhibits, displays, conferences, trade shows, speeches, demonstrations, product launches, anniversaries, sponsorship launches
Sponsorship	Scholarships, awards, sponsorship of not-for-profits and events, alliances
Alliances	Sponsorships, collaboration on other communication pathways and tools

The tools practitioners can use to implement a strategic communication plan are almost endless, and choices about them depend perhaps only on available technology and finance. That is, here's the chance to be creative within the parameters determined by the amount of money available and how practical your idea is. But there is a key to selecting tools: make sure they are appropriate for, and will be effective in, reaching target publics—that is, match them to communication pathways.

Being clear about what you are trying to do in a specific situation helps in making decisions about whether communication should be proactive or reactive, informative or persuasive. Table 10.2 shows how these decisions might be made.

The following questions should be considered when choosing communication tools:

■ Will the tool reach enough people in the identified target public?
   How much information should be provided? How often should it be repeated?
■ Will there be a creative match of message and tool?
   Can the target public be reached in several ways?
■ Can the tools be implemented with the available resources?
   Can delivery of messages be controlled?
■ What communication tools are competitors using—and does it matter?
   Will the tools enable a dialogue and interaction with the target public?

Table 10.2 Content and timing of communication approaches

Approach	Content
Informative	Your communication approach presents the facts; it is objective or neutral.
Persuasive	Your approach engages in a logical argument, based on the facts or the opinions of experts; it makes appeals to reason and also involves emotional appeals and motivating people.
Approach	Timing
Proactive	A program is initiated by the organisation at a time of its choosing (for example, the launch of a product, a community consultation, release of the annual report).
Reactive	A program responds to influences and actions by competitors and other publics in an organisation's market and non-market environments as the need arises (for example, dealing with an issue or a crisis).

FURTHER READING

Hallahan, K. (2010), Public Relations Media, in R.L. Heath (ed.), *The Sage Handbook of Public Relations*, 2nd edn, Sage, Los Angeles, CA, pp. 623–41.

MATCHING PATHWAYS AND COMMUNICATION TOOLS

How might communication tools be matched to communication pathways in given contexts or situations? To identify some examples, let's consider possible needs:

- To *reach* significant numbers of people;
  to deliver *rich* information;
- To *control* the content, timing and distribution of a message, and how often the message needs to be *repeated*.
  Doing as much as possible to ensure messages are *effective* and *efficiently* delivered requires practitioners to think in other dimensions.

REACHING A SIGNIFICANT NUMBER OF PEOPLE

The use of an *uncontrolled media communication pathway* has the potential to reach a lot of people. After all, the mass news media have huge audiences. When an organisation needs to deal with an issue, launch a new product, publicise some interesting research findings, handle a crisis or report a fascinating human-interest story, practitioners almost always default to using an uncontrolled media pathway. Often, this is a proactive approach that is relatively inexpensive in terms of time and money, but it doesn't guarantee coverage, or an increase in awareness, or that understanding will be built or favourable action taken. In responding to a crisis, this pathway is a reactive approach. In both approaches, an acknowledgement of the potential reach available through the mass news media leads to a pragmatic decision to take this path, even though a result is not guaranteed. Tools to implement this pathway include:

- *Media conferences*: the number held would depend on the context: for a product launch, just one; for a public policy issue, maybe a series
  media releases: how many depends on need and the problem or issue being addressed
- *Fact sheets*: these may be about different topics, or may expand the points made in media releases
  backgrounders: these are used to expand on points in media releases, or to provide details about allied topics, like the history of the organisation, the industry or the CEO's career
- *Question and answer sheets*: these can provide information on specific topics, especially in a public policy debate
  briefings: these are a way of providing background information to reporters and commentators
- *Interviews*: allowing individual reporters to interview the CEO or other experts.

A test of reach

Next time you are in a coffee shop, watch the people reading newspapers. There will be some people doing that, despite the wide use of mobile phones and tablets. How often do they just scan the headlines? How often do they concentrate on news stories? Most likely, they skip through the pages of the newspaper reading in detail only those stories that catch their attention in some way: the headline, the topic, the photograph that illustrates it. Then they do the crossword. How many people are using their mobile smartphones to do more than read personal emails or post to their favourite social media sites? That's a bit harder to pick up without being a real snoop. Both observations, though, give a real sense of reach and of the problems inherent in building awareness and understanding and generating action.

THE AMOUNT OF INFORMATION

A *controlled (or own) media communication pathway* uses tools that enable richness of information—that is, include more information than is possible in tools for the mass news media. Tools for this pathway include:

- *Brochures: these hard copy publications contain material about specific topics.*
  a website: this will include all the formal information produced by the communication team and will often be the first point at which people interact with the organisation.

■ *Fact sheets: these contain the same expanded material used in an uncontrolled communication pathway.*
   Podcasts, webinars, videos: these enable extended information.
■ *Speeches: these enable the CEO or other experts to talk directly to target publics and to expand, explain and discuss relevant points.*
   displays: a display in a shopping centre, including one based on social media technology, uses information that is controlled: no one mediates the messages.

CONTROLLING THE DELIVERY OF MESSAGES

Several communication pathways enable practitioners to control message content, timing, and distribution. Planning what message content publics will get without mediation, and when and how this will happen, is the real definition of "control" in this context. Using one or more communication pathways enables a combination of some or all the tools that can be applied to each pathway. For example, demonstrating the organisation's commitment to corporate social-responsibility principles might involve using *controlled, interactive* and *sponsorship* communication pathways with a combination of these tools:

■ A brochure
   a section in the annual report
■ The website
   sponsoring community organisations
■ An interactive shopping mall display
   an open day.

IN THEORY: REPEATING MESSAGES

The so-called "rule of threes" is a theory that suggests that if a target public receives a message three times in three different ways (or from three different people) and in three different periods, they are more likely to understand and accept it. This is a significant principle behind television advertising scheduling. Television advertisements are scheduled to run several times during a number of programs, over a number of days or weeks. Sometimes, an advertising break on television starts with a commercial about, say, a new hair product, which is repeated in a shorter version halfway through the break, and then again at the end of the break. This is also the principle behind the use of experts to support an organisation—third-party endorsement. So, the frequency of message delivery is important. To ensure messages are delivered frequently, practitioners can use a blend of communication pathways and a mix of tools. There are, of course, practical considerations about timing and cost in blending pathways.

Blending communication pathways and their tools can also illustrate theoretical principles in action. Despite the concerns many scholars express about the four communication models proposed by James Grunig and colleagues (see J. Grunig in Heath, 2001, pp. 11–30), professional practice often involves using all four to maximise the possibility that target publics will be reached more than once in a campaign. You can see how this would be effective by thinking about how a government agency promoting citizens' rights and responsibilities in a new health care initiative might disseminate its messages using all four of the models through:

press agentry as an application of an uncontrolled media pathway. The agency would announce the initiative at a media conference and use, among other tools, a media release and backgrounder about the new policy and one-on-one interviews with the agency head.

public information as an application of a controlled media pathway and interactive media pathway. The tools involved in this part of the communication plan would be designed to reach target publics through publications like factsheets distributed through the agency's offices, and perhaps pharmacies, doctors' surgeries and allied health care offices. The agency could also do some press, radio and television advertising, supported by a website and some social media, not to argue a point, but to provide information.

two-way asymmetrical communication using sponsorship and controlled and uncontrolled communication pathways. This would involve tools like sponsoring a sporting event or team, the agency's website, its publications and media relations activity. These would be directed at providing basic information but would not engage in debate or discussion about the initiative.

two-way symmetrical communication applied through interpersonal media, interactive media and special events pathways. Tools like community meetings, face-to-face meetings, social media, personal email and letters and displays are used to engage publics in dialogue by answering enquiries and by providing information in a less formal way.

EFFECTIVENESS

It is axiomatic that strategic communication needs to be effective. That is why clients pay for the expertise practitioners provide. And that is why tools need to be carefully planned to align with communication pathways that match the way in which target publics access information. Controlled and interpersonal pathways with direct and face-to-face communication tools work best at ensuring that messages reach publics to build understanding and action. But these tools are expensive, and time-consuming, so it is important to consider the size of the target public and how gatekeepers can be avoided before using them. For example, it is likely to be financially prohibitive to produce a limited run of an expensive publication for a small target public group—unless a rational decision was made that it was important to do this. When cities bid for the right to host the Olympic Games, they spend huge amounts of money to convince the International Olympic Committee, a small target public, of their suitability. They take a rational decision to commit this money given the potential rewards in terms of investment, jobs, tourism income and the overall economic benefits of being known as an "Olympic city."

EFFICIENCY

Doing something efficiently means making sure available resources are used in the best possible way. That is, making decisions about how messages can be delivered as directly as possible to publics without breaking the available budget (see Chapter 11). A media release that is published in the news is an efficient way of distributing a point of view, because it is cheap and has a large audience. On the other hand, communications tools that match controlled and interpersonal media pathways like direct mail, websites and publications deliver information efficiently but can be expensive in terms of time (for example, the information technology people need to maintain websites and email systems; someone has to keep the site up to date, and that takes time) and distribution. Face-to-face meetings are the best way of providing information or debating a point of view. In that sense, they are efficient, but they are also expensive, because meetings usually involve a relatively small number of people.

COMMUNICATION TOOLS IN PRACTICE

Strategic communication planning requires practitioners to think critically about what they are asked to do. Deciding on tools is not a simple matter: it requires an understanding of what is possible and what best suits the target public you are attempting to reach. This sometimes involves a mix of pathways and tools. Figure 10.1 illustrates how pathways and tools work together to deliver messages to publics—in this case to convince chief executives to support a new policy about shareholders having the full details of the individual salaries and bonuses paid to senior executives. The case example that follows demonstrates the reasoning behind decisions about specific communication pathways and tools.

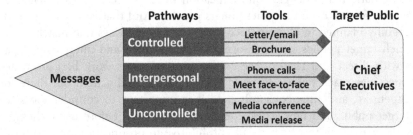

Figure 10.1 Combining communication pathways and tools

CHAPTER EXERCISE: REACHING CHIEF EXECUTIVES

The situation

Assume you are the Public Affairs Director for the (fictitious) National Company Shareholders' Association (NCSA). The NCSA represents small and medium investors, individuals who own shares in companies and who are therefore entitled to vote at company annual general meetings. NCSA members are concerned that salaries and bonuses paid to individual senior executives are not publicly disclosed. At a time of lower dividends during a global financial downturn, the NCSA is concerned that executive salaries still increase, as do their bonuses. The NCSA believes its proposed change would lead to greater transparency the way companies operate and improve ethical decision-making. But first the law governing corporations needs to be changed to allow this kind of disclosure. The NCSA has decided to seek that legislative change. It needs to convince the national corporate regulator to seek a change in the legislation. Before it does that, the NCSA has decided it needs to convince chief executives to support the proposal and has decided on a campaign to generate that support. NCSA knows the change would be widely supported by ordinary shareholders and others in the community but recognises convincing chief executives to support it will be extremely difficult.

The task

You have been tasked with developing the campaign to convince the top ten chief executives in the nation—your primary target public (there are, of course, others)—that the change would be an important way of improving business transparency and company reputations. You have got to focus on the top ten because they are influencers capable of convincing others, but the campaign will also approach as many other CEOs as possible. Having done the research, written a situation analysis and prepared messages, you are thinking through communication pathways and tools. You have decided to use a mind map to help you work this out. Mind maps are diagrams that help organise information in a visual way to show relationships between ideas. They are great for showing how pathways and tools for a communication strategy link up with target publics. The mind map you use to work this out might look something like the one in Figure 10.2. (Commercial software can help you do this—so, too, can word processing and spreadsheet programs. Or you could draw mind map by hand on a large sheet of paper.)

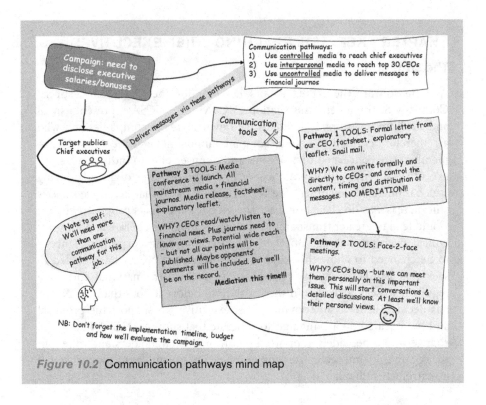

Figure 10.2 Communication pathways mind map

BEING CREATIVE

All practitioners want to produce creative, perhaps award-winning, communication strategies. It is by understanding how tools implement communication pathways to deliver messages that practitioners can be creative.

Sometimes finding a creative way to deliver messages means thinking "outside the box" and trying tools others have not used before. This is the idea behind media "stunts" that are used to attract news media (particularly television) coverage of a product launch or to make a political point like activists do when they hold demonstrations. An example is when politicians visit factories dressed in yellow safety vests and hard hats to hold a media conference about a new policy on workplace safety. Yet thinking outside the box can lead to outcomes that are more meaningful than political stunts, and to tools that are often outside the heat of the 24-hour news cycle: the program.

There are multitude of examples of communication tools that do this for government agencies, not-for-profit organisations, charities, community organisations, commercial businesses and sporting teams. One of the most famous, Red Nose Day, began in Australia more than 30 years ago to raise funds for research into sudden infant death syndrome. The idea was that awareness of the need for research funds could be built by people wearing red, plastic clown noses for a day and using that to promote the cause. It worked and is still an annual event—and the outcome so far has been research funding that led, for example, to six evidence-based steps all parents can take to reduce the risk of their baby dying in their sleep. (see https://www.rednoseday.org.au/about-red-nose-day). Around the world, sporting codes have been strongly supporting causes seeking funds for health research: beanies for brain cancer research, bandanas for research into cancers affecting young people and an annual fun run to raise funds to investigate the causes and possible cures for the childhood disease neuroblastoma. One of the most highly visible creative tools in Australia involves players, officials, spectators and journalists wearing pink hats and other items during the annual Pink Cricket Test Match in Sydney to raise awareness of the need for funding for breast cancer nurses. The cricket balls, stumps and bats are all pink, and the event is preceded by a week of publicity.

Knowing what you need to do, and how you will do it, means you can develop creative tools, sometimes by doing things that have not been tried before. But they will all be based on good research about what tools effectively deliver messages to target publics.

FURTHER READING

Fitch, K. (2009), New Media and Public Relations, in J. Chia and G. Synnott (eds.), *An Introduction to Public Relations: From Theory to Practice*, Oxford University Press, Melbourne, pp. 333–56.

Kent, M.L. (2010), Directions in Social Media for Professionals and Scholars, in R.L. Heath (ed.), *The SAGE Handbook of Public Relations*, 2nd edn, SAGE, Los Angeles, pp. 643–56.

Strategic Plan Checklist: Matching tools and pathways

Using a template

There are two parts to this exercise.

First, reflect on the matrix you prepared in Chapter 9 (see p. 182). Make sure that the communication pathways are still appropriate for the target publics. Now, enter the communication tools to match the pathways and target publics.

Then, when you've matched the tools to publics and pathways, you will be ready to start compiling your strategy. To start this, set up a word-processing document based on the template that follows (see Figure 10.3 below). Leave the executive summary and contents page till later. Remember that there's more to come on this project: the implementation and evaluation sections can be added after they are dealt with in the following chapters. When you complete this first part of the template based on what you've done so far, you should be able to assess whether the decisions you've made relate directly to the issues you identified or are about something else. If you are not on track, revise and amend where appropriate.

Chapter 11 will examine how a strategic communication plan is resourced and managed.

Executive summary

One page maximum

Insert a page break here

CONTENTS	Page
Executive summary	1
Situation analysis	X

Strategy

Insert a page number for each item in the table of contents when you are finished.

Goals	xx
Objectives	xx
Target publics	xx
Messages	xx
Communication pathways	xx
Communication tools	xx

Implementation

Budget	xx
Timeline	xx

Evaluation xx

Insert a page break here.

Situation analysis

Write your situation analysis here.

Insert a page break here.

Strategy

1 Goals

Fill in your goals and objectives below.

Goal 1:

Objective 1:

Objective 2:

Objective 3:

Goal 2:

Objective 1:

Objective 2:

Objective 3:

Insert a page break here.

2 Target publics

List your target publics under each heading, using dot points.

Primary

Secondary

Tertiary

Insert a page break here.

3 Messages

You are listing brief messages here, so use dot points. Write each message in about one sentence.

Insert a page break here.

4 Communication pathways and tools

*Goal:*Write the goal here.

Objective 1: Write the objective here and fill out the cells of the table.

Communication pathways	Target publics	Communication tools

Objective 2: Write the objective here and fill out the cells of the table.

Communication pathways	Target publics	Communication tools

Objective 3: Write the objective here and fill out the cells of the table.

Communication pathways	Target publics	Communication tools

Figure 10.3 Template for a strategic communication plan

CHAPTER EVALUATION

The goal of this chapter was to help you to understand how tools implement communication pathways. This is important, because communication pathways, or message delivery pathways, define how target publics can be reached; communication tools are the packages that deliver messages via pathways, a bit like the postal service delivering snail mail. Pathways and tools reflect what a practitioner wants to achieve: the strategic communication plan's goals and objectives.

To evaluate your understanding of how tools implement communication pathways, reflect on the following questions:

1. Do the tools you've identified for your strategic plan project reflect the communication pathways you identified in the Chapter 9 exercise? In other words, are you sure that the information you added to the matrix in this chapter is appropriate for the pathways and target publics you chose? If not, why not?
2. Can you segment your pathways and tools to deal with issues in the market and non-market environments? Why would the tools be different?
3. How would you redesign your project to deal with current, mid-term and long-term issues?
4. What objectives, publics, pathways and tools would be appropriate for the mid- and long terms?
5. How would you advise a client who wanted to use only news releases and social media in a campaign to introduce new cycle paths in a bushland neighbourhood? What reasons would you give for that advice?

TIME OUT: ON APPLYING PROFESSIONAL PRACTICE SKILLS TO STRATEGY

Sometimes when communication students start internships as part of their degree programs, they are tasked with writing a strategic plan. This is a tough project, especially since many interns have not yet studied the concepts involved in researching and writing a communication strategy. Much of what they have explored so far in their studies will have been based on strategies prepared by others. When they are asked, for example, to prepare material for a case, perhaps one that has won an award, students follow goals and objectives set to reflect situations researched by others. Students work on these cases to give them opportunities to apply their developing practice skills.

Researching and writing a complete strategy from scratch, though, takes practitioners to a new plane, where critical thinking, analysis, theory and creativity are vital. It is here, in this sometimes difficult place, that practitioners wrestle to find big answers to small questions: what issues are important? Why are they important? Who cares about them, and why? What needs to be done about them, and how can we do that? What will it cost? And how will we know that it worked? When they face these questions in an internship, or at the start of a capstone communication strategy unit, students will, for the first time, be able to set the directions for communication activity.

Preparing a strategy is high-level practice, mostly the role of senior people. Many scholars have examined and defined the various levels of professional practice. They describe the technical work of beginning practitioners, the specialist roles of those in areas like media relations, sponsorship and campaign management, and the work of senior practice leaders who advise clients and who prescribe strategic solutions for communication problems or public policy issues. At the top level of practice, it is the expert prescriber, the experienced practitioner, who uses research to work out what needs to be done, and why and how a range of professional skills can help a client solve problems. Think here of "problems" in the sense of mathematical equations that can be solved, rather than in the pejorative sense. Resolving a communication problem means finding the big answer to the small question of how, for instance, a charity could effectively explain the good health outcomes that result from the science it funds so that it can attract more donations. The answer to the "how" question sets the parameters for the communication strategy the charity needs. This involves understanding how and why and with what tools people communicate. It involves more than simply proposing a website or YouTube video post, tweeting a few points, or issuing a media release. They all help, but why would the charity need these tools? A communication strategy would explain why.

Learning to be strategic

When he researched how students assess each other's performances in group assignments during their campaign or strategy classes, Charles Lubbers (2011) noted the work of other scholars who argue strongly about the need for public relations students to understand strategic planning. The goal is to prepare students for success in the workplace. The same is true for students of the other professional communication disciplines. Understanding strategic planning is what economists would call the "value-added" benefit of a communication degree because it adds high-level practice skills.

Strategy classes often involve students in group work as teams resolve communication problems, sometimes by working for real-world clients, sometimes on case studies. Students are not always supportive of group work, mainly because they feel at times that some members do not contribute as much as they should. Group work, however, reflects professional practice in which teams—maybe of only two or three, sometimes more—work on clients' issues by utilising each other's strengths and specialisations. Lubbers (2011) cites some valuable findings from other researchers about the benefits of group work in strategy classes. Researchers found that group work:

- Promotes deep learning
  helps earn higher grades
- Teaches social skills and civic values
  teaches higher order thinking skills
- Promotes personal growth
  develops positive attitudes towards autonomous learning.

All these are vital in professional practice—even the higher grades, which lead to better employment chances.

To read more about Lubbers's research, see C.A. Lubbers (2011), An Assessment of Predictors of Student Peer Evaluations of Team Work in the Capstone Campaigns Course, *Public Relations Review*, 37(5), pp. 492–8.

Planning a strategy is the critical point at which analytical thinking, competency in professional skills, specialisations and an understanding of what is possible intersect. Academics planning new or revised degree sequences often ponder whether strategic communication should be the first unit taught—that is, whether it should precede the teaching and development of professional writing and other practice skills. After all, this approach would set the context in which skills can be developed. The alternative is to teach and develop skills, knowledge of theories about communication, and an understanding of research methodologies first because they all sustain strategic planning. Preparing a situation analysis, for instance, uses skills learnt in research theory and methodology classes. Knowing how specific tools in advertising, public relations, personal selling and sales promotion can work together comes from an understanding of the specific roles each of those disciplines has in integrated communication. Recommending that a client revise a website requires a practitioner to know how this should be done and how to write content for the new site. Senior strategic planners know how to link the specialist expertise of practitioners in each of these areas to generate effective communication. To narrow the example, the strategist at a public relations consultancy engaged to help the charity mentioned above would research all the issues facing the organisation. These would include what potential donors already know about the charity and the medical science research it supports. There would be questions about the tax advantages for donors who contribute to the charity and whether it is possible for these to be made more advantageous. While these public policy questions would be just one part of the practitioners' research and analysis, they would involve working out how to reach potential donors and those who determine the tax regime, and what tools would be needed to do that. Try finding some answers using your own knowledge and by research. How could you reach the people who decide tax policy? If you did not have the specialist knowledge and skills to answer these questions, who in the consultancy might? It is likely that the practitioner would ask the person in the consultancy who specialises in public affairs to help. And at this stage of planning, the practitioner has not even considered what might be done to identify and reach potential donors.

So, basic professional skills learnt in the first years of a degree program are the keys to successful long-term practice. They are taught and developed not just for the duration of the specific subjects in which they are covered; the competencies they involve are for lifetime practice, and what is studied in first year at university applies in final year strategic planning. But what do such skills involve?

In 2011, Bey-Ling Sha reported the results of research on public relations professional competencies and work categories in the United States. These are the same competencies strategic communicators need. Sha (2011) notes that **practising** public relations involves not only individual practitioners' personal competencies but also the various work categories that are needed in public relations. Time Out Table 1 summarises Sha's broad work categories and the activities they involve. These work categories reflect the communication functions discussed in Chapter 4.

Practise regularly perform professional skills, or competencies, in a systematic way. In the sense in which it is used in this book—as in being a *practitioner*—*practising* means doing the things that are involved in working in a profession, in the way that doctors practise medicine and lawyers practise law.

Sha (2011) found that the skills and competencies needed for practitioners to work in these categories are:

- Research, planning, implementation and evaluation
  understanding of public relations ethics and relevant laws
- Application of communication models and theories
  business literacy

- Management skills
  crisis communication skills
- Media relations (including social media)
  use of information technology and social media
- Historical knowledge of public relations
  advanced communication skills.

The skills Sha identified as those needed to work in these categories demonstrate that public relations and strategic communication planning involve multidimensional practice in which professional competencies work in tandem to build successful outcomes.

Time Out Table 1 Work categories and activities in public relations

Work category	Activity focus
Account/client management	Client and customer relationships; coaching and counselling clients; managing expectations
Strategic planning	Developing the overall plan; reputation management; research; goal setting; engaging with customers and key stakeholders; developing messages for specific publics; branding
Program planning	Research; identifying key publics; developing detailed plans; managing marketing communication; evaluation; leveraging interactive elements of a campaign
Project management	Logistics for implementation; creating and managing a budget; resource allocation; managing the team; working with suppliers and contractors like graphic designers, printers, website developers
Media relations	Pitching stories; writing and distributing releases and other tools like factsheets and backgrounders for the mass news media and social media outlets via traditional (hard copy) and social media applications; coordinating publicity; identifying and liaising with appropriate reporters and commentators; monitoring and evaluating media coverage; training people in the organisation to be spokespeople
Social media relations	Utilising web-based social networks; producing in-house or client blogs; advising clients on how to use social media communication channels; measuring social media engagement efforts
Stakeholder relations	For each set of stakeholders: developing strategies and key messages; arranging site inspection tours, conferences, and meetings; establishing strategic partnerships or alliances

Work category	Activity focus
Issues management	Identifying or anticipating and analysing potential mid-term and long-term problems and public policy issues likely to impact on the business; crisis communication planning; providing strategic counsel for clients; resolving conflicts
Crisis management	Reacting to immediate problems; implementing crisis communication plans; coordinating release of information via traditional and social media; training spokespeople; monitoring and analysing media coverage
Internal/employee communication	Communication with employees, management, board members; developing internal communication strategies; producing print and online internal communication tools; developing web content; managing communication during organisational change
Special events	Developing themes for special events; promoting products and services; coordinating event logistics; organising/ managing external promotions
Community relations	Sponsoring community events; managing corporate social-responsibility programs; building alliances; community outreach; using social media applications to engage with communities important to the organisation

Source: Adapted from B.-L. Sha (2011), pp. 187–96.

Chapter 11
Managing a strategic communication plan

Goal: To learn about the roles of budgeting and task scheduling in implementing a strategic communication plan.

Objectives: This chapter will help you to:

- Appreciate the importance of budgets and task schedules in the implementation of a strategic communication plan
  Prepare a basic budget and task schedule for your project
- Understand how a strategic communication plan works in a systematic way.

Principle: Detailed budgets and timelines are essential tools for project management.

Practice: A communication strategy should include a budget and implementation timeline.

Taking a commercial airline flight for a vacation is mostly straightforward, despite almost inevitable airport delays. Passengers research flights, book and pay for tickets, and check in online. At the airport, computer systems produce boarding passes, check in luggage, operate security screening, display departure times and gates and finally scan boarding passes to make sure everyone who has checked in for the flight boards it. And when they fly, passengers can be rewarded with frequent flyer loyalty points. Nothing much has changed in this planning process since commercial airlines began operating, except for increased security and the greater efficiency, despite hiccups, provided by computer-assisted booking, check-in, boarding and satellite navigation. The pilots use set flight paths and follow others set by air traffic control for take-offs and landings. Yet the process passengers experience is only part of managing an airline flight. Behind the scenes, airline staff need to manage everything about a flight, from time scheduling, safety, aircraft availability, crewing, fuelling and loading, to meals (including for special diets), flight paths, arrival times and gates, unloading, cleaning and maintenance—and much more. Airline staff work in a systematic way according to a plan for each flight, so that at every point of that plan—from

DOI: 10.4324/9781003317579-12

when a decision is taken to provide the flight until the crew leaves the aircraft at the destination and hands it over to another team—someone knows exactly what needs to be done.

Implementing a strategic communication project also needs a plan, nowhere near as involved as those for aircraft flights, but nevertheless one that identifies the steps needed to make sure a strategy is delivered on time and within budget. The template you are using for your strategic plan project shows where the implementation details should go.

> **Implement** put a plan or a decision into action. Implementing a strategic communication project involves both a plan and a decision: a plan based on decisions about what needs to be done to resolve a situation or issue is put into action.

An implementation plan is part of a strategic communication system designed to make sure goals and objectives are achieved. The implementation plan sets out the steps and time needed to write, design, produce and distribute the communication tools identified in the strategic plan; to schedule an evaluation; and to prepare a budget. It avoids guesswork, or "flying by the seat of your pants," a phrase that originated in the late 1930s to describe pilots who flew aircraft without using instruments or radios. Practitioners need to use planning "instruments" like budgets, timelines and checklists to make sure that they don't navigate the implementation process by guesswork. For example, to manage annual student graduation ceremonies for the Australian National University, event manager Giles Pickford used an agreed budget, and a 30-page, 12-month combined planning timeline and checklist. The timeline began with an entry that simply noted, "Book Llewellyn Hall for next year." That task was scheduled for the day after the previous annual graduations ended. The timeline then set out the tasks for each of the following 12 months, and for the weeks, days and hours before each ceremony, to make sure they happened on time and budget—and to clarify who was responsible for each task.

A COMMUNICATION PLAN'S IMPLEMENTATION SECTION

The implementation section of a strategic communication plan should set out:

- The budget for the project
  a checklist that has a timeline for the project—this shows in detail what needs to be done and the dates by which things have to happen
- An indication of who is responsible for each part of the plan.

Budget and checklist information is necessary for managing a project. Fraser Seitel (2011) says communication projects should be disciplined by budgetary realities. Laurie Wilson and Joseph Ogden (2008) say that because they are strategic planning tools, checklists and budgets need specific details and must be considered carefully.

Preparing a budget for a project seems an obvious step, but it must be based on the best possible information about costs, and sometimes expected revenue, to give a true assessment of funding requirements.

A checklist should display individual responsibilities and include an indication of the time needed to research, write, produce, implement and evaluate the success of the project. Most in-house communication departments, and consultancy firms, have their own computer-based or hard copy processes for doing this.

USING INFORMATION

Sometimes a practitioner is part of a team, sometimes the team leader and sometimes the sole person on the project. In each role, practitioners must be aware of what needs to be done in their own jobs as well as what the team needs to do, but they do not need to be experts on everything. For example, they don't have to be web designers to manage a project to re-launch an organisation's revised website, but they do need to understand that other professionals involved in their projects have specialist knowledge and skills. It also helps to have a basic knowledge of production processes to understand what designers, printers, audiovisual producers, photographers and other specialists are talking about when tools are being produced. An in-house team redesigning a website may include technical experts, people adept at using social media applications, a web designer, other communication practitioners, someone from the finance section and maybe an internal user who can advise on functionality. An in-house team can sometimes be boosted by including an external specialist to provide specific expertise not available internally. The project leader needs to know how long each person will take to do their part of the project and the sequence in which their output is needed before others can be involved—or which parts can be written and designed at the same time. A project team should meet regularly to discuss progress and the next steps, and to sort out any problems. A checklist is normally part of a progress and review meeting agenda—sometimes the only item. The agenda will also often include reports on spending to indicate how the project is tracking against the approved budget. Tablet, notebook and laptop computers enable the efficient distribution and updating of agendas, checklists and budgets and other web-based data for progress meetings.

When in doubt about something, ask. Designers and printers can advise how long it will take to produce a 24-page, full-colour brochure and the expert constructing a display for the state's major agricultural exhibition can provide a good estimate of how long it will take to build. Experienced practitioners build a working knowledge of these processes over years of professional practice, but beginning practitioners need to research and ask questions.

Implementation plans are based on the answers to the following questions:

- Can we make the communication tools work?
  Can we fund the tools?
- Do we have enough people and the right technology to make them work?
  Will each tool reach enough people in the intended target public group to make this an efficient use of resources? Have we chosen the best communication pathways to do this?
- How much information do we need to provide?
  Can target publics be reached in different ways? How many and at what cost?

The answers will help you to decide whether tools are appropriate and effective for each target public.

CHAPTER EXERCISE: BE SMART WHEN YOU PLAN A PROJECT

People who research and write about project management, and those who manage projects, share a common view: be clear about all aspects of planning and implementation. This includes knowing what must be done and who needs to be informed about progress. Most recommend using the SMART technique for planning project objectives. SMART is an acronym:

S—specific, significant
M—measurable, meaningful, motivational
A—agreed, attainable, acceptable, action-oriented
R—realistic, results-oriented
T—time-based, can be tracked.

SMART is sometimes applied to writing strategic communication objectives—note the similarity with the ideas in Chapter 7. The technique is useful when planning how a strategic plan should be implemented.

For this exercise, write an implementation plan for your project that:

is *specific* about what needs to be done to implement the strategy,
has *meaningful, achievable* and *action-oriented* steps,
is clearly *results-oriented, and*
can be *tracked* and delivered on *time* and on budget.

In this way, your implementation plan should reflect what you planned with your goals and objectives, communication pathways and tools.

ABOUT BUDGETS

Preparing a budget is an essential part of project planning and management because nothing can be implemented unless there is money to pay for it. The budget shows how much money you have for each part of the project, and usually includes an amount for unexpected costs—contingencies. The biggest communication budgets are likely to be those for product advertising, the smallest for public relations. Budgets will be approved and allocated only when clients, or in-house managers, decide they can afford what is proposed in the strategic plan. This brings a sense of reality to practitioners' decisions about tools: can your client afford them?

Communication departments work at two budget levels. First, in-house, the communication department has an overall annual budget which will be prepared during the organisation's business planning cycle, and it will fund each part of the department's yearly program. Second, one-off special projects need a specific budget so the manager of the department will need to identify a funding source. Consultants are generally told how much money a client has for a project. Sometimes, clients ask practitioners to recommend a budget to implement a strategic plan.

CONSULTANCY BUDGETS AND CHARGING

Communication consultancies also operate with budgets. Consultancy principals are acutely aware of cost structures because their company's viability can be adversely affected if they provide unrealistically low quotes for delivering projects. Their fees are thus calculated using a formula that covers the time each consultant on the project devotes to it, as well as the costs of telephone calls, fares and accommodation on business trips for the client and other expenses. Each consultancy has its own formula for calculating fees, but they are normally based on a charge-out rate for consultants' time on a project plus expenses incurred in developing and implementing work they are contracted to produce for a client. Charge-out rates vary according to the seniority of a consultant: fees for the most experienced are higher than those for a beginning practitioner. Charge-out rates are devised to reflect the salaries and on-costs of consultants involved in a project and to ensure that the consultancy makes a profit from a job.

Calculating a charge-out rate

Most banks and accountancy firms provide services to help businesses plan their financial goals. The ANZ Bank New Zealand Ltd advises business customers that they don't need to be "mathematical wizards" to calculate an accurate charge-out rate (see https://www.anz.co.nz/business/bizhub/start/tips-for-calculating-an-accurate-charge-out-rate/). There are some simple steps to follow.

Let's say you need to calculate a charge-out rate for a consultant who is paid US$80,000 a year. This is how you can do it:

1. Decide how much you will pay the consultant.
2. Work out the consultant's "share" of the office's overhead costs.
3. Add the annual costs of the consultant's superannuation.
4. Double the total salary + costs.
5. Add a profit margin for your business.
6. Divide the result by the consultant's annual work hours to calculate the charge-out rate that will cover the consultant's US$80,000 salary.

You can work out the number of hours a consultant spends at work this way:

> **Total year** = 52 weeks × 40 hours = **2,080 hours**
> **Deduct:**
> Holidays = 4 weeks × 40 hours = 160 hours
> Statutory holidays = 2 weeks × 40 hours = 80 hours
> Sickness = 1 week × 40 hours = 40 hours
> Non-chargeable hours = 25% of your time at work = 450 hours
> **Total to deduct** = 730 hours
> **Actual work hours** = 2,080 − 730 hours = **1,350 hours**

This really means that a consultant only officially works for 34 weeks at 40 hours per week in a year for which they are paid an annual salary. However, the consultant needs to generate enough revenue to not only meet their salary, but to cover their office overheads, and on-costs like superannuation. This means they need to generate an additional 30 per cent of their annual salary in revenue for the business. And the consultancy needs to earn enough money to pay for the normal running of the business—like rent, electricity, photocopier, computer, mobile phone and vehicle leases, office cleaning, the salaries and on-costs of support staff, office supplies, new and replacement furniture and many more items. And the consultancy needs to earn a profit. So, in addition to overheads and on-costs, the consultant needs to earn enough from their work to pay for a share of the costs of running the business. That is about another 20 per cent. In other words, a consultant on an annual salary of US$80,000 costs the business another US$40,000 a year. The resulting US$120,000 is a cost to the business. The consultancy needs to make a profit, so individual salaries and on-costs are doubled—and probably 10 per cent added for a safety margin. The following formula is used to calculate each consultant's charge-out rate:

$$\textbf{Charge} - \textbf{out rate} = (\text{Salary} + \text{On} - \text{costs}) \times 2 = \text{TOTAL. Add 10\%.}$$
$$\text{Divide the result by 1350 (total work hours).}$$

That means to pay your US$80,000-a-year consultant, cover your business costs and make a profit, you need to charge a client US$196 (or US$264,000 divided by 1,350) for every hour your consultant works on their account.

CHAPTER EXERCISE

How much would you cost?

Assume you are a consultant. Your consultancy is pitching for some new business—a project you've been assigned. You'll be supported by a beginning practitioner. You need to decide how much you'll put in the budget for the time you'll spend, which you estimate to be about 60 hours for you, and 100 hours for the beginning practitioner. You earn US$100,000 a year and the beginning practitioner US$50,000. On-costs for both of you are an additional 50 per cent of your annual salaries.

Using the information above, work out the hourly rate at which your client will be charged for the work each of you will do on their project.

First, determine how much you each cost the consultancy in annual salary and on-costs.

Second, double those figures. Add 10 per cent.

Using the formula above, calculate how much your normal individual charge-out rate should be to recover these costs and for the consultancy to earn a profit.

Third, multiply the charge-out rate by the estimated number of hours you will each work on the project.

The result may surprise you.

Read the following Chapter Exercise carefully to work out what happens next—there's another step.

WHAT IS IN A BUDGET?

Budgets need to provide the estimated costs of every part of the project. Graphic design and printing costs (yes, some communication tools are still printed), internet service provider fees, IT consultants' charges, display construction and installation costs and mailing costs can be identified by seeking quotations from possible contractors. It is usual to seek two or three quotations from different designers, printers, mailing houses and other contractors like web designers, specialist writers, audiovisual producers or display builders. A competitive quotation process such as this means assessments can be made about the best price for what you need to do, always balanced with the need for quality. Often, especially in government, organisations have lists of "preferred" suppliers, contractors who agree to provide services at specific prices. Using contractors on these lists means that practitioners do not need to seek competitive quotes.

FURTHER READING

Beard, M. (2007), Running a Public Relations Department, 2nd edn, Kogan Page, London, chs. 6 and 7, pp. 55–73.

IN THEORY: FINDING AND CONTROLLING THE MONEY

Everything always comes down to money. Someone must find enough for practitioners to implement their strategies, and that is no easy task; someone also must control spending. Each of these jobs is equally hard.

Anne Gregory (2009a, p. 191) says practitioners have a duty to be effective and efficient when implementing programs. Seitel (2011, p. 120) argues that like any other business activity, public relations programs must be based on sound budgeting; Dennis Wilcox and Glen Cameron (2012, p. 159) point out that no program is complete without a budget. So, budgets are important.

From an organisational management perspective, budgets are about making sure resources (money, people, technology) are available, allocated to a project and spent effectively. Hodge and others (2003) note that without sufficient resources, and proper distribution of them, an organisation would cease to exist, so control of resources is vital. In a public relations context, Mike Beard (2007, p. 63) says that meticulous control of a budget can do more to enhance a practitioner's reputation than any other performance measure. He provides some budget principles for practitioners. They should:

- Demonstrate the link between a strategic plan's objectives, action items (our communication tools) and targeted results, on the one hand, and the proposed budget, on the other
  show outstanding control of a budget once it is approved
- Understand the detail of expenditure
  be able to answer questions from management about expenditure—and never surprise them
- Work closely with the person who produces accounts
  follow the budget-management procedures of the organisation
- Check accounts carefully
  not allow anyone to charge things against the communication area's accounts without approval
- Clearly establish (in writing) who in the team can spend funds and who can approve invoices and other charges.

There will be times when practitioners will be required to spend more than has been allocated in a budget. If the budget contingency does not cover the new costs, formal approval for "over-spending," or for additional funding to cover the unexpected costs, should be sought from management. See Table 11.1 for a simple budget format.

Sometimes projects have tight deadlines and need to be completed quickly. When that happens, designers, printers, mailing houses and others involved in the project need to know the deadlines for their involvement so that they can provide a realistic quote and indicate how long they'll need to do their part of the project. This information helps in selecting the best option in terms of cost, quality and the contractor's ability to meet the deadline. If a celebrity has been proposed as the spokesperson for a campaign, the fee that that person will charge for being involved should be included in the budget. Similarly, the costs of venues, equipment, transport and refreshments for events need to be listed. Include an amount for a contingency in case there is an unexpected increase in costs.

Clients need to know what additional taxes may be incurred for the service provided by consultants and on the production of tools. When in doubt about this, check with the organisation's accountants.

The more complex a project is, the more detailed the budget needs to be. For example, a campaign to attract young people to donate blood would need a budget covering the costs of:

■ A media kit, leaflets and other communication tools included in the project. (And remember, even though it seems axiomatic, these tools must be written,

Table 11.1 Budget items

Budget type	Requirements
Communication department budget	**Prepared in line with the organisation's chart of accounts**
	All regular activities included
	Changes to the total budget determined annually
	Little room for variation
	Priorities set by the senior manager
	Includes details of
	○ salaries and on-costs like superannuation
	○ rent, electricity, telephones, services
	○ allocations for segments of the total regular program (see also "Project budget" below)
	○ contractors
	○ travel and accommodation
	○ revenue, where that is expected
	○ a contingency (an amount set aside for unexpected costs)
Project budget	**Funding–often a fixed amount–for a specific project (such as a special event, maintaining the website, the annual report, an anniversary celebration)**
	Used for regular annual projects implemented by the department as well as for unexpected projects
	Includes details of costs directly related to the project:
	○ producing tools (for example, graphic design, website production, maintaining social media, printing, displays, audiovisuals, printing, distribution)
	○ materials
	○ travel and accommodation related to the project
	○ consultants
	○ salaries and on-costs
	○ revenue where that is expected
	○ a contingency

designed and produced for publication on the website, or for transmission by social media, as well as for hard copies.)
website design, development and testing
- Displays
hiring a venue for the campaign launch (including, if necessary, sound equipment)
- Casual staff costs; overtime for permanent staff
any audiovisual aids
- Refreshments, if these are to be provided for guests
transport, perhaps to bring the campaign spokesperson from interstate.

There are myriad ways of writing a budget. Most computer accounting software has templates for budgeting, and others can be found using search engines. Word processing programs and spreadsheets can also be used for compiling budgets and often have templates for this. Table 11.1 gives details of what is needed in two types of budgets: one for the entire communication department and one for a single project. The amount of detail needed depends both on the complexity of the project and on what is required by an organisation's budgeting system.

USING TIMELINES AND CHECKLISTS

A primary project management tool is a realistic timeline that gives a time frame for implementing each step in the plan. A timeline can be used as a checklist at meetings where progress on a project is regularly reviewed. A more detailed checklist/to-do list that identifies all the steps needed to complete each task is also a useful tool for work-in-progress meetings. Of course, you can add these steps into your timeline.

Preparing an implementation timeline means estimating as accurately as possible how long it will take to:

- Complete any formative research that still needs to be done
finalise the strategic plan (there's always more to do)
- Design and produce each of the tools
approve drafts, final copy, artwork and budgets
- Test and launch the website
post the first social media contributions
- Print materials
deliver material to distribution points or to a mailing house
- Prepare for a launch event or a media conference
issue invitations and get responses
- Decide on and organise catering
set up an event
- Evaluate the project.

Details must be specific. It is pointless listing "website" in a timeline and just giving start and finish times because this means nothing. If the website is new, time needs to be allocated for scoping what it will do and include the time needed to design it, populate it with information, test, revise, get client approvals and so on. If an existing website has to be revised, then say so on the timeline with a simple "website revision" and include the stop and start dates for the revision.

Most of the time senior managers will approve material quickly, but you need to make sure that you schedule approval steps in plenty of time to meet production deadlines and to suit the manager's own work schedule. For example, scheduling a manager to approve a website design on the second day of their overseas trip would mean the project could be delayed.

So, to prepare an implementation timeline, ask about each part of a project:

- How long will it take?
  How can this be managed to ensure it will be completed in the available time?
- How can the team make this happen?
  Start planning by writing down everything you and your team will need to do to produce a successful project. Rearrange this in approximate date order—from the things that need to be done first through to the last items. For example, don't schedule the delivery of refreshments for the day before or after your launch. That sounds like a silly point—but it has happened. Work out how long each step will take. Make realistic assessments and ask contractors like designers and printers for their estimates of the time involved in their part of the project. Identify which steps don't rely on others. If you are planning a launch, one of the first things you could do is identify and book a venue that is available on the date of the event. And the timeline should include a reference to "Hold the event." That's an important point: it means you should schedule all the steps in the implementation by working backwards from this date. If it takes three weeks to design and construct a website, a week to approve it, a week to test it and a day to launch it, the project should start at least five weeks before the launch—plus a day or two as a contingency in case something goes awry.

Sometimes, especially for complicated projects, special software can be used to create a "critical path" to show steps in a timeline. A critical path shows what needs to be completed (like approvals to proceed) before work on other steps can be started. The critical path changes if there's a hold up on a prior step. This kind of software is widely used in the construction industry.

Setting up a timeline

You can find templates for timelines, checklists and to-do lists in standard spreadsheet and word processing software. A simple timeline includes:

- A column showing all the planning and implementation steps as a list, sorted by individual parts of the project
  a column that shows the date on which each step of the project should start

■ A column showing the expected completion date for each step of the project (and sometimes another column to show when the step has been completed) a final column showing who in the team is responsible for that step in the project.

Strategic Plan Checklist: An implementation timeline

Variations on a theme

Just as there is software for budgeting, so there are computer-based tools to show implementation timeline in a more visual way. A Gantt chart, a two-dimensional way of displaying each of the steps involved in an implementation plan, is an example and looks like a wall planner. (Henry Gantt introduced the first chronological chart as a project management system.) Gantt charts show how all the steps in the implementation plan interrelate, and those that need to be done before others are started. They usually have a vertical axis showing the steps involved in the project and a horizontal axis showing the time taken for each. The horizontal axis is filled in with a line covering the months, weeks and days involved in each step of the project. Gantt charts are flexible, and most commercial spreadsheet applications include Gantt chart templates. They can also be compiled using the table function in word processing software. Figure 11.1, an example of a simple Gantt chart with some steps for scoping a new corporate website, was produced using the table function of standard word processing software. Other steps in the development of the site, of course, need to be added. Search the internet for more examples.

Exercise: Review what you have planned for your strategic plan. Work through the section on implementation timelines (above) again and prepare a timeline to show how your plan will be implemented. Choose your own way of showing the implementation steps, but make sure you include all that you will need to take.

Project: New corporate website					Team Leader: Emma S.				
PLANNING TASKS	Week 1	Week 2	Week 3	Week 4	Week 5	Week 6	Week 7	Week 8	Responsible.
1. Project scoping									
Briefing from team leader	▓								Emma
Brainstorm with communication team		▓							All
Set up internal users' reference group		▓							Holly
Reference group meeting on progress			▓						Holly, TJ
Discussion with senior executives				▓					Em, Jorja
Draft scoping paper					▓				Emma, Holly
Recommendations from reference group						▓			Ref group
Write final scoping paper							▓		Emma
Management approval								▓	CEO
IMPLEMENTATION TASKS	Week 1	Week 2	Week 3	Week 4	Week 5	Week 6	Week 7	Week 8	Responsible
2. Website design 3. Populate website 4. Test site 5. Seek feedback 6. Launch website 7. Evaluate project									

Figure 11.1 A simple Gantt

A project manager needs to identify all the steps involved in a project, the time taken to do them, which need to be done first and who is responsible for doing them. Having this information means deadlines can be met. Notes of meeting decisions and about progress should be kept, although there does not need to be a set of formal minutes unless that is an organisational requirement. Sometimes, ticking a box on a checklist will suffice, but it is important to make sure there is a record of decisions. Figure 11.2 is an implementation toolkit with examples of a project meeting report, and a checklist, you can use to manage your project.

In-house communication teams usually work to an annual program calendar, perhaps displayed on a large Gantt chart that sets out the dates on which individual activities will be planned and implemented. The calendar will show, for example, when the factory open day will be held; edition dates for the internal newsletter on the website; when the CEO's speech for the industry association annual conference is due to be written, approved and given; research and production dates for the annual report; when community consultation meetings will happen; and the date for the staff Christmas party. Practitioners responsible for individual activities in the program will have more detailed planning and implementation checklists.

FURTHER READING

Seitel, F.P. (2011), *The Practice of Public Relations*, 11th edn, Pearson, Upper Saddle River, NJ, ch. 5, esp. pp. 120–2.
Wilson, L.J. and Ogden, J.D. (2008), *Strategic Communication Planning for Effective Public Relations and Marketing*, 5th edn, Kendall Hunt, Dubuque, IA, ch. 8.

WORKING WITH CONSULTANTS

Some in-house communication teams are lucky to have graphic and web designers and social media specialists on the staff. They can often seek practical help from other skilled people in their organisation. Practitioners at a manufacturing company may, for example, be able to use the company's apprentices to build a display, or organise the facilities staff to move equipment, or the information technology people to set up the website. Most in-house communication teams, however, need outside specialists for services they cannot source internally.

Adequately briefing external contractors on what precisely is required of them ensures that what is needed is delivered, but also helps you to get an accurate cost for providing the service. A "brief" for external consultants needs to be like a strategic plan. It is like a contract (a formal contract will be signed later) specifying what the consultant must do and whether they will supply materials and arrange other services, like designers. Consultants base their quotes on the brief, so it needs to be accurate. A brief should include information that:

■ Identifies and analyses the situation, summarises research and outlines other activities in the same area that might have been implemented previously outlines goals and objectives

◼ Identifies target publics
   indicates messages
◼ Identifies the time frame in which the consultant's work and the total project need to be completed
   indicates the budget, including whether the organisation is exempt from taxes and other government charges
◼ Sets out how the consultant should respond to the brief, including the format (usually with a written response and a face-to-face presentation) and the time they have been given to prepare their response to the brief
   identifies the people with whom the consultant will most directly work.

Of course, some of this may be the task that the consultant is being engaged to do, but the brief should provide as much information about the situation as possible.

Often more than one consultant will be asked to tender for an organisation's business—a process called a "competitive pitch." Each consultancy should be individually briefed about the job they are pitching for, but the brief and all requirements should be the same. After the consultancies have responded, the decision about which proposal best meets the issues raised in the brief will be based on their creative solutions, the costs involved and, sometimes, how comfortable the client will feel working with the consultancy's team. After a consultant has been chosen, the organisation and the consultancy sign a contract detailing what will be done, by when and for how much.

On creativity

Graphic designers are creative people. That's how they make a living. They know how to translate your ideas into creative and practical solutions for websites, designs for printed material, logos, packaging and all the other material you'll need to produce your communication tools. They build their reputations on these creative solutions. But they do need to know exactly what is required. They can't provide a creative solution, or charge appropriately, if they do not know clearly what is expected of them. It is a good idea to provide a designer with a written brief and to schedule regular meetings to discuss progress.

Working with designers means treating them as fellow professionals who are skilled in their craft. Avoid telling them how to do their job. Tell them in a brief, in as much detail as possible, what you need so that they can use their creative skills to produce that product. A communication practitioner's task is not to design the product but to suggest a possible approach. For example, a communication tool for older target publics about a serious issue may require a classic approach, while something for Gen Zers might need a more relaxed and interactive social media solution. Leave it to the professional designer to interpret how this should be done. A mutually respectful professional relationship means designers will be open to ideas and suggestions for change after practitioners see what they propose.

WORKING THE SYSTEM

After all the research and analysis, development of goals and objectives, identification of target publics and communication pathways and selection of appropriate communication tools, decisions need to be made about:

- The budget and who approves it
  who will research, prepare and coordinate which parts of the implementation plan
- When communication tools will be produced and applied
  who will manage the project
- How it will be evaluated.

To coordinate this process, practitioners do not need to be management experts. But they do need to use common sense and to understand how all parts of a strategy work together in a system. Working the system—a rational sequence of things that need to be done—means that a strategic plan can be researched, developed and implemented in a coordinated way. We've already seen the sequence of strategic planning steps, the actions they involve and what each step involves in Figure 1.1 in Chapter 1. It is worth revisiting Figure 1.1 at this stage of your strategic planning journey.

When planning and writing a strategic communication plan, University of Canberra third-year public relations strategy student Alecia Slocombe highlighted the problems that can arise if the research, development and implementation of a strategy are not coordinated effectively. Alecia analysed an academic journal article based on research into the communication strategy used by the former Australian airline Ansett when it was grounded by aviation authorities in 2001 (Howell, 2006). The company closed shortly after the grounding. The researcher found:

- Ansett's crisis communication strategy was ineffectual, uncoordinated and ignored the company's values as well as original strategy goals.
  The messages that Ansett wanted to convey to its target publics were inconsistent and confusing to tertiary target publics (that is, the media and government)
- An organisation's management should have been united and should have supported a crisis communication strategy for a successful resolution to the problem. Tools were not directed towards important target publics and were a waste of resources.

For her analysis, Alecia used the strategy planning sequence in Figure 11.2 and the research findings to point out that the company appeared to be unprepared for the grounding despite months of safety concerns, and that an inconsistent approach to strategy implementation led to:

- Conflicting information being given by up to six company spokespeople
  a lack of action due to the CEO's absence overseas during the critical period

- Negative media coverage
blame-passing, zero customer service and short-term "fixes"
- Customer mistrust of the company, despite a US$30 million advertising campaign.

The Ansett case illustrates Mike Beard's (2007) point that systematic procedures reduce errors and create good internal and external impressions of the communication department. Beard says public relations managers "should be forward thinking, skilled in ... practice, ... a good manager—of people and resources and proficient at administration. Of course, they may have assistance, that's the essence of teamwork, but there is absolutely no excuse for sloppiness or disinterest in any aspect of work" (2007, p. xi).

TEAM LEADERSHIP

Leading a team can be difficult, especially when you need to ask tough questions or give frank assessments of performance. Effective teams need people to contribute openly to discussions. U.S. training consultant Keith Ferrazzi (2012) researched what helped teams at 50 companies to be candid in expressing views at meetings. Ferrazzi argues that it takes work to create respectful and honest team relationships. As a general approach, the brief recommendations from Ferrazzi's research can guide communication practitioners in leading team meetings:

- Break big meetings into smaller groups to promote brainstorming.
Designate a "Yoda"—someone whose job is to notice and speak up when something is being left unsaid.
- Allow what Ferrazzi described as "caring criticism" to promote positive feedback.

Strategic Plan Checklist: Implementation

Writing the implementation plan

Using the strategy template you started in Chapter 10, add, after Section 4, two new sections: Implementation and Evaluation. The Implementation section should include the budget, checklist and timeline (such as those provided in the implementation toolkit in Figure 11.2)—or the Gantt chart in place of a timeline you produced for the previous Strategic Plan Checklist in this chapter. Complete the Evaluation section when you've worked on the information in Chapter 12.

If you are already working full-time, and your strategy is for a real project, use your organisation's budget and timeline/checklist frameworks, and seek actual quotes from external suppliers for the work you need them to do.

If your strategy is being developed as part of a university assignment, develop these tools from the information in this chapter. There'll be no need for you to seek actual costs from suppliers unless you are instructed to do this.

At the end of this exercise, you should have a realistic implementation plan. All that is needed to complete the strategy is an evaluation plan (see Chapter 12) and for you to write an executive summary—your last task.

The tools in this section can help manage implementation of a communication strategy. Set them up as word processing documents. The budget and checklist templates can be used in your communication strategy project.

1: Project meeting report

Project: **Team leader:**

Meeting date:

Attendance: (Who was at the meeting)

Item/decision/action	Responsible
1: 2: 3: 4: 5: 6:	

Next meeting date:

2: A simple budget format

Project: **Team leader:**

BUDGET $XXXX

COSTS

Tool: Fill in the name of each tactic (e.g. New website) then fill in the appropriate details. Examples are given below.

Scope $XXXX

Design $XXXX

Populate $XXXX

Test $XXXX

Launch $XXXX
Do this for each tool and cost each part of the process. Examples are given below.

Total cost $XXXX

INCOME

Itemise expected revenue. Examples are given below.

Sponsorship $XXXX

Sales of promotional items $XXXX

Total income $XXXX

TOTAL (= Cost minus expected Income) $XXXX

3: Checklist or task list

Make sure every part of each task and the relevant dates are shown in the checklist.

Project: Team leader:

Task	Progress			Responsible
	Start	Due	Completed	
1. Website scoping with internal users. • Brainstorm ideas with communication team. • Establish reference group. • Meet individual users.	1 May	30 May	28 May	William
• Draft scoping paper. • Reference group meets; recommendations. • Submit final scoping paper to team leader.				
2.				
3.				
4.				
5.				
6.				
7.				
8.				
9.				
10.				
11.				
12.				

Figure 11.2 Implementation toolkit

These points are also useful for building and maintaining professionalism and in relationships with clients and contractors.

FURTHER READING

Beard, M. (2007), *Running a Public Relations Department*, 2nd edn, Kogan Page, London, esp. chs. 3 and 4, and the Public Relations Education Trust's training matrix in the Appendix, pp. 149–53.

Ferrazzi, K. (2012), Candor, Criticism, Teamwork, *Harvard Business Review*, 90(12), p. 40.

Howell, G. (2006), Ansett Airlines—Absolutely! Going, Grounded, Gone, *Asia Pacific Public Relations Journal*, 7, pp. 1–19.

Wilcox, D.L. and Cameron, G.T. (2012), *Public Relations Strategies and Tactics*, 10th edn, Pearson Education, Boston, MA, ch. 6, esp. pp. 156–9.

Chapter 12 examines the final formal part of a communication strategy—an evaluation plan—and discusses why it is necessary to evaluate.

CHAPTER EVALUATION

In this chapter, we explored two essential strategic communication implementation tools—budgets and task schedules—and shared some thoughts on managing a strategy.

To check your understanding of this topic, answer the following questions:

1. Why is a budget an important element of a strategic communication plan?
2. What are the important items of a budget? Why?
3. Why does a communication strategy need to include a schedule that shows the timelines for preparing and implementing tools?
4. How does a strategic communication plan work in a systematic way?
5. What skills are needed to manage the implementation of a communication strategy? Why?

TIME OUT: PLANNING COMMUNICATION PATHWAYS AND TOOLS

At this stage of our exploration, it is useful to take time to think about how planning decisions about communication pathways and tools link up to make a strategic plan as effective as possible.

Planning a communication strategy includes researching a situation analysis that sets out what the organisation does, the issues it faces, why they are important and what needs to be done about them (see Chapter 4 and Figure 4.2 on page 73). Having found all that out, the next step is to identify the people (target publics) who are important to your organisation in the context of those issues, and what they need to be told about them. Then you'll need to plan (a) communication goals and objectives that help the organisation deal with the issues you have identified and which link to the organisation's overall business plan, (b) pathways for reaching target publics and (c) tools for carrying messages. Table 9.1 (see page 167) lists factors you need to consider when you plan communication pathways and tools. Time Out Table 1 gives some examples (you could list many more) of pathways and tools that match these factors.

Time Out Table 1 Factors that determine communication pathways and tools

Factor: need to consider	Potential communication	
	Pathways	Tools
Reach: Number of people to receive messages	Uncontrolled media	Media releases
		Media conference
		Fact sheet
		Q and A sheet
		Backgrounder
		One-on-one journalist briefings
		Email
Argument needed to support messages	Controlled media	Own publications
		Website
		Blog
		Speech
		Podcast
		Display
		Email and attachment
Control: Of content, timing and distribution of messages	Controlled media	Own publications
		Website

Factor: need to consider	Potential communication Pathways	Tools
		Social media applications
		Sponsor event/group
		Display
		Speech
		Email and attachment
		Interactive media
		Social media applications
		Website
		Email dialogue
Sponsorship		Sponsor community group
		Sports team sponsorship
		Sponsor art exhibition
		Sponsor fun run/walk
Repetition: Frequency of message delivery	Blend of pathways	Mix tools to pathways
Or how many times publics will hear messages		Consider using Grunig's models (see below)—all, or some, to ensure messages are repeated through different pathways and tools
		You will need to consider timing implications for implementing tools in you planning
Efficiency: Best use of available resources	Uncontrolled media	Media release—potentially wide reach for the message at low cost
	Interpersonal media	Face-to-face meetings for a small target public group
	Controlled media	Using your own website, emails, publications and direct mail means you can reach a specific public, when you want to

Another way to do this could be to just use Grunig's four models. Time Out Table 2 shows examples of how this might work if you used the theory behind one or more of Grunig's models when you plan how you will implement your strategic plan. Remember that some strategic plans use only one of the models while some use all four. A decision about which of the models you want to use depends on the goals and objectives you are trying to achieve and the complexity of the issues with which you are dealing. Are you, for example, engaged in an informative campaign (perhaps supporting the launch of a new watch-like high-tech fitness gizmo linked to smart phones for young people) or a persuasive campaign planned to convince people to donate to a homeless people's charity?

Time Out Table 2 Examples of communication pathways and tools using Grunig's four models

Grunig's model	*Pathways*	*Examples of tools*
Press agentry	Uncontrolled media	Media releases
		Media conferences
		Interviews by journalists
		Fact sheets
		Backgrounders
		Q and A sheets
		Email
Public information	Uncontrolled media	Media releases
		Interviews by journalists
		Fact sheets
		Publications
		Email
	Interactive media	Website—feedback mechanism
		Social media applications
	Controlled media	Publications
		Advertising
		Website
Asymmetrical (or one-way)	Uncontrolled media	Media releases

Grunig's model	Pathways	Examples of tools
Communication		Media interviews
		Q and A sheets
		Static shopping mall display
	Sponsorship	Sponsor local community centre
		Sponsor the national ballet
	Controlled media	Organisation's own publications
		Website
Symmetrical (or two-way) Communication	Interpersonal media	Face-to-face meetings/talks
		Community meetings
		Staff at displays for dialogue
		Email and snail mail
	Interactive media	Social media applications
		Email
	Special events	Community meetings
		Staff at town hall display
		Open house site visits

These are examples only. Given the range of tools practitioners can use, you could list many more in each category. But it is interesting that as communication between an organisation and its publics becomes more symmetrical (or two-way) it enables dialogue. An example is the role of humble email. In press agentry, public information and asymmetrical communication, email is a one-way tool with no expectation that anyone will respond to it. Of course, good organisational media relations practice would mean that if a journalist did respond to your email with a question, you would reply as soon as possible with an answer. When communication is truly two-way and initiates a dialogue, email is a handy device for interaction between and organisation and its target publics. Time Out Table 2 also illustrates how using the mass media is essentially one-way communication practice. That is not to say that news reporting of your information won't start a dialogue. But it does illustrate how campaigns that rely solely on an uncontrolled media communication pathway may not be as effective as they could be.

Chapter 12

The Gemini factor

Evaluating strategic communication projects

Goal: To demonstrate the importance of evaluating strategic communication projects.

Objectives: This chapter will help you to:

■ Understand the need to evaluate strategic communication projects
Familiarise yourself with basic evaluation techniques
■ Write an evaluation plan for your strategic plan.

Principle: Evaluation is an essential component of strategic communication planning.

Practice: Practitioners evaluate the success of their projects in several ways.

For many professional team sports people, a Monday morning video session after the weekend match can be a nightmare, especially if the team lost. At these sessions, the coach replays the game, repeats the horrid bits and uses the video to point out the weaknesses that led to a defeat, or the strengths on which a win was built. At these sessions, just how the team played to, or ignored, the coach's carefully thought-out game plan is dissected, commented on, reviewed and argued about—sometimes with passion, because coaches are rarely entirely happy with a team's performance. After all, they are paid to make it even better next time—and to win the competition. The whole thing starts again later in the week, with a video session analysing the team's next opponent: how they play, their perceived weaknesses, the set-plays they use, who the game-breakers are and how they will be covered and how the new game plan will reflect this analysis.

The concepts on which this kind of review and match planning are based are like those used in strategic communication: that path of research, planning, implementation and **evaluation**. The four points in this path are often shown graphically as a circular timeline, with "research" at the top as the start point. Each point is linked to the previous one by a one-way arrow, the last from "evaluation" to

DOI: 10.4324/9781003317579-13

"research." The timeline demonstrates just how what is achieved in a strategic communication plan informs decisions on what to do next.

Evaluate "assess, appraise"; "find or state the number or amount of"; "find a numerical expression for" (*Australian Concise Oxford Dictionary*, 2004). An *evaluation* (also known as *summative* research) is the result of these activities. Evaluation is important in strategic communication because it assesses how well the project went and attempts to put a value, sometimes numerical, on the result. It is important to remember that an evaluation is research and utilises social sciences research methodologies.

For strategic communication practitioners, explaining how success will be measured is the vital final section of a strategic plan. This chapter discusses the importance of writing an evaluation plan as part of a strategy to demonstrate how outcomes and outputs will be measured against agreed strategic goals and objectives. At its simplest, an evaluation demonstrates how well you achieved your objectives. Evaluation could thus be described as "the Gemini factor," since objectives have twin uses, being both the first and last steps of strategic communication planning.

WHY EVALUATE?

To return to the professional sport analogy, game plans involve teams implementing set-plays, or using the natural talents of individual players to respond to an opposition move. Some teams play to complicated game plans that attempt to have a solution to every situation they are likely to encounter. Others allow players to read the game and respond accordingly. These are objectives set to achieve the goal of winning the match and are the yardstick by which the team is measured.

Nominating the yardstick for evaluating a strategic communication project is vital. This not only informs planning for what needs to be done next time, but it also gives clients and in-house managers assurance that the money they provided for a strategic communication project was effectively and efficiently spent. And if the strategy didn't do what was promised, why didn't it? That is, communicators need to be accountable for the money they are given, and to demonstrate good management (Gregory, 2009a).

The Research Methods Knowledge Base notes that the generic goal of most evaluations is to provide "useful feedback" to sponsors, donors, client groups, administrators, staff and other relevant constituencies, and that most often, feedback is perceived as "useful" if it aids in decision-making. (www.socialresearchmethods.net/kb/intreval.php)

Ronald Smith (2005) says that when evaluation is properly built into a strategy, it can increase effectiveness, an advantage that should appeal to bosses and clients.

Gyorgy Szondi and Rüdiger Theilman (2009) note that evaluation is essential and should be systematic and purposeful. Sadly, this doesn't always happen. Jim Macnamara (2012), who has specialised in evaluation throughout his practice and academic career, and is regarded as a world expert, writes that public relations is notorious for failing to evaluate in a systematic and rigorous way.

In a large organisation that has a corporate communication strategy covering several programs—that is, the programmed communication activities it does regularly every year—evaluations help with budgeting for the following year. Joep Cornelissen (2005) says that communication will continue to play an important role alongside finance and human resources in the overall strategic management of an organisation if it is perceived by senior management to be valuable and accountable.

Evaluation means using appropriate tools to measure what is achieved and to avoid relying on chance, intuition or guesswork. It is the systematic gathering, recording and analysing of data about the image, identity and reputation of the organisation from the perspective of publics who have an interest in it (Oliver, 2007).

PRACTITIONER VIEWS

Most communication practitioners agree that evaluation is necessary. However, Tom Watson and Paul Noble (2007) note considerable confusion about what evaluation means because it is a broad topic, so the use of evaluation and the application of effective techniques vary.

A significant survey of Australian, South African and US practitioners in 1994 by the International Public Relations Association (IPRA, 1994) found evaluation was more talked about than practised. Since then, several researchers (for example, Walker, 1994, 1997; Xavier et al., 2004; Simmons and Watson, 2005) have found an increased focus on evaluation in Australian public relations practice.

When they examined the evaluation techniques reported in 118 Australian award-winning programs, Robina Xavier and her team at the University of Technology in Queensland found that practitioners in Australia used an average of three evaluation methods in each program. However, practitioners appeared to favour *output* evaluation methods over *outcome* methods (see the discussion of outputs and outcomes in Chapter 7). This meant that evaluations were primarily based on media monitoring, response rates such as attendances at meetings, or call centre feedback. Few used communication audits. The most common outcome-evaluation methods were surveying to confirm changes in target public opinions, and activity outcome to measure the result of a program aimed at a particular target public.

Peter Simmons and Tom Watson reported similar findings from their 2005 study. They noted a "media relations–centric focus" to evaluation in Australian public relations practice. However, they also found that practitioners in government agencies were less likely to evaluate outcomes than were those working in consultancies, commercial organisations and not-for-profit groups. Practitioners working in not-for-profit groups were more likely than others to believe in the measurability of their work but, like those in government, were under less pressure to demonstrate results. Consultants were under pressure to evaluate, but they were more confident than other practitioners about the measurability of their work. Simmons and Watson reported that practitioners support evaluation but that the main barriers are time, lack of training and budget limitations. They found that practitioners would welcome:

- Cost-effective standard evaluation measures
  an evaluation model
- An industry-standard tool to measure evaluation of public relations campaigns.

Watson and Noble (2007) argue that effective evaluation needs starting points and objectives to set the basis of comparison between the situation before a campaign and the results a campaign achieves. These must be defined as part of the planning process. Thus, research has illustrated the point IPRA made in 1994: evaluation should be sufficient to prove that an activity is well directed, well implemented and achieves the desired result. Thus, evaluation is complex and varies according to a range of factors:

- There is no magic bullet or simple solution. Evaluation needs a sophisticated approach.
  Effective evaluation starts with effective objectives (see Chapter 7).
- Evaluation is a research-based discipline.
  Focus on impact—what publics do with information.
- Evaluation is user-dependent—performance is judged on criteria important to a client.
  Evaluation is also situation dependent.
- Be realistic—don't waste resources trying to achieve the ideal.

FURTHER READING

Oliver, S. (2007), *Public Relations Strategy*, 2nd edn, Kogan Page, London, ch. 7, pp. 104–18.

Simmons, P. and Watson, T. (2005), Public Relations Evaluation in Australia: Practices and Attitudes across Sectors and Employment Status, *Asia Pacific Public Relations Journal*, 6(2), at www.deakin.edu.au/arts-ed/apprj/vol6no2.php#8

Watson, T. (2006), Evaluation—Let's Get on with It, *PRism*, 4(2), at www.prismjournal.org/fileadmin/Praxis/Files/Journal_Files/Evaluation_Issue/EDITORIAL.pdf

Xavier, R., Mehta, A. and Gregory, A. (2006), Evaluation in Use: The Practitioner View of Effective Evaluation, *PRism*, 4(2), at www.prismjournal.org/fileadmin/Praxis/Files/Journal_Files/Evaluation_Issue/XAVIER_ET_AL_ARTICLE.pdf

Xavier, R., Patel, A. and Johnston, K. (2004), Are We Really Making a Difference? The Gap between Outcomes and Evaluation Research in Public Relations Campaigns, paper presented at the Australian and New Zealand Communication Association annual conference, University of Sydney, 7–9 July, at http://conferences.arts.usyd.edu.au/papers.php?first_letter=X&cf=3

IN THEORY: ON METHODOLOGY

Alan Bryman (2008) says that evaluation research asks whether an intervention (in our case, a communication strategy) achieved its anticipated goals, and he points to the use of both quantitative and qualitative methodologies for evaluation. He notes that while social science researchers have different opinions about using qualitative research in evaluations, there is nevertheless agreement that it is important to have an in-depth understanding of the context in which an intervention occurs. That suggests again that a properly researched situation analysis that provides the context for a communication strategy is vital.

Selecting the right methodology for an evaluation can be a problem. Watson and Noble (2007) suggest why when they identify six "intrinsic" problems in evaluation methodology. In brief, these are that:

- Campaigns are unique and planned for specific purposes
- Comparison groups are difficult to find because clients would not be happy leaving out half a target population to enable comparisons with a control group
- Variables outside a practitioner's control may impact on the target public
- Pre- and post-campaign data is needed for a methodologically sound evaluation
- Sometimes the person managing the campaign also does the evaluation, and this can lead to subjective judgments
- A plethora of techniques are available for evaluation.

What is important, however, is that accurately written objectives, and appropriate target publics, communication pathways and tools lead to an effective evaluation. That is, detailed strategy planning means a client knows how the campaign will be evaluated and what they can expect from it.

FURTHER READING

Bryman, A. (2008), *Social Research Methods*, 3rd edn, Oxford University Press, Oxford.
Macnamara, J. (2012), *Public Relations: Theories, Practices, Critiques*, Pearson, Sydney, pp. 388–404.

WHAT NEEDS TO BE MEASURED?

It is all starting to sound a bit complicated, but consideration of what needs to be measured helps to clarify the task. Communication evaluations measure how well objectives were achieved, responses to messages, and whether pathways and tools were appropriate. Evaluations should be based on four broad measurement categories, all of which work together to build a picture of how well a campaign was implemented. These are:

■ *Input*: the *formative* research and other information that was used in the initial program planning. That research should have directed the situation analysis and the identification of goals, objectives, target publics and messages.

output: a measurement of the frequency with which a program's *communication tools* were used. Output examples are the number of media releases issued, telephone enquiries received, speeches given, number of tweets you made or emails sent, people in an audience, visits to web pages, times the organisation was mentioned on radio or television or in newspapers or people who visited your display at an industry exhibition. Sometimes, practitioners report media coverage of their organisation by assessing whether individual stories were positive, negative or neutral towards the organisation. Measurements like these demonstrate that the work you said you would do was done. However, measuring outputs does not say anything about whether target publics received, processed, understood, accepted or acted on the messages you have written for the program

■ *Outtake*: a measurement of what a public might do with a tool. In other words, people might remember a message ("smoking is bad for your health") but not change their behaviour ("I recall the message, but I enjoy smoking, so I won't quit.")

outcome: the most important category and a measurement that shows whether a public changed its knowledge, attitudes and/or behaviour. Outcomes are the results you planned when you wrote goals and objectives. An example would be a change to a public policy after an organisation identified an issue in its environmental scanning and engaged in a mid- to long-term campaign for that change.

Measuring outcomes is also difficult because changes in knowledge, attitude and behaviour do not generally happen in the short term. It may take weeks, months or years for a practitioner to measure these changes. It is also generally more expensive to measure outcomes because *summative* research can involve in-depth surveying through polling, focus groups or other survey methods.

EVALUATION RESEARCH METHODOLOGY

In The Brief at the start of the book, we looked at 5Ws and H, one-word questions journalists ask about whatever it is they are reporting. To start your evaluation, you might ask questions like,

■ What issues that affect my client's organisation did I identify in the formative research that informed the strategy's approach? Were they relevant and appropriate?

Who were the target publics I identified? Were they the correct publics for the strategy? Are there other publics who are important that I did not identify?

- Where will I find that information?
  What kind of research methods will I need to evaluate the strategic communication plan?
- Why is this evaluation important?
  When will I do the summative, evaluative, research?
- How will the evaluation be used?
  Asking these questions will help you to work out how to approach your evaluation.

To undertake research for, and measure the success of, a communication strategy, it is vital that you have a proper understanding of research methodologies. That is why university communication degrees often include mandatory units that teach research methodologies, and others that encourage critical thinking and analysis. These units help students to understand how to use social science qualitative and quantitative methods to find things out, and to be able to work out what the results mean.

Many commercial research and monitoring firms sell evaluation services. Practitioners can also develop their own effective evaluation tools. However, whatever approach you take, evaluative research should go beyond measuring simple outputs like media coverage by generating data that indicates outcomes from strategic communication activities. That doesn't mean measuring outputs is not necessary, because a complete evaluation should demonstrate whether output objectives were achieved. That is, did you issue as many output tools as you said you would? Were your tools produced at a cost-effective price? And so on.

An understanding of research methodologies helps in planning an evaluation and to interpret the findings, irrespective of whether the research was conducted by an outside consultant. This interpretive role is part of the environmental scanning discussed in the early chapters.

Practitioners sometimes schedule evaluations at key points of an implementation timeline so that a project can be fine-tuned to ensure that it is still on track. Tom Watson and Paul Noble (2007) describe these points as "way stations," stopping places on a journey, and in a communication context the points at which refinements can be made to a campaign. Evaluative measurements taken at these points use the same methodologies applied to formative and summative research.

The British academic Sandra Oliver makes the important point that by using developments in audience and social psychology research tools and technology, evaluation is becoming more scientific (2007). David Dozier proposes a conceptual matrix (Table 12.1) for evaluation that practitioners can use to classify and report the impact of campaigns they manage (in Oliver, 2007).

Figure 12.1 shows a list of methods that can be used for evaluation—and for formative research. It includes the broad scope of areas practitioners can investigate and the range of methods available for this.

Table 12.1 Content and method in evaluation: Dozier's conceptual matrix

| | Content of evaluation | | |
Method	Preparation	Dissemination	Impact
Individualistic	Activities prepared according to professional standards of quality	Message dissemination evaluated by reactions of mass media professionals	PR impact evaluated with subjective qualitative "sense" of publics' reactions
Scientific	Activities prepared by application of scientifically derived knowledge of publics	Message dissemination evaluated by quantified measures of media usage	Public relations impact evaluated with objective quantitative measure of publics' reactions

Source: Adapted from Dozier, as cited in Oliver (2007), p. 105.

Category	Examples of what to measure	Research method examples
Outcomes Research to discover the campaign's outcomes will provide the most important measure of its success	Number who • change behaviours • change attitudes • objectives achieved/not achieved	Formal • quantitative and qualitative surveys • qualitative focus groups • interviews
Outtakes This is research to discover people who recall a campaign's messages but take no action	Number who • understand messages • retain messages • consider messages	Formal • quantitative and qualitative surveys (a mixed method approach) • Interviews Analyse formal feedback Media – including social media • monitoring • content analysis
Outputs Research to assess how successful output objectives were is measuring process, not acceptance of messages, or change	Number and type of messages that • reached publics • were published in news media Number of people who received messages Number of messages sent Costs within/over-Budget? Project delivered on time?	• distribution statistics and circulation numbers • Readership Financial analysis
Inputs This is generally formative research for planning a communication strategy.	What do target publics know, think, feel, need/want? How do publics receive messages? Performance of previous strategic plans • quality of message presentation • how appropriate were communication pathways? • were messages relevant to publics' needs? • Were communication tools appropriate? • were pathways and tools properly matched?	Informal: analysis by • communication specialists • academic experts and from • journal articles/specialist books • formal and informal feedback • secondary data identified by desk research • previous program evaluations • client briefs Formal qualitative/quantitative baseline surveys, focus groups and interviews

Figure 12.1 Research categories, measures and methods

EVALUATING MEDIA COVERAGE

Whether practitioners are working on issues in an organisation's market or non-market environment, in Horizon 1 or Horizons 2 and 3, clients are at the very least keen for mass news media coverage of their organisation's products, achievements, personalities or points of view. They smile when this happens, their colleagues comment about the coverage and egos are stroked. As the discussion about uncontrolled media communication pathways in Chapter 9 argued, generating media coverage is an important, but not the only, task for practitioners. When it happens, there's a requirement to demonstrate what it means beyond the fact that there's a media clipping, a video, a sound recording or a transcript to show off. How did potential readers and audiences react to it? Did the news coverage reach the intended target publics for whom messages were intended? Did anyone take any action? How can any of these be demonstrated? Answering these and other questions is often difficult, often expensive and often not attempted. But effective, in-depth evaluations of media coverage can produce useful data through answers to questions based on the following:

Share of voice: Was your organisation's point of view the first point made in the story? How much of the story reported the organisation's message? Was your organisation's view included in the story (sometimes it is not)? How much space or time was given to an opponent's views, or to background, compared with the organisation's views?

Opportunities to see (reach): What is the potential readership for this newspaper, or audience for the television or radio program? Did the relevant websites carry the story? Data about newspaper, television and radio readership and audiences is publicly available (through frequent television and radio ratings surveys, for example) or from media monitoring companies.

Target-to-story ratio: What was the ratio of a planned distribution of a release to what appeared, or was broadcast, or included on a website? Did the outlets that were targeted publish material from your release?

Prominence: How prominent was the story? Did it run on page 1 of the newspapers, or page 8? Was it broadcast early in the news bulletin, or did it get a tiny mention towards the end? Did the website run the story on the home page, or on another section?

Focus: Were the news frames used in the media coverage aligned with the organisation's point of view, or was the coverage framed by opponents' views?

Tonal analysis: Was media coverage positive towards the organisation, negative or neutral? Was there a difference in tone between coverage in newspapers, on television, posted to websites and on radio? Which was more favourable, which the most negative? Why would news publishers take that stance?

Behaviour, awareness and attitudinal analysis: Was there any change? Measuring how target publics change behaviour, awareness and attitudes requires opinion polling and analysis. However, it is possible, with some dedicated work, to analyse whether changes like these occurred in media coverage during the course of a campaign. For example, did media commentators who took an opposing view to that of the organisation before the campaign change their opinions during or after it? Did their attitude soften—that is, did they publish less critical opinions after hearing the organisation's view? Did more positive letters to the editor appear after the campaign than before it? Were blog posts less trenchant and more supportive?

Answering these questions takes time and effort, but it can be done. Media monitoring companies will do it for a fee; practitioners can set up a simple database or spreadsheet to do it (see the exercise at the end of this section).

The value added for clients from collecting these answers is determined by how you match them up in a report. For example, linking ("cross-tabbing" in database-speak) target-to-story ratios with a tonal analysis, prominence and share-of-voice data can produce a rich assessment of the media relations effort. You might be able to report that

> 95 per cent of the media releases issued were carried in the media outlets selected for the campaign [target-to-story ratio]. Of these, 60 per cent were positive and only 10 per cent negative [tonal analysis], but all were carried in the first three pages of newspapers, and in the early part of news broadcasts on radio and television [prominence] and in all but 5 per cent of coverage Ideal Widgets' view on this issue was the dominant share of voice (averaging 85% share of voice).

A report like that, including additional analysis based on other cross-tabs, would delight a client by delivering rich details about the campaign's success and would be far more valuable, and a better demonstration of your accountability and management, than a simple measure of the possible cost of media coverage (see the following box).

A big no-no: putting a financial value on media coverage

Sometimes clients ask practitioners how much it would cost them if they had to pay for the space given to coverage of a media release in the newspaper, on television or on radio. This is known as an "advertising value equivalent" (AVE)— an "equivalent" because clients don't pay for that media coverage. An AVE is calculated by multiplying the number of column centimetres, or seconds, the release was given by what it would cost for that space or time. Clients and managers understand that financial value and think this is a great way of showing how good coverage from a media release is: all that free publicity that would have cost them a lot if they'd had to pay for an advertisement. And after all, so many people read a newspaper, or watch the telly (reach) that they would have all read or watched the story.

However, this "evaluation measure" is at best an indication of output only and is widely criticised by scholars and senior practitioners because it doesn't prove anything except a potential cost. Good coverage of a media release, or a speech, or an event, or a product launch, can be valuable and effective. AVEs, however, do not prove the coverage was effective as they do not answer any of the questions posed in the previous section. Evaluating via AVEs is invalid, undermines the worth of professional communication and borders on being unethical.

FURTHER READING

Johnston, J., and Glenny, L. (2021), *Strategic Communication: Public Relations at work, Routledge*, London, esp. chp. 6.

Watson, T. and Noble, P. (2007), *Evaluating Public Relations: A Best Practice Guide to Public Relations Planning, Research and Evaluation*, Kogan Page, London, esp. ch. 2.

MAKING AN EVALUATION WORK

Knowing what to measure well before it is measured is the key to evaluation. That theme was pursued by Patti Nelson Andrews, an American academic, who used her accountancy background to research how several key US companies judged the effectiveness of their communication efforts. While her research was conducted a long time ago, it is nevertheless still useful when thinking about how to make the evaluation of a strategic communication plan work. Andrews (1985) found that most of the companies investigated in the research had public relations goals that could be classified into three distinct categories:

■ To gain and maintain credibility and legitimacy
   to facilitate timely and appropriate responses
■ To have a positive financial impact.

Andrews proposed that an evaluation of a communication plan should:

■ Be rational, understandable and simple
   take account of the dilemma that communication directors have more responsibility than authority
■ Deal explicitly with the difficulty of knowing with confidence that there is a true cause and effect between action and results
   be flexible and recognise that the communication time horizon can vary from a few days for a crisis to many years for an intractable issue.

Andrews' last point is true for strategic communication planned to deal with emerging issues over the mid- to long-terms.

Andrews' approach demonstrates the importance of writing meaningful goals and precise, measurable objectives. That means an evaluation will be rational, understandable and simple. Equally important is the link between objectives and *communication pathways* and *tools*. Remember that a communication pathway is the way an organisation will deliver the important information it wants to give to its publics; tools are the "packages" by which those messages will be delivered. If an objective is to increase awareness of an organisation's views on climate change, pathways and tools should be selected for specific publics who have an interest in that issue and can take action to determine an outcome or influence other publics. That means assessing whether pathways and tools were appropriate to achieving the objective.

WRITING AN EVALUATION PLAN

An evaluation plan need not be long, but it does need to identify how you will analyse success by describing how you will measure outputs, outtakes and outcomes. You need to consider why there'll be an evaluation and what will be measured. See Figure 12.1.

The plan may involve qualitative and quantitative methods and include desk research (perhaps a content analysis of daily media clippings to generate output and outcome data) or a series of post-campaign focus groups using an external expert to determine whether there has been a change in awareness, understanding, attitude or behaviour.

When you write your evaluation plan, you need to decide which of these methods, or combination of methods, is appropriate for what you need to measure. Objectives that deal with *reputation*, *relationships* and *tasks* may require different evaluation methods.

Table 12.2 illustrates a simple way of preparing an evaluation plan using one objective as an example—and assuming your project has more than one goal and associated objectives. Add it as the next element in the strategic plan matrix you have been developing.

A mix of *qualitative* and *quantitative* methods will enhance an evaluation. Where possible, use quantitative methods to demonstrate percentage changes and other outcomes and qualitative feedback to explain the changes. Include output measures—it is legitimate to report that you did the things you said you would do within budget and on time. Comments from journalists about how quickly you responded to their questions are a valid qualitative measure. So, too, are unsolicited comments about the campaign you are evaluating. It is important that you include negative findings and comments in an evaluation. This is ethical practice,

Table 12.2 Evaluation plan example

Goal 1: *(Write goal here)*

Objectives	Proposed evaluation method
To increase awareness among primary target publics [identify them] of the organisation's views on this issue by 50 per cent in three months	1. Repeat benchmark survey of target publics to determine whether awareness increased by 30 per cent. 2. Conduct focus groups with primary publics to determine their level of knowledge about this issue 3. Monitor mass news media to assess positive/negative/neutral coverage and the organisation's share of voice 4. Audit campaign material to assess whether it was appropriate for target publics
[Write objective 2 here.] [Write objective 3 here.]	

---

it provides balance, and often legitimate reasons why something didn't work. And knowing why something didn't work is a valuable lesson for the next project.

EVALUATING A CORPORATE STRATEGIC COMMUNICATION PLAN

An evaluation of each goal and its objectives links with those for other goals and objectives, thus building a total picture of how successful the whole project has been. This concept is equally important for evaluating a corporate strategic communication plan. This is the coordinated program of regular activities implemented each year, often reflected in the way the communication area is functionally organised. For example, the Director, Corporate Communication may be responsible for a department comprising separate staff for media relations, publications, the website and social media, advertising, community relations, customer services, special events and research and strategic planning. Often CEOs and other senior managers don't have time to drill down into the details of how successful each individual project was over the course of a year. Their time will be limited to a report about how the overall department performed, information that they will use when it comes to setting annual budgets and assessing managers'—and your—work performances. There is a need, then, to evaluate the whole communication department's performance.

Patti Nelson Andrews' (1985) schema for doing this is a useful guide. Her approach is to divide the total number of activities into discrete levels—we called them Program, Components and Activities in Table 4.3 (Chapter 4).

This reflects "program budgeting," in which departments or business units (programs) are funded as a whole and it is the responsibility of the program manager to allocate specific component and activity budgets. It is also a useful way of showing how the department's work team is structured.

In this approach, each level should have its own "mini" strategic plan, linked to the corporate communication strategy which will reflect the overall strategic goals and objectives of the organisation. That is, each level contributes not only to the success of the strategic communication plan, but also to the overall success of the organisation.

Andrews proposes that the individual evaluations of *activities* (or tools) could be combined to deliver an evaluation of the *component* to which they belong. All results for *components* could in turn be combined to produce an overall assessment of the performance of the *program*. A range of quantitative and qualitative measures (like those identified in Figure 12.1) can be used to evaluate each level of the framework.

EVALUATION PUZZLES

Scholars regularly research questions about how often and how well practitioners evaluate. Findings from some of this research are cited earlier in this chapter, along with the relevant readings. The concept of "return on investment" as an evaluation measure has been a research puzzle. How can practitioners, particularly in public relations, demonstrate a financial return for the funding provided for that activity? Similarly, how can the impact of social media use be measured? What does the impact of social media on the way in which news is gathered mean for communication practice? Often, marketing and advertising practitioners can identify bottom-line dollar impacts of what they do. An increase in sales of a new breakfast cereal during and after an advertising campaign suggests the campaign worked. Regularly reading discipline-specific academic journals can help identify the latest research. Examples of research related to these evaluation puzzles are listed in the further reading below.

FURTHER READING

Bajkiewicz, T.E., Kraus, J.J. and Hong, S.Y. (2011), The Impact of Newsroom Changes and the Rise of Social Media on the Practice of Public Relations, *Public Relations Review*, 37(3), pp. 329–31.

DiStaso, M.W., McCorkindale, T. and Wright, D.K. (2011), How Public Relations Executives Perceive and Measure the Impact of Social Media in their Organizations, *Public Relations Review*, 37(3), pp. 325–8.

A useful site for exploring case studies and evaluative techniques is the World Advertising Research Centre's, at www.warc.com.

Chapter 13 will draw the themes of this book together by exploring the role of strategic communication counsellors. This role, usually a function of the communication director, or practice leader, is responsible for strategic planning for each of the horizons to deal with issues in the market and non-market environments.

Strategic Plan Checklist: Evaluation

Write your evaluation plan

This exercise is designed to help you develop an evaluation plan for your strategic communication project. It builds on the exercises you've completed in previous chapters.

First, answer these questions:

1. Why is this project being evaluated?
2. Who wants to know whether the project was successful or not?
3. What specific questions need to be answered?
4. How should the information needed for the evaluation be collected and analysed?
5. What resources (money, people, technology) are available for this task?

Second, using Table 12.2 as a guide, set up a document you can include in your plan. Enter the goals and objectives.

Use the answers to the questions to rewrite your objectives into positive statements that, step by step, provide a method for collecting the data you need after your project is implemented to show how successful it was. These statements show how you will measure the changes you want to achieve by using the methods you identify in your answer to question 4 above, as illustrated by the example in Table 12.2.

When you have completed this exercise, add it to your plan based on the template in Chapter 10.

You should now have a complete communication strategy. But it will need an executive summary and you'll need to fill in the page numbers in the table of contents.

Write an executive summary for your plan by *summarising*:

- The issue the plan deals with and why it is important
- Research findings—briefly
- What you are trying to achieve based on the research: what is the plan is trying to do
- The timeline and budget for implementation.

Limit your executive summary to one page of clear and concise language that deals only with the important points.

CHAPTER EVALUATION

This chapter was designed to demonstrate the importance of evaluation, and the need to include a plan for doing this in a communication strategy.

Review your understanding of this topic by answering:

1. What principles should guide the evaluation of a strategic communication plan?
2. Why would a mix of quantitative and qualitative research results enhance an evaluation of a strategic communication project?
3. What information can be used to assess the impact of media coverage?
4. What are six research methods that could be used for an evaluation?
5. What are the most important results that an evaluation should measure? Why?
6. Why do AVEs provide only basic information in an evaluation?
7. Would using AVEs in an evaluation be ethical practice? Why or why not?

Chapter 13
Strategic communication counselling

Goal: To explore the role of a strategic communication counsellor.

Objectives: This chapter will help you to:

- ■ Understand the importance of counselling as a strategic communication function
- ■ Recognise different levels of communication practice
- ■ Explain the strategic direction of your planning project.

Principle: Chief executives and other managers regularly seek communication advice from senior practitioners.

Practice: Communication counsellors need to understand management and organisational environments.

Most senior practitioners, the leaders who head up communication teams, spend a great deal of time giving advice. Unlike the people in their teams who write a lot, plan, meet clients and contractors, set up events and talk to journalists, senior practitioners interact directly, and daily, with the corporate management team. It is not that senior practitioners don't write, organise events, brief journalists or deal with clients. They do, but their experience and knowledge of the organisation and its internal and external environments, or client's business and issues, mean they have a special role. Someone always needs advice on how to promote a product, handle an issue, resolve a crisis, understand cultural diversity (including the need to consider minorities) and decide if, when and how to speak to the media. In consultancies, practice leaders identify new business opportunities and liaise with existing clients. Often in-house communication practice leaders become their organisations' representative at industry forums, at conferences and community meetings, and with politicians and bureaucrats. Their role spans the organisation and its external environments. Often, a senior practitioner will have an office on the corporate floor, not far from the chief executive. They know the top people in the organisation: its board directors, its executive and its main operational managers. They are comfortable in the rarefied environment of the executive suite because they understand how it works and the pressures it imposes on everyone who works there, or who needs to work with this dominant coalition. They'll know a virtual "who's who" of people who matter in the industry, and the external stakeholders who are vital to the organisation's success, like politicians, regulators, media commentators, activists and the leaders of the communities in which the organisation has facilities. It is likely they also know the security guards; those who run the warehouse, maintain the organisation's infrastructure and clean the offices; and many of those who produce its products.

Counsellor a professional who is trained to advise others. Lawyers, psychologists, social workers and accountants give guidance and advice in the special areas of expertise. In the United States, barristers are described as counsellors. In professional strategic communication practice, advice given to chief executives and other managers about dealing with issues can be described as counselling. People "take counsel" when they ask for advice.

THE COMMUNICATION COUNSELLOR'S ROLE

Senior practitioners have a special relationship with chief executives. It is a relationship built on trust. Lynette McDonald and Aparna Hebbani (2011) say these relationships determine whether practitioners are viewed as skilled technicians or strategic **counsellors**. Many practitioners in these roles comment about how their chief executives often just want someone to talk to about things in general, or to use them as sounding boards, and sometimes as confessors. They often become the confidants of the chief executive, in much the same way that coaches do for their teams, and media advisers do for politicians. This is a role not always shared by others in the management team, even by those who are functionally senior to the communication director. It is a privileged relationship built on a practitioner's professional and interpersonal communication abilities, reputation, knowledge of what works and what doesn't, critical analysis skills, awareness of how the wider world "ticks" and ability to keep confidences. A sound knowledge of communication theory and the nature of the organisation's publics, and how and when to segment them, is vital. They get on with people, but they know how to debate, often taking an opposing view to that of other executives, especially the lawyers, when that is needed to protect or advance the organisation's interests. Above all, counsellors know how to listen.

Working in these roles is not easy. Delivering good news to the executive suite doesn't require courage; announcing bad news does, and that happens, especially in issues management. It is often said that the counselling role of senior practitioners means they are the "devil's advocate" of an organisation, the person who takes a particular position in a discussion to test the validity of the original argument. Although clichéd, it is nevertheless an apt description for a job that involves advising top people on how to handle public policy issues that impact on the organisation's reputation, credibility and corporate social responsibilities, or an issue that is emerging as something the organisation has not before contemplated.

In 1935, the famous British philosopher Bertrand Russell published his *Sceptical Essays* (1966), one of which explored his reflections about whether people could act rationally. Russell thought that to hold a rational opinion involved taking account of all relevant evidence before adopting a belief. He argued that differences of opinion on practical matters came about first because people had different desires about outcomes, and second because of variations in how they believed those desires could be achieved. Thus, some people persuade themselves to act in ways in which they would not act if they did not have a particular desire, and which are contrary to how someone without that desire would act. In many ways, Russell was describing the challenge counsellors face when they are required to advise the dominant coalition on a course of action. There are almost always senior people in those conversations who have different views and different solutions, sometimes because they have different goals (Russell's "desires"), and often because they regard themselves as communication experts, even though they have no qualifications. That is the kind of tricky situation that counsellors must negotiate.

Communication counsellors thus need to be detached and well informed, and to have a good network of contacts. They need to be brave when they raise issues and pass on information and advice. Writing about public relations, Jim Macnamara (2012), an academic who has worked in senior practice roles, describes counselling as one of the oldest models for that discipline and, with press agentry, one of the "bookends" of practice. Macnamara says requirements for the job are:

- Understanding of management and negotiation skills
  ability to mediate and to synthesise diverse, sometimes conflicting, interests
- Sound knowledge of communication studies.

So, theory counts as much as professional skills and the ability to engage in critical analysis when practitioners take on counselling roles, especially when they are interpreting an organisation's non-market environment, the space in which public policy issues play out. Successful counsellors are knowledgeable about:

- The business and the industry of which it is a part
  the organisation's competitors
- People who are important to it
  issues the organisation faces and may need to deal with in the mid- and long terms.

They advise on how communication strategy and practice can help to deal with all these.

PROFESSIONAL PRACTICE: VENUS OR MARS?

In the world of professional practice—where a common pragmatic view is that we need to do the job, so do it and forget theory—not everyone agrees with the idea that scholarship can help. Academics are interested in what drives professional practice and explaining the frameworks, or paradigms, in which practitioners work. They ask the simple "why" and "how" questions about professional practice and try to explain the answers in terms of what is known about how and why people communicate, and how management theory can help explain all this.

A strategic counselling role reflects one of two **paradigms** for public relations practice, defined by James Grunig (2009) as either:

- An *interpretive or symbolic paradigm*, which takes a tactical approach to influencing how publics interpret organisations, and which emphasises messages, publicity and media relations, or
  a *strategic management or behavioural, paradigm*, which focuses on communication executives' participation in decision-making, and which emphasises two-way communication and a consideration of the problems of publics and management in that decision-making.

Paradigm "an example or pattern, especially one underlying a theory or methodology" (*Australian Concise Oxford Dictionary*, 2004).

Larissa Grunig (2008) uses the metaphor of a "thinking heart" to describe how public relations people legitimate the concerns of internal and external publics, and argues that thinking through plans, and how they'll measure effectiveness, is an approach that builds practitioner credibility.

Each of these paradigms and the views of many scholars and commentators about professional practice are based on theoretical approaches developed from sustained research. Yet it seems that technical and tactical practice, rather than strategic practice developed from research, dominates the way the communication profession goes about its daily tasks. Mahoney (2022) argued it was curious that this modern "normative approach" to professional communication practice was "... tactical alchemy which does not resolve long-term issues" (p. 52).

Dutch scholar Betteke van Ruler (2005) investigated the puzzle of why practitioners did not seek support from academics, especially to help build higher standards of public relations practice. Van Ruler suggests, in a play on the title of a famous relationship manual, that this gap might mean practitioners come from Venus while scholars are Martian. Nevertheless, van Ruler uses four historical models of professionalisation (see Table 13.1) to develop a **typology** that illustrates who decides what knowledge is needed for each professionalisation model (see Figure 13.1).

Typology the study of "types." So, van Ruler's (2005) typology shows four types, or models, of professional practice. All the discussion about strategy and professional practice in this book can be defined by van Ruler's "knowledge model" (see Table 13.1).

Table 13.1 Van Ruler's four historical models of professionalism

Model	View of professionalism
Knowledge	Professionalisation is seen as the development of an organised group of experts who implement scientifically developed knowledge through a cluster of tasks defined by the professional group to deliver a unique contribution to the well-being of the client and the progress of society.
Status	Professionalisation is seen as the development of an organised elite, who use general and specific knowledge on a cluster of tasks defined by the professional group to gain status, power and autonomy for their profession.
Competition	Professionalisation is seen as the development of experts who gain value for their clients by implementing those scientifically developed models that match the demands of the client and the determinants of the problem through a cluster of tasks negotiated with the client, and in permanent competition with other professionals.
Personality	Professionalisation is seen as the development of experts who gain value for their clients by their commitment and their personality, their creativity and their enthusiasm for a cluster of tasks negotiated with the client.

Source: Adapted from van Ruler (2005), p. 161.

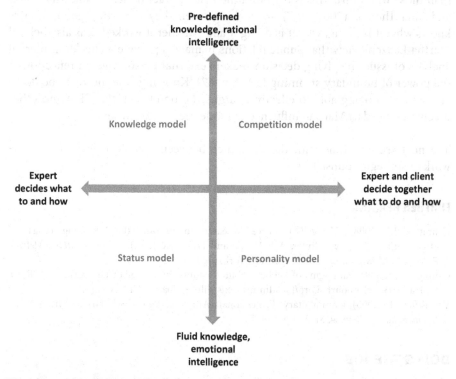

Figure 13.1 Van Ruler's typology of professionalism models

Source: Adapted from van Ruler (2005), p. 165.

Strategic Communication's approach to planning and writing a communication strategy is firmly grounded in the knowledge model quadrant of Van Ruler's typology. This is also the quadrant that reflects the essential nature of successful strategic communication counsel and David Dozier's (in Oliver, 2007, p. 105) evaluation methodology based on a scientific approach matrix (see Chapter 12, Table 12.1). Understanding what van Ruler's typology and Dozier's matrix mean are essential if practitioners are to be effective strategic counsellors. That is, chief executives and other senior managers look for sound, evidence-based advice, not gut feelings. Practising this vital senior role on the basis of the "knowledge model" means a strategic counsellor will have the facts about a situation and provide advice accordingly. It works effectively with the approach defined in the "competition model" and both will deliver sound, informed, strategic advice and outcomes that can be properly evaluated. The arguments of both van Ruler and Dozier are important examples of how a theory based on scholarly research can inform professional practice.

Despite what might happen on Venus, success in convincing the dominant coalition about a course of action to address an issue in the non-market environment, and for horizons 1 and 2, requires more than technical skill. Communication counsellors who are knowledgeable about theoretical perspectives, and who use that knowledge to support practice decisions, are more likely to be successful than those who don't. This is the point the British practitioners Frank Albrighton and Julia Thomas (2001, p. 7) are making when they write that good practice knows what it is doing, why it is doing it and whether it worked. It is also behind Martha Lauzen's view that public relations managers provide a check on internal analysis of issues by giving decision-makers external perspectives, a reflection of the power of boundary spanning (1997, p. 67). Knowing what needs to be done, and why, and being able to effectively argue the point with the CEO and other executives, needs a Martian influence to moderate practice from Venus.

The next section deals with the difference between technical practice and the work of strategic counsellors.

FURTHER READING

Grunig, L.E. (2008), Using Qualitative Research to Become the 'Thinking Heart' of Organisations, in B. van Ruler, A.T. Verčič and D. Verčič (eds.), *Public Relations Metrics: Research and Evaluation*, Routledge, New York, pp. 120–36.

Grunig, J.E. (2009), Paradigms of Global Public Relations in an Age of Digitalisation, *PRism*, 6(2), at www.prismjournal.org/fileadmin/Praxis/Files/globalPR/GRUNIG.pdf

Van Ruler, B. (2005), Commentary: Professionals Are from Venus, Scholars Are from Mars, *Public Relations Review*, 31(2), pp. 159–73.

DOING THE JOB

Giving high-level strategic advice is only part of the job of those who take on practice leadership roles. Senior practitioners need to manage a team—and to plan and write the communication strategy. It is useful, then, to look at the technical and management functions.

Technical practice

Delphi research in which experts in a field discuss an issue several times with the goal of reaching a consensus about it. Delphi research usually takes longer than other research techniques, and participants generally do not know the specific views of others.

Beginning practitioners leave university with skills to take on their first jobs as communication technicians, in which they prepare the tools that implement pathways: researching for and writing and editing collateral, producing the staff newsletter, managing the website, posting to the blog and various social media, organising events and answering questions from publics. First jobs often mean working in integrated marketing communication and delivering on strategic plans prepared by others. More senior practitioners specialise in functions that can also be described as technical practice. These include media relations, in which practitioners manage relationships with external media people, and provide advice on devising and implementing uncontrolled media communication pathways. Others take on roles in which they manage communication pathways and tools between the organisation and its external publics through community consultation and major events.

Senior practice

Working at senior levels, either in house or in a consultancy, involves professional and skills leadership, managing people and issues and program planning. People at this level:

- Prescribe solutions to communication problems based on boundary spanning and environmental scanning
  interpret issues
- Mediate between the organisation and its publics
  advise management.

Technical and senior practice roles are not always discrete or delineated. Often one practitioner in a small organisation combines the functions of both, seeking help from external consultants when it is needed.

Michael Seibert and Michael Harris (2004) developed a list of 34 competencies that people who counsel small-to-medium business enterprises (SMEs) should hold. They developed their list using a modified version of the **Delphi technique** with a group of SME management-counselling experts. The competencies they identified relate to knowledge, skills and attitudes, and many are applicable to the

Table 13.2 Strategic communication counselling competencies

Skills	Knowledge	Attitudes
Listening and questioning	Strategic management	Integrity, trust, and credibility
Relationship management	General business knowledge	
Critical thinking	Environmental scanning	Collaborative with peers and clients
Strategic thinking	(And, we should add knowledge of communication theory, practice, and strategic planning; research methods)	Self-directive learner
Goal and objective setting		Empathetic towards client
External scanning		
Team building		Positive and open-minded
SWOT analysis		

work of strategic communication counsellors. Table 13.2 distils the broad competencies required by strategic communication counsellors from the framework identified by Seibert and Harris.

FURTHER READING

McDonald, L.M. and Hebbani, A.G. (2011), Back to the Future: Is Strategic Management (Re) emerging as Public Relations' Dominant Paradigm? *PRism*, 8(1), at www.prismjournal.org/fileadmin/8_1/mcdonald_hebbani.pdf

Seibert, M. and Harris, M. (2004), The Identification of Strategic Management Counseling Competencies Essential for Small Business Counsellors: An Exploratory Study, in United States Association for Small Business and Entrepreneurship, *2006 Proceedings*, at usasbe.org/knowledge/proceedings/proceedingsDocs/USASBE2006proceedings-Seibert%20-%20ESO.pdf

Sison, M.D. (2009b), Whose Cultural Values? Exploring Public Relations' Approaches to Understanding Audiences, *PRism*, 6(2), at www.prismjournal.org/fileadmin/Praxis/Files/globalPR/SISON.pdf

COUNSELLING FOR THE NON-MARKET ENVIRONMENT

A key role of counsellors is to advise on how the organisation should manage issues that arise in the non-market environment. These are generally public policy issues that occur outside an organisation's direct market of customers, suppliers and competitors but nevertheless impact on its ability to achieve its goals (see Chapter 2).

Dealing with non-market issues often means finding communication solutions for day-to-day implementation (Horizon 1). Organisations attain a value-added benefit from strategic counselling for the longer term through the identification and analysis of issues in their non-market environments in the mid- and long terms (Horizons 1 and 2). That's because this kind of analysis alerts organisations to issues well ahead of when they'll emerge and so enables planning to deal with them. That in turn often prevents a crisis. For example, a state government might propose amendments to the building code to tighten the rules about acceptable standards for roof trusses in manufacturing plants. A prudent strategic counsellor for a manufacturer would flag that as an emerging issue that might impact on the company. That would lead to some research about the security of the manufacturer's factory roofs and the preparation of a communication plan to deal with this public policy issue before it becomes a safety problem for the company.

Van Ruler's knowledge model and the counselling competencies identified by Seibert and Harris illustrate what is needed for issue analysis in the non-market environment. The key words are:

- *Knowledge*: of the environment and the business flowing from environmental scanning and SWOT analysis; of professional communication
  skills: to decide what needs to be done and how it should be done, based on strategic thinking and critical analysis, listening and questioning and an understanding of developed knowledge
- *Attitudes*: integrity, a commitment to ethical and collaborative practice, professionalism.

A SENSE OF ACHIEVEMENT

Working as a senior communication counsellor brings significant job satisfaction. Daily tasks are rarely mundane; situations are constantly changing and often challenging; the focus is on supporting senior colleagues and guiding others, and there's always a sense of making a positive difference as part of the management function. That sense of achievement comes from knowing a job well done is based on an understanding of:

- Issues and target public attitudes, and their actual, or potential, impact on the organisation
  how to generate changes in opinions and behaviours
- The ways in which public policy issues are debated and resolved in society
  how to research, plan and implement strategic communication
- The role of evaluation to demonstrate success
  a communication counsellor's privileged role.

This chapter has discussed the role of senior counsellors who advise the dominant coalition on responses to issues and in planning and leading the implementation of communication strategies. This is the final step in this exploration of the practical process for preparing strategic communication plans. That process is based on theoretical principles applied in the context of how public policy issues emerge and impact on organisations in mid- to long-term business planning horizons. Dealing with current issues is an essential *tactical* role of professional communication practice, and the process explored here helps in that, but thinking and planning *strategically* builds a framework for sustained success.

CHAPTER EXERCISE

How would you counsel this client?

You are the communication director of an international travel company, Top Notch Tours, which specialises in arranging overseas holidays for young people who have just graduated from university. Top Notch has its headquarters in your capital city. For many years, one of the favourite your young clients wanted to visit was Maya Bay in Thailand. This is not surprising, given the beautiful beach in this serene cove. And it has been one of Thailand's most popular tourist destinations.

However, Maya Bay was described as the beach that was loved to death, such was the impact of tourists on the beach, coral and the waters of the cove. When they became concerned about damage to the Bay in 2018, Thai authorities closed it for tourism so it could be rehabilitated. Maya Bay re-opened for tourism in 2020.

You CEO wants advice on how Top Notch Tours can responsibly and ethically re-start its business taking university graduates to Maya Bay. Research the issue by first reading the story at https://edition.cnn.com/travel/article/maya-bay-thailand-recovery-c2e-spc-intl/index.html

Find out more about Maya Bay and tourism with further desk research.

Then, to prepare your advice to the CEO, answer these questions:

1. What should we tell our customers about Maya Bay's recent environmental history?
2. Should we offer advice on how customers should behave at the Bay?
3. Do we have a professional ethics requirement to explain as much as we can about the Bay's history of environmental damage?
4. How should we tell our customers?
5. Would Top Notch's reputation be damaged if we did not disclose what has happened to Maya Bay, and why?
6. How serious would that damage be—and how long would it take to repair that reputational damage? What would we need to do to repair the damage?

CHAPTER EVALUATION

All the Chapter Evaluations in *Strategic Communication* have been examples of a qualitative methodology: seeking your opinion. For the last evaluation, assess your understanding of the role of strategic communication counsellors, by answering the following questions:

1. How does strategic communication counselling add to an organisation's ability to respond to issues?
2. Why do senior counsellors need to understand the different levels of communication practice?
3. What personal competencies would assist a strategic communication counsellor to advise senior management on a public policy issue?
4. Why do chief executives and other managers regularly seek communication advice from senior practitioners?
5. Why is it important for communication counsellors to understand management and organisational environments?

A reflection

So, we've done it—completed a journey exploring strategic communication and attempted to write a plan for the case your selected right at the start of the book. Now is the time to reflect on what it all means.

To start that reflection, let's think about the plots of John Le Carré's spy novels. They are rarely simple. To understand what his principal character, the clever and cerebral spymaster George Smiley, is doing and experiencing as the stories weave through plot and sub-plot takes concentration, almost at the level Smiley himself applies. Smiley is, of course, trying to unravel and explain mysterious, sometimes traitorous, situations. Unlike his opponents, he does it mostly without force, but always through research, analysis, deduction, intuition, historical knowledge and hard work.

Then issues we've dealt with in this exploration have not been in Le Carré's league. But resolving them requires similar skills to those Smiley uses on his cases. The issues organisations face can be mysterious until they are investigated and unravelled. Conducting research and analysis to understand what issues mean in each situation is the starting point for strategic communication planning. The results of research, analysis and historical knowledge of an organisation and how the world outside it works lead to informed decisions about how to communicate about the issues it faces.

Here we've examined why decisions to communicate are made, how messages can be effectively given to people who share issues with organisations, what techniques can best do that, when they should be applied and how we'll know they've worked. In doing that, we have, almost Smiley-like, delved deeper to think about strategic communication in a new way: how it works in the mid- and long-term time frames, or horizons, of business planning. This approach derives from the notion that communication strategies should be linked to corporate business goals and objectives to be effective. If they are to be so linked, then why not plan communication strategies in the time frames senior executives use to develop their business strategies? We'd at least be on the same time frames as senior executives and thinking, talking and counselling about matters, and in a way, they understand. We've located that approach to strategic communication in a specific part of an organisation's environment—that area where discussion and debate about issues happens and where they are resolved: the non-market environment.

DOI: 10.4324/9781003317579-15

In a sense, this exploration has led us, like Smiley, into a mysterious situation, for defining strategic communication as part of the non-market environment departs from some traditional views about strategic communication and the pathways and tools it applies. These are often defined as applying in the market environment, and of course pathways and tools are important there. But the mystery we've unravelled is that strategic communication is about more than enhancing the bottom line. It is about communication that deals with longer-term topics like reputation, issues management, lobbying, credibility, corporate social responsibility, organisational positioning and strategic counselling.

Success means understanding the times, as Machiavelli put it in his advice on statecraft to the Florentine "prince" Lorenzo de' Medici. For strategic communicators, "understanding the times" means understanding issues that are important, interpreting what they mean for the organisation and applying professional skills to address them. A communication strategy is the result of that understanding.

A strategy provides reasons and directions for doing things, just as a business plan does for the whole organisation. The founder of the web marketing company HubSpot, Dharmesh Shah, uses various social media platforms to great effect. The *Harvard Business Review* (in January and February 2012) reported that social media platforms are not just fun tools to keep Shah linked to friends. His use of social media in a planned way answers the communication strategy "why" question: to consult broadly, gather information and influence people. Shah is focused on enhancing his business' reputation, specialisations and network position.

At the end of it all, Smiley's research, analysis, deduction, intuition, historical knowledge and tradecraft work triumph. He always finds the answer to the mystery he's pursuing. This exploration has guided you in taking a quantum leap from skill development and writing tools to strategic thinking, planning and ethical practice. That will be vital knowledge.

In his Distinguished Lecture to the Institute for Public Relations in November way back in 2010, Richard Edelman, founder and CEO of one of the world's major consultancies, noted that the profession was the discipline that paid most attention to the broad interests of the corporation. Edelman talked about communication being "public engagement" in which business participates in global conversations about trust, changed corporate behaviour and deeper communities (see Edelman, 2011). Edelman argued that one of four principles that should guide public engagement is that communication executives must help fashion companies' operating strategies. He was not wrong then, and, like all informed commentary, his views are equally relevant today. These are the practical links between business planning and strategic communication that have been our focus throughout the book: the organisation's interests and strategic planning.

Glossary

Advocacy advertising   Advertising that deals with an organisation's position on public policy issues.

Alliance   'A union, or an agreement to cooperate'; 'a relationship resulting from an affinity in nature or qualities' (*Australian Concise Oxford Dictionary*, 2004).

Analyse   Systematically examine something's constituent parts. An *analysis* is the result of this examination. Things are analysed to explain why they are the way they are. For example, when pathologists analyse blood tests, they can explain why someone is healthy or sick by identifying whether they have high cholesterol, or dangerous sugar levels that might lead to diabetes. When geologists analyse rocks, they can tell whether the ground they have been investigating contains gold, or copper, or tin—or even all these minerals. For strategic communication, analysing issues means practitioners can understand them, including how they might impact on an organisation, and thus why those issues are important.

Boundary spanning   What practitioners do when they identify, monitor and analyse external and internal issues to understand and interpret the opportunities and threats they pose for organisations.

Business   The core activities of organisations. Definitions of business in the *Australian Concise Oxford Dictionary*, 2004, include 'a thing that is one's concern', 'a task or duty', 'serious work or activity', and 'a thing or series of things needing to be dealt with'. In these senses, all organisations—whether in commerce, government, or the not-for-profit sector—engage in business.

Communication pathway   *How* a message will be delivered (as opposed to its format or packaging). This is sometimes called a message delivery strategy or a communication channel. A metaphor for a communication pathway is the role that the postal service plays in delivering a snail-mail letter. You write a letter (a message) to your grandfather, seal it an envelope and post it; the postal service delivers the message to your grandfather's house (the communication pathway); he opens the envelope and reads your message. Communication pathways, then, indicate how a message is delivered, not the format of the message.

Communication system   The overall structure or system through which an organisation communicates with target publics, and in which each piece fits with others to make up the overall picture, a bit like a jigsaw puzzle. Effective communication systems are integrated so that people working on each part follow the same goals and objectives and use the same messages.

Complexity theory The idea—derived from the physical sciences—that all systems, natural and human-made, are continually changing, often in small ways. Some scholars use complexity theory to study interactions and relationships in organisations.

Context 'The circumstances relevant to something under consideration', so that something that is *out of context* is 'without the surrounding words or circumstances and so not fully understandable' (*Australian Concise Oxford Dictionary*, 2004).

Contingency theory An attempt to explain how internal and external factors (independent variables) influence organisations' abilities to do what they do. It is used by scholars to explore how such factors influence communication.

Control The power to direct, to command, to restrain or to regulate. The *Australian Concise Oxford Dictionary*, 2004, explains that 'controls' may also be the switches and other devices that control vehicles. Former Australian prime minister Paul Keating was fond of saying he had control of the levers that drove the economy. These are the concepts embedded in a controlled media communication pathway: practitioners pull the levers that drive the content, timing and delivery method of messages; no one else has that role.

Corporate advertising Advertising that promotes the organisation itself rather than its products.

Counselling What senior practitioners do when they advise top management on communication solutions to current, emerging, or potential issues.

Counsellor A professional who is trained to advise others. Lawyers, psychologists, social workers, and accountants give guidance and advice in the special areas of expertise. In the United States, barristers are described as 'counsellors'. In professional strategic communication practice, advice given to chief executives and other managers about dealing with issues can be described as counselling. If someone 'takes counsel', they are consulting an adviser (*Australian Concise Oxford Dictionary*, 2004).

Culture 'The customs, civilisation and achievements of a particular time or people' (*Australian Concise Oxford Dictionary*, 2004). Some people, perhaps migrants, suffer 'culture shock' when they experience an unfamiliar culture or way of life. *Multiculturalism* means the existence of many culturally distinct groups in a society.

Delphi research Research in which experts in a field discuss an issue several times with the goal of reaching a consensus about it. Delphi research usually extends over a longer time than other research techniques, and paricipants generally do not know the specific views of others.

Demographics Statistical data about groups in the general population.

Desk research Informal research that involves using secondary sources from the internet or books and reports that are directly available.

Diffusion theory A theory that proposes that people go through a five-step process before they decide whether they will adopt an idea or buy a product. The steps are: awareness, interest, evaluation, trial and adoption.

Dominant coalition The most influential people in an organisation in a specific situation.

Dynamic Changing and evolving, sometimes over a long period; not static.

Elaboration likelihood model (ELM) A theory that suggests that people process, or elaborate, information in two ways: via 'central route' and 'peripheral route' processing. Central route processing involves careful, rational thinking about information (or 'elaborating'), leading to considered decisions. Peripheral route processing occurs when people are less motivated to elaborate and instead take decisions based on peripheral clues, perhaps the perceived credibility of an information source.

Environmental scanning Identifying and interpreting complex and changing environments—or business contexts—for clients. This kind of analysis is part of strategic issues management. It identifies changes in the environment in which an organisation operates and how these changes will affect the organisation and its activities.

Evaluate 'Assess, appraise'; 'find or state the number or amount of'; 'find a numerical expression for' (*Australian Concise Oxford Dictionary*, 2004). An *evaluation* (also known as *summative* research) is the result of these activities. Evaluation is important in strategic communication because it assesses how well the project went and attempts to put a value, sometimes numerical, on the result. It is important to remember that an evaluation is research and utilises social sciences research methodologies.

Expectancy The probability that target publics will make an effort to understand the organisation's point of view on an issue, or consider buying its products.

Expectancy theory A theory proposed by Victor Vroom as a way of predicting or explaining the effort a person uses to deal with tasks. Expectancy theory deals with work motivation and it is applied in communication as a way of assessing people's willingness to buy a product or accept an idea. This is an important theoretical concept in public policy discourses in the non-market environment.

Formal structure A hierarchy or ordered system that identifies the ways in which an organisation is managed. Each organisation has a structure designed to best meet its needs and objectives. Large organisations generally have more complicated structures than smaller ones.

Formative research Finding out about an organisation, what it does, its business environment, its plans, how its internal systems work, and the communication issues it faces.

Goals Broad statements that deal with what must be done. Goals are about building *reputation*, about *relationships* and about *tasks*. Wilson and Ogden (2008) describe goals as statements of the end to be achieved to resolve the core problem. In their view, goals are a positive restatement of that core problem. They warn that it is dangerous to set strategic communication goals in isolation from the organisation's overall goals.

Hierarchy See *formal structure*.

Implement Put a decision or a plan into effect. In strategic communication, implementation means deciding what needs to be done, writing a plan to do that, working out the resources—money, people, and technology—that are required, and preparing a timeline showing the dates by which all the activities will be completed and who will be responsible for them.

Industry associations Organisations set up to represent the common interests of all the businesses in one industry. Sometimes they are formed as interest groups (e.g. environmental activists) to give them a united and stronger voice in public debates.

Instrumentality The probability that the target public will do something about the message, or buy the product.

Interactive Acting reciprocally; or acting on or influencing each other; allowing a two-way flow of information between people via computer technology (*Australian Concise Oxford Dictionary*, 2004). Interactivity includes the notion of *feedback*, and it is one of the principles behind Grunig's (2009) argument that social media can enhance his concept of two-way symmetrical communication.

Issue 'A point in question; an important subject of debate' (*Australian Concise Oxford Dictionary*, 2004).

Lobby Attempt to influence someone or convert them to a particular point of view. Lobbying often happens in political contexts and involves meetings with bureaucrats and politicians about issues; submissions to formal inquiries; media releases on the organisation's views; and other public relations tasks.

Lobbyist Specialist communication practitioner, often with experience in politics, who engages in lobbying on behalf of individual organisations and industry associations.

Market environment Relationships with customers, suppliers, and competitors.

Measure 'To work out the extent or quantity of something by comparing it with something that is fixed or of a known size' (*Australian Concise Oxford Dictionary*, 2004).

Media effects theory The idea that the mass media have a powerful direct influence on people's awareness and understanding of an issue, and that people change their behaviour as a result of exposure to messages delivered via this communication channel.

Messages The key themes that guide the content of tools like websites, brochures, meetings, displays, media releases, speeches, and podcasts. *Informative* messages provide facts objectively. *Persuasive* messages seek to influence publics by presenting an argument. Messages can be re-crafted into summary briefing notes for people from the organisation when they are interviewed by journalists or when they represent the organisation at meetings.

Mission A person's task or goal; the general principles that an organisation says guide its operations (adapted from *Australian Concise Oxford Dictionary*, 2004).

Non-market environment All the relationships an organisation has beyond the market that nevertheless affect its ability to reach its objectives. Non-market issues are social, political, and economic.

Objectives Precise, measurable statements that indicate the steps needed to achieve goals. Objectives deal with change, such as increasing awareness, acceptance or understanding, or generating action. Objectives are mostly outcome specific. However, just as goals can be about processes, like doing tasks, so too can objectives deal with outputs, such as producing a website, launching a Facebook page or issuing media releases during a campaign. Objectives back up a goal; they are the steps needed to achieve the goal. There should always be more objectives in a strategy than goals.

Organisational values   The beliefs on which the organisation bases its policies and actions.

Paradigm   'An example or pattern, especially one underlying a theory or methodology' (*Australian Concise Oxford Dictionary*, 2004).

Practise   Regularly perform professional skills, or competencies, in a systematic way. In the sense in which it is used in this book—as in being a *practitioner*—*practising* means doing the things that are involved in working in a profession, in the way that doctors practise medicine and lawyers practise the law.

Psychographics   The study of people's attitudes and aspirations.

Public affairs   A communication specialty that primarily deals with issues management. Like many such terms, there is no one, clear definition.

Public policy   The decisions governments make about issues that are important to the way a society functions. In most countries public policies deal with, for example, health care, pensions, immigration, industrial relations, and education. These are all issues that relate to an organisation's external environment, which is why strategic communicators are interested in them, and their impact on organisations. And it is why organisations contribute to discourses on public policy issues in their role as 'social actors'.

Qualitative research   Research that is concerned with finding people's attitudes and opinions about something. It can be used to explain quantitative results.

Quantitative research   Research that reports its results as numbers.

Relationship-management theory   An explanation of the different ways in which organisations and their publics relate to each other. Working out the nature of the relationships that target publics have with an organisation provides important information for a situation analysis.

Resource dependency theory   The idea that organisations depend on, and manage, external resources to do the things they do. In strategic communication, building good relationships with suppliers (of electricity, water, and raw materials, for example) assists in the acquisition of resources.

Salient   Prominent, conspicuous, or pertinent; important or significant. Salience in strategic communication refers to how target publics process information; whether that information is significant to them, whether goals, objectives, message delivery pathways and tools are pertinent.

Segment   To divide something into several parts. Think of the structure of a peeled orange; each segment is a part of the whole. For communicators, target publics are the segments of a stakeholder group.

Situation analysis   Narrative that provides a detailed analysis of the communication issues and opportunities facing an organisation. The analysis is based on formative research.

Situational theory A theory that predicts when publics will actively seek information and how they will process it. It suggests that publics can be identified by the context in which they are aware of a problem and the extent to which they do something about the problem. The theory suggests there are three independent variables in relation to how they do this (problem recognition, constraint recognition and level of involvement) and two dependent variables (information seeking and information processing). Situational theory helps to explain why some people become activists on an issue while others do not and may even be apathetic towards the issue.

Social actors People who participate in public discussions about social, economic, and political issues.

Social exchange theory The idea that people make a kind of 'what's-in-it-for-me' economic judgment on the benefits and costs of them behaving in a certain way. They want to maximise the benefit of what they are being asked to do but keep the costs of doing it low.

Stakeholder 'Someone with an interest or concern in something' (*Australian Concise Oxford Dictionary*, 2004). Stakeholders are those who help the organisation to go about its business or have an interest in (or receive a benefit from) what it produces, or regulate it, or have some impact on its market and non-market environments.

Strategic communication plan A document that describes how an organisation will achieve its communication goals and objectives.

Strategy The term used to describe what organisations or individuals will do to achieve goals, usually over the long term.

Summative research The research you conduct at the end of a campaign to work out whether you achieved its goals and objectives.

SWOT chart A simple analytical tool whereby an organisation or program is assessed in terms of its strengths, weaknesses, opportunities, and threats.

System A set of connected things, or parts, that function as a whole. The *Australian Concise Oxford Dictionary* explains systems using, as examples, the human body, and the group of related hardware and program units that make up a computer.

Systems theory A theory that regards organisations as systems that adapt to their environments; changes in the economic, social, or political environments in which an organisation operates impact on that organisation.

Tools The means by which a strategy is carried out. In professional communication, tools are the things practitioners produce to implement a strategy.

Target public The people who receive messages to raise awareness, generate acceptance and promote action. Formative research for a public relations plan will help you to identify your client's target publics.

Typology The study of types. So, van Ruler's (2005) typology shows four types, or models, of professional practice. All the discussion about strategy and professional practice in this book can be defined by van Ruler's 'knowledge model'.

Valence The value that a target public will put on the message or the product. For example, do they see it as desirable or undesirable?

References

Albrighton, F. and Thomas, J. (2001), *Managing External Relations*, Open University Press, Buckingham.

Alexander, D. (2006), Reframing Leadership Communication: Consequences for Organisational Leaders Resulting from Communication Failure: An Australian Case Study, *Empowerment, Creativity and Innovation: Challenging Media and Communication in the 21st Century* (ANZCA and University of Adelaide). http://researchoutput.csu.edu.au/R/?func=dbin-jump-full&object_id=7224&local_base=GEN01-CSU01

Allert, J. and Zawawi, C. (2004), Strategy, Planning and Scheduling, in J. Johnston and C. Zawawi (eds.), *Public Relations: Theory and Practice*, Allen & Unwin, Sydney, pp. 169–96.

Andrews, P.N. (1985), The Sticky Wicket of Evaluating Public Affairs: Thoughts about a Framework, *Public Affairs Review*, 6(3), pp. 94–105.

Argenti, P., Howell, R.A. and Beck, K.A. (2005), The Strategic Communication Imperative, *MIT Sloan Management Review*, 46(3), pp. 82–9. https://sloanreview.mit.edu/article/the-strategic-communication-imperative/

Austin, E.W. and Pinkleton, B.E. (2006), *Strategic Public Relations Management*, Informa, New York.

Bach, D. and Allen, D.B. (2010), What Every CEO Needs to Know about *Nonmarket* Strategy, *MIT Sloan Management Review*, 51(3), pp. 41–8 retrieved on 1 April 2013 from http://www.management-issues.com/2007/10/3/mentors/david-bach-on-nonmarket-strategy.asp on 1 April 2013

Baghai, M., Coley, S. and White, D. (2000), *The Alchemy of Growth: Practical Insights for Building the Enduring Enterprise*, Basic, New York

Bajkiewicz, T.E., Kraus, J.J. and Hong, S.Y. (2011), The Impact of Newsroom Changes and the Rise of Social Media on the Practice of Public Relations, *Public Relations Review*, 37(3), pp. 329–31. https://doi.org/10.1016/j.pubrev.2011.05.001

Beard, M. (2007), *Running a Public Relations Department*, 2nd edn, Kogan Page, London.

Beinhocker, E.D. (1999), On the Origin of Strategies, *The McKinsey Quarterly*, (4), pp. 47–57.

Bouzon, A. and Devillard, J. (2009), Changes in Contemporary Organisations and Interculturality: From Orchestrated Communication to Confidence, *PRism*, 6(2), at www.prismjournal.org/fileadmin/Praxis/Files/globalPR/BOUZON_DEVILLARD.pdf. https://doi.org/10.1002/pa.117

Brønn, P.S. and Brønn, C. (2002), Issues Management as a Basis for Strategic Direction, *Journal of Public Affairs*, 2(4), pp. 247–58. https://doi.org/10.1002/pa.117

Bryman, A. (2008), *Social Research Methods*, 3rd edn, Oxford University Press, Oxford.

Burr, A. (2022). OAK Plus extends Panthers' partnership, Panthers Media, retrieved on 26 October 2022 from https://www.penrithpanthers.com.au/news/2022/10/26/oak-plus-extends-panthers-partnership/

Cacioppo, J.T and Petty, R.E. (1984), The Elaboration Likelihood Model of Persuasion, in T.C. Kinnear (ed.), *Advances in Consumer Research Volume 11*, Association for Consumer Research, Ann Arbor, pp. 673–5.

Cancel, A.E., Cameron, G.T., Sallot, L.M. and Mitrook, M.A. (1997), It Depends: A Contingency Theory of Accommodation in Public Relations, *Journal of Public Relations Research*, 9(1), pp. 31–63. https://doi.org/10.1207/s1532754xjprr0901_02

Chia, J. (2009), Understanding Twenty-First Century Public Relations, in J. Chia and G. Synnott (eds.), *An Introduction to Public Relations: From Theory to Practice*, Oxford University Press, Melbourne, pp. 3–30.

Conley, D. and Lamble, S. (2006), *The Daily Miracle: An Introduction to Journalism*, 3rd edn, Oxford University Press, Melbourne.

Coombs, W.T. and Holladay, S.J. (2009), Further Explorations of Post-Crisis Communication: Effects of Media and Response Strategies on Perceptions and Intentions, *Public Relations Review*, 35(1), pp. 1–6. https://doi.org/10.1016/j.pubrev.2008.09.011

Cornelissen, J.P. (2000), Toward an Understanding of the Use of Academic Theories in Public Relations Practice, *Public Relations Review*, 26(3), pp. 315–26. https://doi.org/10.1016/S0363-8111(00)00050-3

Cornelissen, J.P. (2005), *Corporate Communications: Theory and Practice*, Sage, London.

Crawshaw, B. (2021), The end of the end, Letters to the Editor, *The Canberra Times*, 3 September 2021. Retrieved on 3 September 2021 from https://www.canberratimes.com.au/story/7411939/teacher-shortages-are-forcing-dedicated-educators-to-leave/

Cutlip, S.M., Center, A.H. and Broom, G.M. (2006), *Effective Public Relations*, 9th edn, Pearson, Upper Saddle River, NJ.

Dilenschneider, R.L. (1989), Keynote Address: Communication, in S.A. White (ed.), *Values and Communication*, Longman Professional, Melbourne, pp. 17–21.

Dougall, E. (2008), Issues Management, *The Science beneath the Art of Public Relations*, Institute for Public Relations' online topics at http://www.instituteforpr.org/topics/issues-management/, accessed 28 December 2013.

Edelman, R. (2011), Reimagining Our Profession: Public Relations for a Complex World, *The Public Relations Strategist*, winter, pp. 28–30.

Falkheimer, J. and Heide, M. (2018). *Strategic Communication: An Introduction*, Routlege, Milton Park.

Fawkes, J. (2006), Can Ethics Save Public Relations from the Charge of Propaganda? *Ethical Space, Journal of the Institute of Communication Ethics*, 3(1), Troubadour Publishing, Leicester, pp. 32–42.

Fawkes, J. (2009), Public Relations, Propaganda and the Psychology of Persuasion, in R. Tench and L. Yeomans (eds.), *Exploring Public Relations*, 2nd edn, Prentice Hall, Harlow, pp. 252–72.

Ferrazzi, K. (2012), Candor, Criticism, Teamwork, *Harvard Business Review*, 90(1/2), p. 40.

Fitch, K. (2009), New Media and Public Relations, in J. Chia and G. Synnott (eds.), *An Introduction to Public Relations: From Theory to Practice*, Oxford University Press, Melbourne, pp. 333–56.

Gabbot, M. and Clulow, V. (1999), The Elaboration Likelihood Model of Persuasive Communication, in P.J. Kitchen (ed.), *Marketing Communications: Principles and Practice*, Thomson, London, pp. 172–88.

Gavetti, G. (2011), The New Psychology of Strategic Leadership, *Harvard Business Review*, 89(7–8), pp. 118–25.

Gibson, J.L., Ivancevich, J.M., Donnelly, J.H. and Konopaske, R. (2003), *Organizations: Behaviour, Structure, Processes*, 11th edn, McGraw-Hill Irwin, Boston.

Gower, K.K. (2006), Public Relations Research at the Crossroads, *Journal of Public Relations Research*, 18(2), pp. 177–83. https://doi.org/10.1207/s1532754xjprr1802_6

Gregory, A. (2000), Systems Theories and Public Relations Practice, *Journal of Communication Management*, 4(3), pp. 266–77. https://doi.org/10.1108/eb023525

Gregory, A. (ed.) (2005), *Public Relations in Practice*, 2nd edn, Chartered Institute of Public Relations/Kogan Page, London.

Gregory, A. (2006), Public Relations as Planned Communication, in R. Tench and L. Yeomans (ed), *Exploring Public Relations*, Pearson Education, Harlow, Essex, pp. 174–221.

Gregory, A. (2009a), Public Relations as Planned Communication, in R. Tench and L. Yeomans (eds), *Exploring Public Relations*, 2nd edn, Prentice Hall, Harlow, pp. 174–97.

Grunig, J.E. (ed.) (1992), *Excellence in Public Relations and Communication Management*, Lawrence Erlbaum Associates, Hillsdale, NJ.

Grunig, J.E. (2001), Two-way Symmetrical Public Relations: Past, Present, and Future, in R.L. Heath (ed.), *Handbook of Public Relations*, SAGE, Thousand Oaks, CA, pp. 11–30.

Grunig, J.E. (2006), Furnishing the Edifice: Ongoing Research on Public Relations as a Strategic Management Function, *Journal of Public Relations Research*, 18(2), pp. 151–76. https://doi.org/10.1207/s1532754xjprr1802_5

Grunig, J.E. (2009), Paradigms of Global Public Relations in an Age of Digitalization, *PRism*, 6(2), at http://praxis.massey.ac.nz/fileadmin/Praxis/Files/globalPR/GRUNIG.pdf

Grunig, J.E. and Hunt, T. (1984), *Managing Public Relations*, Holt, Rinehart & Winston, Fort Worth, TX.

Grunig, J.E. and Repper, F.C. (1992), Strategic Management, Publics, and Issues, in J.E. Grunig (ed.), *Excellence in Public Relations and Communication Management*, Lawrence Erlbaum Associates, Hillside, NJ, pp. 109–16.

Grunig, L. (2008), Using Qualitative Research to Become the 'Thinking Heart' of Organisations, in B. van Ruler, A.T. Verčič and D Verčič (eds), *Public Relations Metrics: Research and Evaluation*, Routledge, New York, pp. 120–36.

Guth, D.W. and Marsh, C. (2006), *Public Relations: A Values-Driven Approach*, 3rd edn, Pearson, Boston, MA.

Hallahan, K. (1999), Seven Models of Framing: Implications for Public Relations, *Journal of Public Relations Research*, 11(3), pp. 205–42. https://doi.org/10.1207/s1532754xjprr1103_02

Hallahan, K. (2000), Inactive Publics: The Forgotten Publics in Public Relations, *Public Relations Review*, 26(4), pp. 499–515. https://doi.org/10.1016/s0363-8111(00)00061-8

Hallahan, K. (2001), The Dynamics of Issues Activation and Response: An Issues Process Model, *Journal of Public Relations Research*, 13(1), pp. 27–59. https://doi.org/10.1207/s1532754xjprr1301_3

Hallahan, K. (2010), Public Relations Media, in R.L. Heath (ed.), *The Sage Handbook of Public Relations*, 2nd edn, Sage, Los Angeles, CA, pp. 623–41.

Hallahan, K., Holtzhausen, D., Van Ruler, B., Verčič, D., and Sriramesh, K. (2007), Defining Strategic Communication, *International Journal of Strategic Communication*, 1(1), pp. 3–35. https://doi.org/10.1080/15531180701285244

Hamel, G. (1996), Strategy as Revolution, *Harvard Business Review*, 74(4), pp. 69–82.

Hamrefors, S. (2010), Communicative Leadership, *Journal of Communication Management*, 14(2), pp. 141–52. https://doi.org/10.1108/13632541011034592

Harvard Business School (2006), *The Essentials of Corporate Communications and Public Relations*, Harvard Business School Press, Boston, MA.

Heath, R.L. (ed.) (2001), *Handbook of Public Relations*, Sage, Thousand Oaks, CA.

Heath, R.L. (2001), A Rhetorical Enactment Rationale for Public Relations: The Good Organisation Communicating Well, in R.L. Heath (ed.), *Handbook of Public Relations*, Sage, Thousand Oaks, CA, pp. 31–50. https://doi.org/10.4135/9781452220727.n2

Heath, R.L. and Palenchar, M.J. (2009), *Strategic Issues Management: Organisations and Public Policy Challenges*, 2nd edn, Sage, Los Angeles, CA.

Heath, R.L. (ed.), (2010), *The Sage Handbook of Public Relations*, 2nd edn, Sage, Los Angeles, CA.

Hodge, B.J., Anthony, W.P. and Gales, L.M. (2003), *Organization Theory: A Strategic Approach*, 6th edn, Prentice Hall, Upper Saddle River, NJ.

Howell, G. (2006), Ansett Airlines—Absolutely! Going, Grounded, Gone, *Asia Pacific Public Relations Journal*, 7, pp. 1–19. http://handle.uws.edu.au:8081/1959.7/34007

IPRA (International Public Relations Association) (1994), *Gold Paper No 11, Public Relations Evaluation: Professional Accountability*, International Public Relations Association, Geneva.

Jaques, T. (2009a), Integrating Issue Management and Strategic Planning: Unfulfilled Promise or Future Opportunity? *International Journal of Strategic Communication*, 3(1), pp. 19–33. https://doi.org/10.1080/15531180802606539

Jaques, T. (2009b), Issue and Crisis Management: Quicksand in the Definitional Landscape, *Public Relations Review*, 35(3), pp. 280–6. https://doi.org/10.1016/j.pubrev.2009.03.003

Jaques, T. (2014), *Issue and Crisis Management: Exploring Issues, Crises, Risk and Reputation*, Oxford University Press, Melbourne.

Johnston, J. (2007), *Media Relations: Issues and Strategies*, Allen & Unwin, Crows Nest.

Johnston, J. and Glenny, L. (2021), *Strategic Communication: Public Relations at work*, Routledge, London

Johnston, J. and Zawawi. C. (eds.) (2009), *Public Relations Theory and Practice*, 3rd edn, Allen & Unwin, Sydney.

Kang, J. and Cheng, I.-H. (2008), Application of Contingency Theory Frameworks to Issue Management: A Case Study of the Restaurant Industry's Obesity Issues Management, paper presented at the annual meeting of the National Communication Association, 94th Annual Convention, San Diego, CA, 20 November 2008.

Kent, M.L. (2010), Directions in Social Media for Professionals and Scholars, in R.L. Heath (ed.), *The SAGE Handbook of Public Relations*, 2nd edn, SAGE, Los Angeles, CA, pp. 643–56.

Kent, M.L. and Taylor, M. (2002), Toward a Dialogic Theory of Public Relations, *Public Relations Review*, 28(1), pp. 21–37. https://doi.org/10.1016/s0363-8111(02)00108-x

Kim, J-N. and Ni, L. (2010), Seeing the Forest through the Trees: The Behavioural, Strategic Management Paradigm in Public Relations and its Future, in R.L. Heath (ed.), *The SAGE Handbook of Public Relations*, 2nd edn, SAGE, Los Angeles, CA, pp. 35–58.

Kim, S. and Rader, S. (2010), What They Can Do Versus How Much They Care: Assessing Corporate Communication Strategies on *Fortune 500* Web Sites, *Journal of Communication Management*, 14(1), pp. 59–80. https://doi.org/10.1108/13632541011017816

Kitchen, P.J. (1999), *Marketing Communications: Principles and Practice*, Thomson, London.

Lattimore, D., Baskin, O., Heiman, S., Toth, E. and van Leuven, J. (2004), *Public Relations: The Profession and the Practice*, McGraw-Hill, Boston, MA.

Lauzen, M.M. (1997), Understanding the Relation between Public Relations and Issues Management, *Journal of Public Relations Research*, 9(1), pp. 65–82. https://doi.org/10.1207/s1532754xjprr0901_03

Lubbers, C.A. (2011), An Assessment of Predictors of Student Peer Evaluations of Team Work in the Capstone Campaigns Course, *Public Relations Review*, 37(5), pp. 492–8. https://doi.org/10.1016/j.pubrev.2011.09.013

McDonald, L.M. and Hebbani, A.G. (2011), Back to the Future: Is Strategic Management (Re)emerging as Public Relations' Dominant Paradigm? *PRism*, 8(1), at www.prismjournal.org/fileadmin/8_1/mcdonald_hebbani.pdf

McGrath, C., Moss, D. and Harris, P. (2010), The Evolving Discipline of Public Affairs, *Journal of Public Affairs*, 10(4), pp. 335–52. https://doi.org/10.1002/pa.369

Mackey, S. (2004), Theoretical Perspectives, in J. Johnston and C. Zawawi (eds.), *Public Relations: Theory and Practice*, Allen & Unwin, Sydney, pp. 43–71.

Mackey, S. (2009), Public Relations Theory, in J. Johnston and C. Zawawi (eds.), *Public Relations Theory and Practice*, 3rd edn, Allen & Unwin, Sydney, pp. 47–77.

Macnamara, J. (2010), 'Emergent' Media and Public Communication: Understanding the Changing Mediascape, *Public Communication Review*, 1(2). https://doi.org/10.5130/pcr.v1i2.1867

Macnamara, J. (2012), *Public Relations Theories, Practices and Critiques*, Pearson, Sydney.

Mahoney, J. (2010a), Strategic Communication and Anti-smoking Campaigns, *Public Communication Review*, 1(2). https://doi.org/10.5130/pcr.v1i2.1868

Mahoney, J. (2010b), Strategic Communication: Making Sense of Issues Management, Communication Policy Research Forum, Sydney, November, at www.networkinsight.org/verve/_resources/CPRF_2010_papers.pdf

Mahoney, J. (2011), Horizons in Strategic Communication: Theorising a Paradigm Shift, *International Journal of Strategic Communication*, 5(3), pp. 143–53. http://dx.doi.org/10.1080/1553118X.2011.53760

Mahoney, J. (2022), *The Strategic Communication Imperative For Mid- and Long-Term Issues Management*, Routledge, Milton Park, Oxon and New York.

Mahoney, J. and Burrell, A. (2007), *A Puff of Smoke: The Effectiveness of Anti-Smoking Campaigns among Young Canberrans*, a pilot study for the ACT Department of Health.

Marx, T.G. (1986), Integrating Public Affairs and Strategic Planning, *California Management Review*, 29(1), pp. 141–7. https://doi.org/10.2307/41165232

Marx, T.G. (1990), Strategic Planning for Public Affairs, *Long Range Planning*, 23(1), pp. 9–16. https://doi.org/10.1016/0024-6301(90)90003-m

Moloney, K. (2006), *Rethinking Public Relations: PR Propaganda and Democracy*, 2nd edn, Routledge, Milton Park, Oxon.

Murphy, P. (2000), Symmetry, Contingency, Complexity: Accommodating Uncertainty in Public Relations Theory, *Public Relations Review*, 26(4), pp. 447–62. https://doi.org/10.1016/s0363-8111(00)00058-8

Nash, L. (1995), The Real Truth about Corporate 'Values', *The Public Relations Strategist*, 1(2), pp. 7–13.

Northhaft, H. (2010), Communication Management as a Second-Order Management Function: Roles and Functions of the Communication Executive—Results from a Shadowing Study, *Journal of Communication Management*, 14(2), pp. 127–40. https://doi.org/10.1108/13632541011034583

Oestreicher, P. (2011), Arthur: King, Leader, PR Professional—Modern lessons from Camelot and the Round Table, *The Public Relations Strategist*, 17(4), pp. 17–9.

Oliver, S. (2007), *Public Relations Strategy*, 2nd edn, Kogan Page, London.

Pang, A., Jin, Y. and Cameron, G.T. (2010), Strategic Management of Communication: Insights from the Contingency Theory of Strategic Conflict Management, in R.L. Heath (ed.), (2010), *The SAGE Handbook of Public Relations*, 2nd edn, SAGE, Los Angeles, CA, pp. 17–34.

Paul, A.M. (2012), Your Head Is in the Cloud, *TIME*, 12 March, pp. 42–3.

Peters, T.J. and Waterman, R.H. (1984), *In Search of Excellence: Lesson from America's Best-Run Companies*, Harper & Row, Sydney.

Petty, R.E., Cacioppo, J.T. and Schumann, D. (1983), Central and Peripheral Routers to Advertising Effectiveness: The Moderating Role of Involvement, *Journal of Consumer Research*, 10(2), pp. 135–46. https://doi.org/10.1086/208954

Porter, M.E. (2008), The Five Competitive Forces that Shape Strategy, *Harvard Business Review*, January, pp. 79–93.

Reber, B.H. and Cameron, G.T. (2003), Measuring Contingencies: Using Scales to Measure Public Relations Practitioner Limits to Accommodation, *Journalism and Mass Communication Quarterly*, 80(2), pp. 431–46. https://doi.org/10.1177/107769900308000212

Rumelt, R. (2011), The Perils of Bad Strategy, *McKinsey Quarterly*, June, retrieved on 28 June 2011 from www.mckinseyquarterly.com/The_perils_of_bad_strategy_2826

Russell, B. (1966), *Sceptical Essays*, Unwin Books, London.

Ryan, M. (2022), What Strategic Options Do Ukrainians Have as They Go Head-to-Head with Russia in the East? *ABC News Online*, retrieved on 12 April 2022 from https://www.abc.net.au/news/2022-04-12/ukraines-strategic-options-as-russian-war-moves-east/100981886

Sandhu, S. (2009), Strategic Communication: An Institutional Perspective, *International Journal of Strategic Communication*, 3(2), pp. 72–92. https://doi.org/10.1080/15531180902805429

Seibert, M. and Harris, M. (2004), The Identification of Strategic Management Counseling Competencies Essential for Small Business Counsellors: An Exploratory Study, in United States Association for Small Business and Entrepreneurship, *2006 Proceedings*, at usasbe.org/knowledge/proceedings/proceedingsDocs/USASBE2006proceedings-Seibert%20-%20ESO.pdf

Seitel, F.P. (2007), *The Practice of Public Relations*, 10th edn, Pearson, Upper Saddle River, NJ.

Seitel, F.P. (2011), *The Practice of Public Relations*, 11th edn, Pearson, Upper Saddle River, NJ.

Sha, B-L. (2011), 2010 Practice Analysis: Professional Competencies and Work Categories in Public Relations Today, *Public Relations Review*, 37(3), pp. 187–96. https://doi.org/10.1016/j.pubrev.2011.04.005

Shin, J.-H., Cameron, G.T. and Cropp, F. (2006), Occam's Razor in the Contingency Theory: A National Survey on 86 Contingent Variables, *Public Relations Review*, 32(3), pp. 282–6. https://doi.org/10.1016/j.pubrev.2006.05.005

Silver, D. (2011), Overcoming Groupthink in the Boardroom, *The Public Relations Strategist*, 17(1), spring, pp. 25–6.

Simmons, P. and Watson, T. (2005), Public Relations Evaluation in Australia: Practices and Attitudes across Sectors and Employment Status, *Asia Pacific Public Relations Journal*, 6(2), at www.deakin.edu.au/arts-ed/apprj/vol6no2.php#8

Sison, M.D. (2009a), Theoretical Contexts, in J. Chia and G. Synnott (eds.), *An Introduction to Public Relations: From Theory to Practice*, Oxford University Press, Melbourne, pp. 54–89.

Sison, M.D. (2009b), Whose Cultural Values? Exploring Public Relations' Approaches to Understanding Audiences, *PRism*, 6(2), at www.prismjournal.org/fileadmin/Praxis/Files/globalPR/SISON.pdf

Smith, R.D. (2002), *Strategic Planning for Public Relations*, Lawrence Erlbaum Associates, Mahwah, NJ.

Smith, R.D. (2005), *Strategic Planning for Public Relations*, 2nd edn, Lawrence Erlbaum Associates, Mahwah, NJ.

Sollis, B. and Breakenridge, D. (2009), *Putting the Public Back in Public Relations: How Social Media is Reinventing the Ageing Business of PR*, Pearson Education, Upper Saddle River, NJ.

Sparrow, B. (2011), Study Finds That Memory Works Differently in the Age of Google, *Columbia News* at http://news.columbia.edu/googlememory

Sriramesh, K. (2007), The Relationship Between Culture and Public Relations, in E.L. Toth (ed.), *The Future of Excellence in Public Relations and Communication Management:*

Challenges for the Next Generation, Lawrence Erlbaum Associates, Mahwah, NJ, pp. 507–26.

Steyn, B. and Niemann, L. (2010), Enterprise Strategy: A Concept that Explicates Corporate Communication's Strategic Contribution at the Macro-Organisational Level, *Journal of Communication Management*, 14(2), pp. 106–26. https://doi.org/10.1108/13632541011034574

Ströh, U. (2006), The Impact of Organisational Change Communication Approaches on Employee Relationships: An Experimental Study, *Asia Pacific Public Relations Journal*, 7, pp. 247–76. Not digitised.

Szondi, G. (2009), International Context of Public Relations, in R. Tench and L. Yeomans (eds.), *Exploring Public Relations*, Prentice Hall, Harlow, pp. 117–46.

Szondi, G. and Theilman, R. (2009), Public Relations Research and Evaluation, in R. Tench and L. Yeomans (eds.), *Exploring Public Relations*, 2nd edn, Prentice Hall, Harlow, pp. 198–221.

Tench, R. and Yeomans, L. (eds.) (2006), *Exploring Public Relations*, Pearson Education, Harlow.

Tench, R. and Yeomans, L. (eds.) (2009), *Exploring Public Relations*, 2nd edn, Prentice Hall, Harlow.

Toth, E.L. (ed.) (2007), *The Future of Excellence in Public Relations and Communication Management: Challenges for the Next Generation*, Lawrence Erlbaum Associates, Mahwah, NJ.

Tymson, C., Lazar, P. and Lazar, R. (2006), *The Australian and New Zealand Public Relations Manual*, Tymson Communications, Sydney.

Van Riel, C.B.M. and Fombrun, C.J. (2008), *Essentials of Corporate Communication: Implementing Practices for Effective Reputation Management*, Routledge, London.

Van Ruler, B. (2005), Commentary: Professionals Are from Venus, Scholars Are from Mars, *Public Relations Review*, 31(2), pp. 159–73. https://doi.org/10.1016/j.pubrev.2005.02.022

Vaughn, R. and Cody, S. (2007), Seize the Day: Dynamics That Will Raise the Profile of Public Relations in 2007, *Public Relations Tactics*, 8 January, at www.prsa.org/searchresults/view/782/105/seize_the_day_dynamics_that_will_raise_the_profile

Wakefield, R.I. (2010), Why Culture Is Still Essential in Discussions about Global Public Relations, in R.L. Heath (ed.), (2010), *The SAGE Handbook of Public Relations*, 2nd edn, SAGE, Los Angeles, CA, pp. 659–173.

Walker, G.F. (1994), Communicating Public Relations Research, *Journal of Public Relations Research*, 6(3), pp. 141–61. https://doi.org/10.1207/s1532754xjprr0603_01

Walker, G.F. (1997), Public Relations Practitioners' Use of Research, Measurement and Evaluation, *Australian Journal of Communication*, 24(2), pp. 97–113.

Watson, T. (2006), Evaluation—Let's Get on with It, *PRism*, 4(2), at www.prismjournal.org/fileadmin/Praxis/Files/Journal_Files/Evaluation_Issue/EDITORIAL.pdf

Watson, T. and Noble, P. (2007), *Evaluating Public Relations: A Best Practice Guide to Public Relations Planning, Research and Evaluation*, Chartered Institute of Public Relations and Kogan Page, London.

White, S.A. (ed.) (1989), *Values and Communication*, Longman Professional, Melbourne.

Wilcox, D.L. and Cameron, G.T. (2006), *Public Relations Strategies and Tactics*, 8th edn, Pearson Education, Boston.

Wilcox, D.L. and Cameron, G.T. (2012), *Public Relations Strategies and Tactics*, 10th edn, Pearson, Glenview, IL.

Wilson, L.J. (1994), Excellent Companies and Coalition-Building among the Fortune 500: A Value- and Relationship-based Theory, *Public Relations Review*, 20(4), pp. 333–43. https://doi.org/10.1016/0363-8111(94)90094-9

Wilson, L.J. and Ogden, J.D. (2008), *Strategic Communication Planning for Effective Public Relations and Marketing*, 5th edn, Kendall Hunt, Dubuque, IA.

Wood, E. (2009), Corporate Communication, in R. Tench and L. Yeomans (eds), (2009), *Exploring Public Relations*, 2nd edn, Prentice Hall, Harlow, pp. 539–59.

Xavier, R., Mehta, A. and Gregory, A. (2006), Evaluation in Use: The Practitioner View of Effective Evaluation, *PRism*, 4(2), at www.prismjournal.org/fileadmin/Praxis/Files/Journal_Files/Evaluation_Issue/XAVIER_ET_AL_ARTICLE.pdf

Xavier, R., Patel, A. and Johnston, K. (2004), Are We Really Making a Difference? The Gap between Outcomes and Evaluation Research in Public Relations Campaigns, paper presented at the Australian and New Zealand Communication Association annual conference, University of Sydney, 7–9 July, at http://conferences.arts.usyd.edu.au/papers.php?first_letter=X&cf=3

Zerfass, A. (2009), Institutionalising Strategic Communication: Theoretical Analysis and Empirical Evidence, *International Journal of Strategic Communication*, 3(2), pp. 69–71. https://doi.org/10.1080/15531180902810205

Zerfass, A. and Huck, S. (2007), Innovations, Communication, and Leadership: New Developments in Strategic Communication, *International Journal of Strategic Communication*, 1(2), pp. 107–22. https://doi.org/10.1080/15531180701298908

Index

Note: **Bold** page numbers refer to tables and *italic* page numbers refer to figures.

Printed in the United States
by Baker & Taylor Publisher Services

Printed in the United States
by Baker & Taylor Publisher Services